From Valor to Pedigree

FROM VALOR TO PEDIGREE
Ideas of Nobility in France in the Sixteenth and Seventeenth Centuries

by Ellery Schalk

PRINCETON UNIVERSITY PRESS
PRINCETON, NEW JERSEY

Copyright © 1986 by Princeton University Press

Published by Princeton University Press, 41 William Street,
Princeton, New Jersey 08540
In the United Kingdom: Princeton University Press, Guildford, Surrey

All Rights Reserved
Library of Congress Cataloging in Publication Data will be found
on the last printed page of this book

ISBN 0-691-05460-6

Publication of this book has been aided by a grant from the
Ira O. Wade Fund of Princeton University Press

This book has been composed in Linotron Bembo

Clothbound editions of Princeton University Press books
are printed on acid-free paper, and binding materials are chosen
for strength and durability

Printed in the United States of America
by Princeton University Press, Princeton, New Jersey

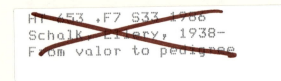

To the memory of my mother and to my father

Contents

Preface

Nobility in our society is only a memory, but it is a memory that continues to attract us. Antiquarians, amateur historians, conservative dreamers, and modern critical historians all study the nobility. Almost everyone else has an opinion on the question, or at the least simply wonders how something so seemingly irrational as nobility could have existed and been so important for so long. It was a similar sort of curiosity that first led me to the subject. I wanted to do a study of collective mentalities on a topic in sixteenth-century French history for a doctoral dissertation, and the idea of nobility seemed a good, if large and challenging, one. Because of its connections to the larger history of the nobility, I felt that this particular study of collective attitudes and opinions could have more direct significance for social history than other topics might have. This has certainly turned out to be the case, although the result has been a far more extensive work than I envisioned when I began. For, while researching the dissertation, which focused on the period of the Religious Wars and of Henry IV, I came to realize that nobility in the 1570s and 1580s was viewed in rather strange ways that seemed quite different from the way it is viewed today and the way most people assume it was viewed in the sixteenth century. At the same time I found more familiar and "modern" ideas concerning nobility in the early seventeenth century, which encouraged me to try to uncover the process of change leading from one view to the other. To present these findings in a preliminary fashion became the task of my dissertation; to attempt to understand them and their implications better, and to refine them and put them into the larger context of the history of early modern France and the history of the idea of nobility has been my task since then. In order to explain the meanings of what people of the time were

saying about nobility from the 1570s through the first decades of the seventeenth century, I found it necessary to go
back into the early sixteenth century and go forward through
the middle of the seventeenth century, and to tie sixteenth-
and seventeenth-century developments to even earlier and later
periods. The present study, then, looks back toward the
Middle Ages, on the one hand, and forward past the 1650s
toward the later ancien régime and the Revolution, on the
other hand.

Many scholars and friends, colleagues, students, and institutions have helped me in the preparation of this book, and
it is possible to mention only a few of them here. To begin
with, I would like to thank the French Government, the Ful-
bright Commission, the American Philosophical Society, and
the Faculty Research Institute of The University of Texas at
El Paso for helping to support indispensable research trips to
France. The College of Liberal Arts of the University kindly
provided typing services. The librarians and archivists of the
Bibliothèque Nationale (B.N.) and the Archives Nationales
(A.N.) were not only thoroughly competent and knowledgeable but also always kind and helpful. Fernand Braudel,
Gene Brucker, the late William F. Church, Kenton Clymer,
Florence Dick, George Huppert, Carl Schorske, and William
Sewell have all helped in important ways. Miriam Chrisman, Natalie Davis, Richard Fischer, David Hackett, Sandra
Harding, and John McKay have each read at least one of the
different versions of the manuscript, offering extremely helpful
and timely criticisms. William J. Bouwsma, who directed my
dissertation at the University of California at Berkeley and
from whom I learned an enormous amount as a graduate
student, has continued to remain interested in my work and
has followed the development of this book with encouragement and interest; I am deeply grateful to him for all that he
has done.

If Professor Bouwsma has supplied the main inspiration and
direction from the point of view of intellectual history, Denis
Richet of the Ecole des Hautes Etudes en Sciences Sociales in

Paris has done so, in more recent years, from the point of view of social history. Through his seminar at the Ecole, and through his work and that of his colleagues in that seminar, I have come to learn at least a little about some of the best of social history today. And I have also, more specifically, learned much that has helped me to work out some of the implications of what I had found in my earlier researches. My wife Ninon helped prepare the translations—they are our joint work, in fact; but far beyond that, in sharing all the main stages of this work with me, she has stood by throughout all of them, offering just the right amount of perspective, humor when necessary, and encouragement.

May 1985

Introduction

In trying to understand how people of the sixteenth century viewed their world socially, historians in the nineteenth and twentieth centuries have not, as a rule, had an easy time of it. Much of what was said about society in the period, apart from the usual clichés about the three estates, appears to lack not only perception but is also confused, contradictory, and naive. When trying to understand the meaning of the concept of nobility, modern historians—with a few recent and very interesting exceptions[1]—have simply tended to rely on more contemporary conceptions of society and social structure, and have used them, consciously or unconsciously, as a comparative standard or model by which to understand the earlier period. This approach has produced some very significant results and, from a number of perspectives, has broadened our knowledge of how nobility was viewed at the time.[2] Among others, Huizinga (for the fourteenth and fifteenth centuries)[3] and Febvre (for the sixteenth century),[4]

[1] Cf. Arlette Jouanna, *L'idée de race en France au xvie siècle et au début du xviie siècle (1498–1614)*, 3 vols. (Paris, 1976), especially her discussion of nobility and virtue; see also the still unpublished researches of Miriam Chrisman on the concepts of vocation and obligation in the early sixteenth century, in which she has found a close relationship between profession and social class, or estate. I am grateful to Professor Chrisman for having supplied me with copies of some of her work in this area.

[2] See, for instance, Davis Bitton, *The French Nobility in Crisis, 1560–1640* (Stanford, Calif., 1969); André Devyver, *Le sang épuré: Les préjugés de race chez les gentilshommes français de l'ancien régime (1560–1720)* (Brussels, 1973); and George Huppert, *Les Bourgeois Gentilshommes: An Essay on the Definition of Elites* (Chicago and London, 1977).

[3] J. Huizinga, *The Waning of the Middle Ages: A Study of the Forms of Life, Thought and Art in France and the Netherlands in the XIVth and XVth Centuries* (London, 1924).

[4] Lucien Febvre, *Le problème de l'incroyance au xvie siècle: La religion de Rabelais* (Paris, 1942).

however, have also taught us that immersing oneself in the past and trying to see and understand the world as directly as possible through the eyes of the people of the period—without, of course, forgetting modern critical methods—can often bring an added perspective and perhaps even a fuller understanding of the actual historical realities of the time.

I used this latter approach in the early stages of this study, and it has produced the study's most surprising conclusions. When I employed these methods to study the concepts of "noble" and "nobility" in sixteenth-century France, it became clear to me that nobility was viewed quite differently then from what most scholars have assumed: it was thought of much more as a profession or function—something one did—rather than something one inherited. The profession was of course the military. In addition, according to the understanding of the people of the period, in order to maintain nobility—to fulfill one's profession as the society's military force—one had to act virtuously; virtue and not birth was what mattered. Furthermore, it was the nobles above all others who emphasized that virtue was their main basis and function. Later study has made it clear that these odd conclusions were not isolated phenomena, no simple repetition of convention, but they reflected instead the basic assumptions of literate society of that time. In some ways, at least until the 1570s and 1580s, there turned out to be no exceptions to the rule.

These conclusions are at variance with most standard assumptions that nobility through birth was a constant in the past, and some historians may have trouble accepting them. However, the evidence presented in the coming chapters, when confronted directly, is very hard to dismiss. At the same time, these conclusions also lead us directly into some interesting problems concerning the relationship between social reality and collective attitudes. For nobility, *in reality*, was certainly not based upon virtuous actions. Most sixteenth-century nobles were noble because they had been born so and remained so no matter what they did—whether they fought, were virtuous, or otherwise. The reality, then, was that nobility was largely an hereditary status. At the same time, the evidence shows that almost without exception, people continued to believe differently. Thus there is a big gap between social and political realities and conceptions and attitudes. The changing relationship between the two across time—by the mid-seventeenth century, for instance, the gap is not as wide— is an important theme throughout this book.

Much of chapters 1 through 3 and parts of chapters 4 and 5 present evidence and explain the origins and dominance of this different view of nobility, which turned out to be essentially medieval. An interesting and even dramatic story also unfolds here: for if during much of the sixteenth century nobility was perceived as virtuous action, by the early to mid-seventeenth century it had acquired a different meaning, one more familiar or "modern" (the latter meaning the standard accepted views of nobility held by most nineteenth- and twentieth-century Westerners, in particular the idea that nobility is based on birth). An important change in collective attitudes took place at that time, and the later parts of this study recount the story of that very important change. As I have brought to bear the implications of a change that had previously eluded historians, several new perspectives on some of the larger problems of French history in the late sixteenth and early seventeenth centuries—for instance on the effects of the Wars of Religion, the role of the popular rebellions of the 1590s, and the consequences of implementing the new absolutist state in the early seventeenth century—have emerged. The later parts of chapter 9 briefly carry the story up to the French Revolution. Here I look briefly at the attitudes about nobility in the late seventeenth and eighteenth centuries and attempt to connect the change of the late sixteenth and early seventeenth centuries with these later attitudes and with the revisionist views about the relative unimportance of the difference between noble and nonnoble in the later ancien régime and during the French Revolution.

Anthropologists and some historians have long used

methods by which they doubt all accepted wisdom on a subject, immerse themselves in the time period, and try to gain an understanding of the times through the eyes of the people of the period. These methods were often useful in this work, despite the difficulties and problems inherent in them[5] and despite the difficulties of trying to escape from the overwhelming nature of the mental constructs of one's own time. As the study progressed, however, it became clear that other theoretical models, while interesting and provocative, could not really be applied to the information I uncovered. What has emerged, instead, is a complex relationship between the changing material reality on the one hand, and the development of new ideas on the other, which does not readily fit the theoretical frameworks of Marx, Weber, Roland Mousnier,[6] or others.

To carry out this study I have consulted treatises, memoirs, letters, political pamphlets, essays, novels, plays, and the like. I have also referred to legal documents and royal ordinances, although here I relied more on existing works by other scholars. When dealing with the almost unknown academies

[5] For an astute analysis of some of these limitations and problems, see Clifford Geertz, "From the Native's Point of View: On the Nature of Anthropological Understanding," in *Local Knowledge: Further Essays on Interpretive Anthropology* (New York, 1983), pp. 55–70.

[6] I am indebted, nevertheless, to Professor Mousnier, who has argued long and eloquently for the existence of major differences between sixteenth- and early seventeenth-century conceptions of social reality and more modern ones, as we move, in his well-known scheme—a scheme that differs substantially, however, from my findings—from a society of orders to a society of "classes." The list of his many important works is well known. For a beginning, see R. Mousnier, J.-P. Labatut, and Y. Durand, eds., *Problèmes de stratification sociale; Deux cahiers de la noblesse pour les Etats Généraux de 1649–1651* (Paris, 1965). Also see Roland Mousnier, *Les hiérarchies sociales de 1450 à nos jours* (Paris, 1969); "Les concepts d'"ordres,' d'"états,' de 'fidélité' et de 'monarchie absolue' en France de la fin du xvie siècle à la fin du xviiie," *Revue historique* 247 (1972), 289–312; *The Institutions of France under the Absolute Monarchy, 1598–1789, Society and the State*, trans. Brian Pearce (Chicago, 1979), French edition 1974; and *Recherches sur la stratification sociale à Paris aux xviie et xviiie siècles, L'échantillon de 1634, 1635, 1636* (Paris, 1976).

for nobles founded in the late sixteenth and early seventeenth centuries, and at other times in my research, I found it necessary to go into the archives to obtain key information that is not available elsewhere. Finally, I have relied heavily on a variety of secondary works to round out the picture and to develop the context in which my story could be told. There remains, of course, much unread and unconsulted material, but I used as wide a range of sources as was possible for one individual to use. Even so, this vast, amorphous, and fascinating subject remains open to even further reading and research.

PART ONE

Medieval Views in the
Sixteenth Century

I

The Military Profession
As a Social Class in the Sixteenth Century

To talk of nobility as a profession or function is in some ways not new. Max Weber, for instance, also at times considered nobility a sort of profession. Nobility stood for or represented a ruling or dominant class, and with the inherited position of nobles went a whole series of rights of rulership and rights of action and authority.[1] In this sense nobility was more than just inherited privilege and represented a kind of function in society, as it indeed did, in different ways, for Marx. But views like Weber's and Marx's are products of later times, and sixteenth-century people simply did not view nobles that way. Their view of nobility tended to be a more focused and narrow one, and it had to do almost entirely with military matters. For them, nobility was indeed a profession or function—it was something you did—and to be noble you had to fight. Action is involved in the matter, but not as seen by nineteenth- and twentieth-century observers like Marx and Weber. In this chapter I will discuss this sixteenth-century understanding of nobility as a profession through an examination of a number of sources of the time, and try to test its plausibility by relating it to military realities and, briefly, to the situation in other countries.

This view of nobility in sixteenth-century France was in fact very rarely stated clearly or theoretically, but it can nevertheless be found in a wide range of literary and other

[1] This is suggested, for instance, at key points throughout his well-known essay, "Politics as a Vocation." Cf. *From Max Weber: Essays in Sociology*, trans. and ed. H. H. Gerth and C. Wright Mills (New York, 1946), pp. 77–128.

sources. It is especially clear in writings that discuss nobility only indirectly or in passing, suggesting that the view was accepted and needed no further explanation. Montaigne, for instance, reflects this attitude well, even if he is not usually explicit about it. He often refers throughout the *Essais* to his "profession" when talking of other matters, without elaborating further, and just assumes the reader will understand he means the military—for example, "A man of my profession has these problems."[2] His direct identification with the military profession may seem strange when one thinks of Montaigne as a noble but not necessarily as a military man. Other sources that are more explicit help clarify what Montaigne means here.

The famous political pamphlet the *Dialogue d'entre le Maheustre et le Manant* states this view of nobility more clearly. Here the term *noblesse* is used not to define a social class—at least not in terms of its being a fixed status—but to define a profession, the military one, the way *justice* is used to define the legal profession. The *Manant* speaks of *noblesse* the way one might speak of a number of troops today:

> As for the nobility, few of them are following our party for Religion's sake, for it has been more than fifty years as far as I know, that the Nobility has not recognized or understood wherein lay the honor of God and piety toward His people, from which has resulted their freedom and ambition which has led them to become ignorant of their origins; as for the very few who joined our party it has been for money, and when it happened to be lacking, *we had no more Nobility* [nous n'avons plus eu de Noblesse]; and what is worse, some of them after receiving our payments, acted as traitors toward us, and went over to your party, making a virtue of betraying and cheating us after they received our money. *So much so that your No-*

[2] For instance, Michel de Montaigne, *Les essais*, ed. Pierre Villey (Paris, 1965), Book I, chap. 3, p. 19, and Book III, chap. 9, p. 963.

bility follows heresy and ours money [Tellement que vostre Noblesse suit l'hérésie et la nostre l'argent].[3]

The *Maheustre* answers that the *Manant* should not complain about the nobility and the king's party in general, and "especially about the Nobility and the Law or Legal Profession, inasmuch as *our Nobility fights gallantly and goes willingly to war, and our Law or Legal profession is rigorous and vigilant toward our enemies.*"[4] Thus there are two professions, *noblesse* and *justice*—fighting and law. This view may have had little to do with the reality of the situation, but it nevertheless seems to have been a basic part of the mentality of the people of the time. A little later, when the *Maheustre* says, "Tesmoin la Noblesse du Lyonnois, Dauphiné et d'Auvergne, qui s'estans adonnée aux Princes . . .,"[5] he does not mean that the nobility had issued a proclamation supporting the princes, the way a political figure might come out in support of a candidate; he means that the princes have gained a fighting force, that those people who do the main or important fighting have decided to fight for them.

Other indications of this attitude are found in the sources of the time. It is especially clear in François de L'Alouëte, for instance. In the preface to his treatise of 1577 on the nobility,

---

[3] François Cromé, *Dialogue d'entre le Maheustre et le Manant . . .* (n.p., 1593), p. 75. The emphasis is mine. The term "profession" in the sixteenth century, according to Wartburg in his *Etymologisches Wörterbuch* and Huguet in the *Dictionnaire de la langue française du seizième siècle*, seems to have had not only *métier*, or calling, as one of its dominant meanings, but also closely associated with that, *état*, or condition. The other dominant meaning of the time involves its teaching or educational aspects. See especially Walter von Wartburg, *Französisches etymologisches Wörterbuch*, vol. 9, p. 429.

[4] Ibid., pp. 77–78: ". . . spécialment de la Noblesse et de la Justice, d'autant que nostre Noblesse combat bien, et va bien, à la guerre; et nostre Justice est exacte et vigilante contre nos ennemis." The emphasis is again mine.

[5] Ibid., p. 79: "Witness the Nobility of Lyonnais, Dauphiné, and Auvergne who had joined the Princes."

after referring to the *noblesse* as those "faisant profession d'armes," he gives his reasons for writing:

> . . . more precisely I want to lead and form the Child to whom this [book] is dedicated into *true Nobility and perfect virtue* [vraie Noblesse et parfaite vertu], and with him all *other Nobles* who might wish to profit from it and to acquire some dexterity *for the practice of their vocation* [pour l'exercice de leur vacation].[6]

It is clearly understood from the context that their "vocation" is the profession of arms. Later in the work he is even more explicit:

> This is the origin of all Nobles and thus of the French *gentilshommes* [or nobles] also, *all of whom have been schooled and formed in virtue* [qui tous ont été forméz et rencontréz en la Vertu] . . . so that they later devote their lifetime in following faithfully this great and beautiful virtue, which, thanks to the action of the Spirit of God, inspired the Kings when choosing and selecting them over others; and under this duty and condition they were given the title of Nobles, and *their vocation (thus limited and consisting in the practice of this virtue)* has been called *Noblesse* [et leur vacation (ainsi limitée et consistant en l'exercice de cette vertu) a été appellée Noblesse].[7]

Here nobility is conceived of as the vocation or profession of virtue, or of the virtuous, suggesting a close relationship between virtue and profession. Indeed, one could, according to L'Alouëte and his contemporaries, make a "profession de noblesse," which was basically the same as making a "profession of virtue." And the profession of nobility was, of course, essentially that of arms, and in particular it implied a special sort of valor and superiority in arms that placed

---

[6] François de L'Alouëte, *Traité des nobles et des vertus dont ils sont formés* (Paris, 1577), p. iii. The emphasis is mine.
[7] Ibid., p. 22v. The emphasis is again mine.

one above the ordinary soldier. The expression "faire profession de noblesse" appears often in the texts of the time. For instance, L'Alouëte writes elsewhere that fiefs should not be alienated since they "have been solely attributed in return for the practice of arms, and very precisely assigned and attached to the persons of Nobles *who make their profession Nobility* [qui font profession de Noblesse]."[8]

The noble or nobles who wrote the *Harangue pour la noblesse* in 1574 also understood the society in terms of profession or calling:

> Those are the three things that kings should wish for: to have religion, that is to say, sound consciences, the Nobility to fight for their defense, and justice to take care of their subjects, so much so that if together we devote ourselves to this goal according to the vocation we each have been called into by the Lord [selon la vacation, à laquelle Dieu l'a appellé]. . . .[9]

The implication here is that regardless of one's legal designation of belonging to one social group or another, a person is really defined by his profession. In other words, a "noble" who does not fight but instead carries out *justice* (or enters the Church) would not really be, in this particular framework of thought, a part of the *noblesse* and belongs instead with those "qui font profession de Justice."

François de La Noue also reflects this view in his writings. For instance, he speaks often of the "gentilshommes et leur profession."[10] More indirectly, when offering exceptions to his attack on the reading by nobles of the Amadis of Gaul books, he writes: "Now, within this discussion I do not include the exercises at arms that are one of the favorite pas-

[8] Ibid., p. 53. The emphasis is again mine.

[9] *La harangue par [pour] la noblesse de toute la France . . .* (Paris, 1574), p. 18v.

[10] François de La Noue, *Discours politiques et militaires* (Geneva, 1967), 1st ed. 1587, for instance p. 133.

times of our Nobility in times of peace."[11] He means, in other words, these are the pastimes of "our leading fighting men" in times of peace. Monluc also seems to have thought of himself as carrying out the profession of nobility. In his writings, *gentilhomme*, or noble, was usually equal to *capitaine*, and the two terms tended to be used interchangeably. Those *capitaines* were then generally contrasted or set off against the *gens de pied*, or the ordinary foot soldiers—those who would not, in his view, be nobles. He makes such a distinction when appealing to his *capitaines* to treat them as men: "Si nous sommes gentils-hommes, ils sont soldats."[12] He also says, in reference to a particular accomplishment of his: "Had I not acted thus, I would have provoked a rising of the whole nobility together with all the soldiers against the king."[13] He could have said that it would have caused all the leading fighters (but not necessarily all the officers) and all the regular soldiers to revolt against the king; he apparently did not need to, because everyone knew what he meant by *noblesse*.

In his poems of 1574 Jean de La Taille presents a similar idea from a slightly different point of view. With the military part of his *métier* comes the duty to be a courtier—a duty which he despises and which has led him to write in the first place. He was born of noble blood (". . . saches donc que/Je suis de sang noble conçeu"), but he would almost have preferred to have been born an *artisan* or a *bûcheron* than to have had to be a courtier. Then he continues:

> When I was young I was taught the classics along with how to handle horses, and have them obey; I had lessons in fencing, in how to perform on horseback, in singing and

[11] Ibid., p. 176: "Or, en ce que je dis icy, je ne comprends pas les exercitations aux armes qui sont les passetemps de nostre noblesse en temps de paix."

[12] Blaise de Monluc, *Commentaires*, 3 vols. (Paris, 1911–1925), I, 32: "If we are nobles, they are soldiers."

[13] Ibid., p. 9: "Si je n'eusse faict cella, je revoltais toute la noblesse et tous les soldats contre le Roy."

playing ball, in running races, and how to talk properly, in doing everything that is *proper to any gentilhomme*. *In short I knew everything about the profession of fighting*—so unhappy a profession!—[De faire ce qui est propre à tout gentilhomme. Des armes sachant donc tout le mestier en somme—Mestier tant malheureux!—] and then was sent to the Court, and I curse that day, that month, that year and even the hour it happened.[14]

Thus, being a noble, he must follow his *métier*, which is that of arms, of being a *gentilhomme*, but which in this case included the other related activities he cites, such as fencing, racing, and the rest.

The kings also seem to have viewed nobility essentially as a profession. Henry III in his letters, for instance, uses *gentilshommes* and *noblesse* when referring to those who are doing the fighting. The Protestants have "managed in various ways and with various means to attract into their party several Catholic *gentilshommes*,"[15] that is to say, several important fighting men have gone over to the other side in the Civil Wars. Or again, in the same letter, which was written to his *baillis, sénéchaux*, and governors after the escape of the Duc d'Alençon, he writes: "They have no better way to have [themselves] known than by surrendering quickly [and I speak of], *those of our noblesse* [ceux de nostre noblesse], of our companies and other men at arms in the places that we have ordered them to."[16] It is clear from the passages cited earlier, and from the context here, that Henry III is not using the term *noblesse* the way a king would usually use it when referring to a group of his subjects, but that he means a specific tactical factor in the military balance between the two sides in the Civil War.

[14] Jean de La Taille, "Le courtisan retiré" (1574), in *Oeuvres*, ed. René de Maulde, 4 vols. (Paris, 1878), IV, 24. The emphasis is mine.
[15] Henry III, *Lettres*, ed. Michel François, 2 vols. (Paris, 1959, 1965), II, 244.
[16] Ibid. The emphasis is mine.

As late as the early seventeenth century, nobility was still referred to as a vocation. For example, in 1612 Flurance-Rivault in defending his proposal for an academy for training young noblemen, said: "For even when the young *gentilhomme*, put on the path of honor right from the cradle, and who has been called to this path by his family and *his profession* [par le voeu de ses parens et de sa profession], was to acquire . . . "[17]; he was naturally assuming what the profession of a *gentilhomme* will be. It is significant that Flurance-Rivault said *his* profession, thus implying that there is only one profession of the nobility. In 1608 La Béraudière stated that it is possible for a nonnoble to become a noble because, as he explains,

> Nobility which has been acquired by virtue can be exercised by the nonnoble as well as the noble [car la noblesse a esté acquise par la vertu qui peut aussi-tost estre exercée du roturier que du noble], and if the nonnoble is made noble it continues for him and his family, if he has any, because it could happen that he would have poor ancestors who would not have *followed this vocation* [qui n'auroient suivy ceste vacation].[18]

That is to say, he might have had parents or relatives, who, even if they were born nobles, were too poor to practice— at its higher levels, anyway—the profession of arms, which theoretically defined their nobility. In this case, one is judged noble by what one does—by the profession one follows— rather than by one's heredity.

Montaigne is particularly revealing on the question in a part of his *Essais* where he goes beyond the ordinary clichés to give a clear and precise statement of the view. In discussing the term *vertu*, which, he points out, means "valor" for the French as well as for the Romans, he goes on to say, in a

[17] David de Rivault de Flurance, *Le dessin d'une académie et de l'introduction d'icelle en la cour* (Paris, 1612), p. 5v. The emphasis is again mine.
[18] Marc de La Béraudière, *Le combat de seul à seul en camp clos* (Paris, 1608), p. 91. The emphasis is again mine.

passage that has been cited often but can now perhaps be interpreted a little differently: "La forme propre, et seule et essencielle, de noblesse en France, c'est la vacation militaire."[19] Montaigne often writes about how much he loves to ride, to be on horseback, to be on campaign,[20] and one tends to forget that according to him, his profession was not that of a writer, nor of a lawyer, but that of a noble, or a fighter on horseback.

People thus often referred to nobility as a tactical factor in the wars—the way one might, for instance, talk of having so many tanks before a battle—while nobles themselves tended to view their special status as something that had to be fulfilled and justified through action, or through fighting. Modern social scientists have often pointed out that profession is an indication of status; but with these writers the roles are in a sense reversed: status, or the status of nobility at least, is *simply* a profession—the profession comes first and determines the status. This is the old, premodern view of nobility. The new, "modern" view, dating from the early to mid-seventeenth century on, is the more familiar one in which nobility reflects a particular status in society that is determined by birth, and the profession—doctor, lawyer, military person, or whatever—is a personal choice that can enhance the prestige of that status and can even, in very recent times, determine it to a high degree.

To state that nobility was viewed essentially as the military profession in the sixteenth century is to suggest the fundamental importance of military realities in understanding the question of nobility. André Corvisier has already raised some of the key questions of the relation between nobility and the

[19] Montaigne, *Essais*, Book II, chap. 7, p. 384: "The proper, the only, the essential form of nobility in France is the military profession." The translation is by Donald Frame in *The Complete Essays of Montaigne* (Stanford, 1957).
[20] For instance, Montaigne, *Essais*, Book I, chap. 48, p. 289; Book III, chap. 9, pp. 974, 978; Book III, chap. 13, p. 1096.

military for early modern France.[21] Unfortunately, the rarity of good sources and the lack of a comprehensive study of the sixteenth-century military, such as Philippe Contamine's for the fourteenth and fifteenth centuries,[22] leave us with many unanswered questions. Nevertheless, Contamine's work still suggests some basic paths for dealing with this problem in the sixteenth century.[23]

For example, we now know that the nobility and the army were inextricably bound together in the fourteenth and fifteenth centuries. Contamine has shown that throughout the fifteenth century an increasing percentage of nobles served in the royal armies and assumed that this was the norm.[24] As the foundation of the new royal army was being laid, nobility and fighting for the king became synonymous in people's minds. John Bell Henneman has a slightly different perspective, but has also shown the military importance of the nobility for the late fourteenth and early fifteenth centuries.[25] The loyalty of the military nobility was a basic prerequisite for the success of any political movement or for political reform, not especially because of the nobility's economic importance, but because of their military importance; indeed, Henneman calls them the "military class." The king had to win them over in order to govern the country well: "If the successful monarch needed regular taxes in order to finance an army, he also needed the loyalty and collaboration of the

[21] André Corvisier, "La noblesse militaire: Aspects militaires de la noblesse française du xve et [au] xviiie siècles; état des questions," *Histoire sociale—Social History* 11 (1978), 336–355.

[22] Philippe Contamine, *Guerre, état et société à la fin du Moyen-Age: Etudes sur les armées des rois de France, 1337–1494* (Paris and The Hague, 1972).

[23] Cf., for instance, Corvisier's conclusion in "La noblesse militaire" (p. 342): "Unfortunately a study similar to that of Ph. Contamine has not yet been done for the sixteenth century. It appears, however, that the noble remained the central element [l'élément pilote] of the army as well as of society."

[24] Contamine, *Guerre, état et société.*

[25] John Bell Henneman, "The Military Class and the French Monarchy in the Late Middle Ages," *American Historical Review* 83 (1978), 946–965.

12

military class [the nobles], on which that army, and indeed the entire structure of government, depended."[26]

There is real evidence in the fourteenth and fifteenth centuries thus to link the nobility with the military, but for the sixteenth century it is not so obvious. On the one hand, we do know, for instance, that numerous nonnobles fought in the army, especially in the local militias, although exact figures are not available;[27] we also know that many nobles never fought at all, yet never seem to have had their status challenged because of it.[28] On the other hand, most of the top positions in the army seem to have been held by nobles, and, in rare cases, if someone was not already noble, he would automatically be ennobled by the position, which suggests that these positions were assumed to be held by nobles.[29]

[26] Ibid., p. 965.

[27] For instance, Roger Doucet, *Les institutions de la France au xvie siècle*, 2 vols. (Paris, 1948), II, 608–651; Gaston Zeller, *Les institutions de la France au xvie siècle* (Paris, 1948), pp. 297–330; and the work of Robert Descimon, now in progress, on the Paris militia in the sixteenth and seventeenth centuries.

[28] This fact has been and can be documented in numerous ways. The lack of effectiveness of the *ban* and *arrière-ban*, for instance, which when used would theoretically have led to all nobles serving, has been studied by Pierre Deyon in "A propos des rapports entre la noblesse française et la monarchie absolue pendant la première moitié du xviie siècle," *Revue historique* 231 (1964), 341–356, especially 349–350. Added to this could be the individual example of the Sire de Gouberville, who was called and did not go (*Le journal du Sire de Gouberville*, ed. E. de Robillard de Beaurepaire [Caen, 1892], pp. 780–783). Bitton's material in *The French Nobility*. pp. 27–41, also backs up such a conclusion, as do the figures in the two recent and important local studies of the nobility during this period done by Jean-Marie Constant and James Wood. Constant's figures for the Beauce, for instance, are especially low for the number of nobles who actually served in the military: cf. *Nobles et paysans en Beauce au xvie et xviie siècles* (Université de Lille III, Service de Reproduction des Thèses, 1981), pp. 158–185, and especially p. 159. Wood's figures for the *élection* of Bayeux, on the other hand, are a good deal higher, but still more than half of the nobles apparently never served at all: cf. *The Nobility of the Election of Bayeux, 1463–1666: Continuity through Change* (Princeton, N.J., 1980), pp. 81–90.

[29] While signaling some of the changes away from an all-noble army, J.-R. Bloch, *L'anoblissement en France au temps de François Ier: Essai d'une défini-

Robert Harding's recent study of the *gouverneurs* in the six-teenth and early seventeenth centuries suggests that contemporaries may have been correct in continuing to take the military importance of the nobles seriously. Harding has shown how the sixteenth-century system of provincial administration was closely allied to the military function of the governors; and the military basis, function, and prestige of these noble governors continued through much of the sixteenth century, and did not begin to change and modify until the end of that century.[30]

From a technical point of view, the military-nobility question is equally complex, even though more information is available in this area. The actual military role in the sixteenth century of the single man on horseback—the medieval, feudal noble-knight—is central. Contemporaries had mixed feelings about the effectiveness of this single rider with lance.[31] We know quite well the composition of a number of armies and the way that certain battles were fought, however,[32] and

---

tion de la condition juridique et sociale de la noblesse au début du xvie siècle (Paris, 1934), summarizes (pp. 96–97): "Certainly the governors of the provinces and the captains of the *gens d'armes des ordonnances du roi* could hardly be anything but noble, and in the case of one of those offices being given to a nonnoble, the latter would simply have changed his condition." Constant has found ennoblement for military reasons relatively prevalent in the province of Beauce in the sixteenth century—suggesting a conclusion similar to Bloch's—while it declines substantially in the seventeenth century: cf. *Nobles et paysans*, especially pp. 46–47; and see also Fleury Vindry, *Dictionnaire de l'état-major français au xvie siècle*, part 1, *Gendarmerie* (Bergerac, 1901).

[30] Robert R. Harding, *Anatomy of a Power Elite: The Provincial Governors of Early Modern France* (New Haven and London, 1978), in particular pp. 21–31 and 71–80.

[31] See, for instance, the comments of La Noue in his *Discours politiques et militaires*, pp. 355–362, and also Etienne Vaucheret, *Le fait de la guerre: Témoignages et réflexions de Jean d'Autun à Monluc*, thèse de Doctorat ès Lettres (unpublished) (Sorbonne, 1977).

[32] Particularly useful for what follows have been Geoffrey Parker, *The Army of Flanders and the Spanish Road (1567–1659); The Logistics of Spanish Victory and Defeat in the Low Countries* (Cambridge, 1972); H. A. Lloyd, *The Rouen Campaign, 1590–2; Politics, Warfare and the Early Modern State* (Oxford, 1973);

the evidence indicates that knights did not come riding at each other to fight in single combat. Infantry men of various sorts such as pikemen, riders with pistols, and others such as those involved with the artillery made up a major part of the army, along with the so-called "lances" on horseback. The number of these lances within a particular army was a relatively small percentage of the whole, and they alone did not play a decisive role.

On the whole, the military situation was fluid and variable and in a process of readjustment to changing technical realities and to social and political trends. The importance, and indeed indispensability, of the infantry had long been recognized—at least since the defeat of Charles the Bold in the 1470s, if not sooner. This period of Michael Roberts's "military revolution"[33] saw a trend toward larger armies with a greater role of the infantry, when the role of the cavalry was transformed and integrated much more into the whole. But the period remained one of technical transformation and flux, and one where ideas and strategy, as Geoffrey Parker has pointed out,[34] seemed outdated and not in line with technical change. The "modern" army of the absolute monarchs did not yet exist in any precise form.

In a sense, then, there was in reality an army that was neither "medieval" nor "modern." The leaders and those in the top military positions would almost invariably be noble; but these nobles did not do the major fighting, and, outside of their leadership positions, they did not seem to play a crucial or dominant role. On the other hand, the view of the people of the time, which assumed almost an equivalency between the nobility and the military, remained decidedly medieval.

---

and Ferdinand Lot, *Recherches sur les effectifs des armées françaises des guerres d'Italie aux Guerres de Religion (1494–1562)* (Paris, 1962).

[33] Cf. Michael Roberts, "The Military Revolution, 1560–1660," in *Essays in Swedish History* (Minneapolis, 1967), pp. 195–225, 1st ed. 1956, and Geoffrey Parker, "The Military Revolution, 1560–1660—a Myth?" *Journal of Modern History* 48 (1976), 195–213.

[34] Parker, *The Army of Flanders*, especially pp. xi–xii.

Technical and social changes had indeed been taking place in the military in the fifteenth and sixteenth centuries, and these were working to make this medieval view obsolete; however, contemporaries seem to have been basically unaware of the effects of these changes. They assumed that having *noblesse* formed an indispensable part of any successful military venture. Just as today one might say that without airplanes one could not win, in the sixteenth century one would say that without *noblesse* one could not win.

Since sixteenth-century French people seemed to assume, even if wrongly, the military primacy of the nobility, it could be useful to look at some of the social and political struggles of the sixteenth century from this perspective. For instance, the members of the radical *Ligue*—about which a good deal of scholarly debate has taken place recently[35]—would seem to have been hesitant or even unable to attack the nobility as a *whole*, believing that without a nobility, they would be without an army and therefore could not succeed in carrying out their programs. Michel François has indeed shown that in the second half of the sixteenth century, when the Protestants had to act as a political movement, they recognized the value of having the *noblesse* on their side for military reasons.[36] Perhaps the nobles were simply considered to be too important—because of their supposed military function—so any serious organized movement could not have been totally antinoble.

In short, nobility was viewed as a *function* in sixteenth-century France. In a sense, this conclusion simply confirms the close relationship already observed by scholars between nobility and the military in the early modern period.[37] None of

[35] See chap. 5 and the works cited there in note 13.

[36] Michel François, "Noblesse, réforme et gouvernement du royaume de France dans la deuxième moitié du xvième siècle," in *L'Amiral de Coligny et son temps: Actes du colloque du 24–28 octobre 1972* (Paris, 1974), pp. 301–312.

[37] As, for instance, in comparative surveys like those of André Corvisier, *Armées et sociétés en Europe de 1494 à 1789* (Paris, 1975); Jean-Pierre Labatut, *Les noblesses européennes de la fin du xve siècle à la fin du xviiie siècle* (Paris,

them has gone so far as to arrive at the same conclusions that I have, perhaps because most if not all of them have focused on the later period of the ancien régime when the relationship between the two had already changed, with nobility no longer thought of as a profession, even if an important connection between the nobility and military continued.[38] On the other hand, one historian of the middle of the eighteenth century, the Président (as he was called) Charles-Jean-François Hénault, seems to have understood that nobility had once—indeed as late as the sixteenth century—been a sort of profession of arms. He wrote in his very popular and widely read history,

All of the *hommes d'armes* at the time of Louis XII [1498-1515] were *gentilshommes* or nobles. By "hommes d'armes" I mean all those who made up the *compagnies d'ordonnance*. But one must not confuse *gentilshommes* or nobles of that period with *gentilshommes* of noble race; for it was enough at that time for a man, born in the third estate, to be accepted as noble if he carried out solely the profession of arms without exercising any other vocation.

He goes on to point out how Henry IV put an end to this state of affairs with his famous edict on the *taille* of 1600.[39]

1973); and Jean Meyer, *Noblesses et pouvoirs dans l'Europe d'ancien régime* (Paris, 1973), especially pp. 43–44. For important comments on this relationship, see also Helmuth Rössler, ed., *Deutscher Adel, 1430–1555* and *Deutscher Adel, 1555–1740* (Darmstadt, 1965), especially Rainer Wohlfeil's articles, "Adel und neues Heerwesen," I, 203–233, and "Adel und Heerwesen," II, 315–343.

[38] See chap. 9. In trying to understand this relationship in the later period of early modern Europe, the connecting role of the horse has often been recognized, as, for instance, in this statement by Albert Babeau, in *La vie militaire sous l'ancien régime: Les officiers* (Paris, 1890), p. 5: "The horse is, so to speak, the moving pedestal of the *gentilhomme*, and the first titles of nobility are derived form this animal that people have itself qualified as noble: *chevaliers, écuyers, connétables, and maréchaux* all draw their name from the horse and the cares that are given to this useful and sometimes superb auxiliary of the warrior."

[39] Charles-Jean-François Hénault, *Nouvel abrégé chronologique de l'histoire de France*, 5th ed., 2 vols. (Paris, 1756), II, 573–574. I am indebted to Jean-

Closer to the time, then, some people, though they lived in a period in which the modern concept of nobility had already become the dominant one, did remember the old situation, if with some surprise that it could have existed. From another perspective, the view of nobility as a function projects into the sixteenth century the same view that some historians have of the situation in the Middle Ages. For example, Michael Howard has written:

"To bear arms," to have a crest on one's helmet and symbols on one's shield instantly recognizable in the heart of battle, became in European society for a thousand years a symbol of nobility. For what it is worth it still is. But in the Middle Ages it was a symbol of *function* and available to all who performed that function. The nobility was not yet a close[d] hereditary caste; war was still a career open to the talents.[40]

As we shall see in the next chapter, which explores the medieval-feudal origins of the sixteenth-century concept of nobility, Howard's statement is typical of how some of today's medievalists understand the situation.

To test the assumptions made in this chapter about the sixteenth century, we can study the prevalence of similar views in other parts of Europe at that time. Preliminary investigations in Germany,[41] Spain,[42] and England[43] have turned up

---

Marie Constant, who first indicated this passage to me. The original of the later part is as follows: ". . . il ne faut pas entendre par les gentilshommes d'alors, les gentilshommes issus de race noble, il suffoisait pour être réputé tel, qu'un homme né dans le tiers-état fît uniquement profession des armes sans exercer aucun autre emploi."

[40] Michael Howard, *War in European History* (Oxford, 1976), p. 4; the emphasis on the word "function" is Howard's.

[41] Examined, for instance, were Johannes Agricola, *Die Sprichwörter-Sammlungen*, 2 vols. (Berlin and New York, 1971), especially I, 201–203; Hajo Holborn, *Ulrich von Hutten and the German Reformation*, Harper Torchbook (New York, 1966), especially the letter of Hutten cited on pp. 18–19; Sebastian Brant, *The Ship of Fools*, trans. and ed. Edwin H. Zeydel (New York, 1944), especially pp. 252–253; Sebastian Franck, *Spiegel und Bildnis*

some interesting results. Not only, for instance, do people perceive a close relationship between the military and nobility, but, at least in the case of the first two countries, they have some conceptions that closely resemble those of the French. For example, Stuart Schwartz found that when Spanish nonnobles came to the New World in the sixteenth century and wished to obtain nobility, they would find themselves a horse and try to develop a military function.[44] And Johannes Agricola, writing in Germany in the early sixteenth century, stated quite plainly that "A person's estate is his calling, his profession, his way of life."[45] It appears, indeed, that in most early sixteenth-century areas of Western

---

des ganzen Erdbodens (Tübingen, 1534), especially p. 44, as cited in Holborn, *Ulrich von Hutten*, p. 21; and the two volumes edited by Rössler cited above in note 37, especially Wohlfeil's two articles, in particular p. 323 of the second one.

[42] Consulted here, for instance, were Bartolomé Bennassar, "Etre noble en Espagne, Contribution à l'étude des comportements de longue durée," in *Histoire économique du monde méditerranéen, 1450–1650: Mélanges en l'honneur de Fernand Braudel* (Toulouse, 1973), I, 95–196; Stuart B. Schwartz, "New World Nobility: Social Aspirations and Nobility in the Conquest and Colonization of Spanish America," in Miriam Usher Chrisman and Otto Gründler, eds., *Social Groups and Religious Ideas in the Sixteenth Century* (Kalamazoo, Michigan, 1978), pp. 23–37 and 154–158; J. B. Owens, "Diana at the Bar: Hunting, Aristocrats and the Law in Renaissance Castile," *Sixteenth Century Journal* VIII, 1 (1977), 17–35; Peter Russell, "Arms Versus Letters: Towards a Definition of Spanish Fifteenth-Century Humanism," in *Aspects of the Renaissance: A Symposium*, ed. Archibald R. Lewis (Austin and London, 1967), pp. 47–58.

[43] For instance, Thomas Elyot, *The Book Named the Governor*, ed. S. E. Lehmberg (London and New York, 1962), 1st ed. 1531; Lawrence Humphrey, *The Nobles or of Nobilitye* (Amsterdam and New York, 1973), facsimile of the 1563 edition; and the Chrisman work in progress cited in note 1 of the Introduction.

[44] Schwartz, "New World Nobility," and also comments when the paper was first presented at the Twelfth Conference on Medieval Studies, in Kalamazoo, Michigan, on May 6, 1977.

[45] Agricola, *Die Sprichwörter-Sammlungen*, I, 201. The translation is by Gerald Strauss in *Manifestations of Discontent on the Eve of the Reformation* (Bloomington, Indiana, and London, 1971), p. 208.

19

and central Europe, where feudalism, understood as a military system based upon homage and the fief, had left its mark, nobility was viewed as essentially military.

These sixteenth-century views of nobility reflect fundamental and important assumptions of the people of the time. Discovering how they grew directly out of the earlier medieval views and how they are tied to the concept of nobility as virtue will provide the evidence we need to accept this conclusion and to understand its significance. In the following chapter I will attempt to do this by presenting the background of the view of virtue and discussing its main implications.

2

Nobility As Virtue
and the Medieval Origins of the
"Feudal-Military" View

If nobility in the sixteenth century was conceived of as a function, that function was to act virtuously. The concept of *vertu* is indeed a crucial part of this view. For the people of sixteenth-century France, it served to include all the qualities associated with being noble. These included courage and prowess in battle as well as personal qualities such as uprightness, selflessness when defending the weak and poor, loyalty to one's monarch or one's military leader or superior, honesty, and adherence to the morals of the time. To contemporaries, and above all to nobles, nobility was the profession of virtue or of the virtuous, the *profession de la vertu*.[1]

In this context, the traditional debate about whether virtue or birth should be considered the basis of nobility was out of place. The debate did exist, to be sure, under certain circumstances and in a limited way; but so long as there was

---

[1] For some pioneering comments on the concept of virtue seen in relationship to the history of the nobility in early modern Austria, see Otto Brunner, *Adeliges Landleben und Europäischer Geist: Leben und Werk Wolf Helmhards von Hohberg, 1612–1688* (Salzburg, 1949). For some preliminary and tentative remarks on the subject in France, see my article, "The Appearance and Reality of Nobility in France during the Wars of Religion: An Example of How Collective Attitudes Can Change," *Journal of Modern History* 48 (1976), 19–31. Arlette Jouanna is one of the few scholars of French history to recognize, to some extent at least, the importance of the concept of *vertu* as a primary ingredient of the way nobles—and indeed most of the rest of society—viewed nobility. See, for example, *L'idée de race*, pp. 728–754, 213–215, 625–630.

no one to argue against virtue or for birth, such a debate could not have any particular social significance. It could not, for instance, form the basis of an attack of nonnobles against nobles, since it was the nobles themselves who argued most strongly for virtue and assumed it to be at the foundation of nobility. Only when it became clear that it was no longer relevant, logical, or sensible for nobles to hold such a view could the more traditional discussion take on real social significance. Such a change of conceptions did take place at the very end of the sixteenth and early in the seventeenth centuries, making possible the emergence of a more modern view of nobility in France. But until that time the older view prevailed, and this view set the framework for and the limits on social action, to the extent that such conceptions actually affected social action.

There is little doubt that the sixteenth-century views were a continuation of views that had their origins in the medieval period. The feudal Middle Ages, as Marc Bloch pointed out many years ago, developed a new understanding of nobility.[2] This new understanding seems to have grown up naturally during the process of formation of what Bloch saw as the new feudal and military aristocracy in the tenth and eleventh centuries, "the period of spontaneous formation," as he called it.[3] During this period, courage and virtue and success in fighting—what one does and not what one inherits from one's parents—were usually the reasons for gaining and holding a dominant position in society. Accompanying this formation of a new aristocracy of talent was the "transformation from the old conception of nobility as a sacred race to the new conception of it as consisting in a mode of life."[4] There was a breakdown in the Roman tradition of an aristocracy of birth, as Georges Duby has more recently shown

[2] Marc Bloch, *Feudal Society*, 2 vols., trans. L. A. Mangon, 1st French ed. 1939–1940 (Chicago, 1961), II, 283–344.
[3] Ibid., p. 335.
[4] Ibid., p. 289.

for the area around Macon.[5] Nobility had become a sort of function, and people tended to see it as that. "He [the noble knight] was committed body and soul to his particular function—that of warrior," and ". . . fighting was for them [the nobles] not merely an occasional duty to be performed for the sake of their lord, or king, or family. It represented much more—their whole purpose in life."[6] Nobility as an hereditary class simply did not exist. As Bloch wrote,

> In this sense [that is, as an hereditary caste] nobility made its appearance relatively late in Western Europe. The first lineaments of the institution did not begin to emerge before the twelfth century, and it took shape only in the following century when the fief and vassalage were already in decline. Throughout the first feudal age, and the period immediately preceding it, it was unknown.[7]

Bloch's work seems to have helped inspire a large number of excellent regional and local studies of the medieval French nobility.[8] (In a sense this is ironic, since the documentation available for that period is almost invariably far less abundant than that available for the much less studied sixteenth and early seventeenth centuries, for which works of a similar kind are just beginning to appear.)[9] In any case, the medieval regional studies have tended to reinforce Bloch's framework and periodization, while modifying it some and enriching it a good deal. For instance, most scholars no longer see a radical break such as Bloch did between the Carolingian aristoc-

[5] Georges Duby, *La société au xie et xiie siècles dans la région maconnaise*, 2nd ed. (Paris, 1971), and "Lignage, noblesse et chevalerie au xiie siècle dans la région maconnaise: Une révision," *Annales: Economies, sociétés, civilisations* 27 (1972), 803–823.

[6] Bloch, *Feudal Society,* II, 289, 292.

[7] Ibid., 283.

[8] The most important of these are discussed in Philippe Contamine's very useful "Introduction" in the volume he edited, *La noblesse au Moyen-Age, xie-xve siècles: Essais à la mémoire de Robert Boutrouche* (Paris, 1976).

[9] Cf. Constant, *Nobles et paysans*, and Wood, *Nobility of Bayeux*.

racy and the aristocracy of the "first feudal age."[10] In testing—particularly through the study of genealogical literature—whether Bloch was right in not finding a traditional *noblesse* in the early feudal period, scholars have found some signs of hereditary feeling at the top levels; but as R. Fossier summed up for Picardie, "In truth, there was no noble class [in the eleventh century] but an 'état' still open to very many."[11]

The relative stability of Western European society from the eleventh century onward made it possible for most of these noble warriors to pass on to their children their privileges and the power of their position regardless of the fighting ability—or any other ability, for that matter—of these children. Recent research has helped broaden and enrich our understanding of this process, also described by Bloch, but the general outline once again appears accurate, at least for France.[12] The nobility as a whole became more and more an hereditary group and differences between the more powerful lords, who were usually of territorial importance, and the less important ones, whose main function was to fight, tended to become blurred. The terms *noblesse* and *gentilshommes* came

---

[10]Contamine, "Introduction," pp. 19–20; and, for a recent example arguing for some continuity from Carolingian times and a good deal of mobility and rejuvenation, see Constance B. Bouchard, "The Origins of the French Nobility: A Reassessment," *American Historical Review* 86 (1981), 501–532.

[11]R. Fossier, *La terre et les hommes en Picardie jusqu'à la fin du xiiiͤ siècle* (Paris and Louvain, 1968), II, 537, as quoted in Contamine, "Introduction," p. 22. See also, Contamine, "Introduction," pp. 20–21, and the articles concerning the nobility by Georges Duby brought together in *Hommes et structures du Moyen-Age: Recueil d'articles* (Paris and The Hague, 1973). For instance, in his article entitled "Situation de la noblesse en France au début du xiiiͤ siècle," Duby makes the following observation (p. 352): "At the center of aristocratic structures, and at the center of the idea of nobility, remains, in the twelfth century still as in the eleventh century, the glorious and striking and eminent and *ennobling* [emphasis mine] value which is knighthood [la chevalerie]." Duby also sets the theoretical background in *The Three Orders, Feudal Society Imagined*, trans. Arthur Goldhammer (Chicago and London, 1980).

[12]Contamine, "Introduction," pp. 22–31.

to be used interchangeably to designate this group, and by the early fourteenth century it is even possible to estimate their numbers and their percentage of the total population.[13] By this time, then, the *noblesse* as a social group, in large part legally defined as hereditary, existed. Judging from sixteenth-century sources, however, it seems that most people had still not stopped *believing* that nobility was essentially a function.

The problem from the early fourteenth century on becomes one of determining the actual military function of this now relatively well-defined social group. Thanks to Contamine's thesis[14] we know a good deal about this question. Nobles continued to be the main military power, if under changed conditions, during the fourteenth and fifteenth centuries. The relation between the nobility and the central government changed as the monarchy laid the basis for its new standing army by introducing mercenaries in place of purely feudal armies, but the role of the nobility continued to be essential. Military power shifted to the king, but that military power was still exemplified by the nobles. Nobles continued to be those who did the main fighting in the new army. Nobility and fighting for the king came to be connected in people's minds. To build from Contamine, it seems that by the end of the fifteenth century, *noblesse* simply meant much more fighting for the king, in his army, than simply fighting for oneself or for one's immediate lord. At the same time, the movement toward more precise legal definition of the nobility seems to have continued during this period.[15]

The fourteenth and fifteenth centuries were also the great

---

[13] Ibid., p. 31. Between 1 and 2 percent of the total population, or between 40,000 and 50,000 families for the years 1300–1340.

[14] Contamine, *Guerre, état, et société.*

[15] Cf., along with Contamine, Jean Dravasa, " 'Vivre noblement'—Recherches sur la dérogeance de noblesse du xive au xvie siècle," *Revue juridique et économique du sud-ouest* 16 (1965), 135–193, and Jan Rogozinski, *Power, Caste and Law: Social Conflict in Fourteenth-Century Montpellier* (Cambridge, Mass., 1982).

age of French chivalry.[16] During this period, in which nobles continued to be the main military force in the country,
the early feudal concepts and justifications for nobility and
the military predominance which went with it were changed
and added to and built upon. The underlying assumptions
concerning nobility as a function served (in a process about
which we still have a lot to learn) as a foundation for the
elaborate creations of chivalric codes and honors. Thus the
emphasis upon the virtue and the virtuous obligations and
duties of the nobles were worked out, developed, and emphasized. Nobility became not just the profession of fighting
but, as it was to be in the sixteenth century, the profession
of the virtuous. We find that to be the case already with Olivier de La Marche in 1436, if without quite as much emphasis as a century later.[17] The twentieth century's most original
and undoubtedly most distinguished student of chivalry
understood it well when he wrote, "The ideal of chivalry
implied, after all, two ideas . . . namely that true nobility is
based on virtue and that all men are equal."[18]

By the early sixteenth century nobility had, on the one
hand, become a fairly well legally defined social group that
was relatively hereditary, and nobles were still essentially the

[16] Sidney Painter shows the significance of these centuries well, for instance, in his *French Chivalry, Chivalric Ideas and Practices in Mediaeval France*
(Baltimore, 1940), and they are, of course, the main focus in Huizinga's
Waning of the Middle Ages. See also Maurice Keen, *Chivalry* (New Haven
and London, 1984), for some perceptive insights and some useful additions
and elaborations to these older studies.

[17] Cf. the assumptions of virtue underlying nobility expressed in La Marche's
discussion of *gentillesse* and *noblesse* in Olivier de La Marche, *Traités du duel
judiciaire: Relations de pas d'armes et tournois*, 1st ed. 1436, ed. Bernard Prost
(Paris, 1872), pp. 45–46. See also Charity Cannon Willard, "The Concept
of True Nobility at the Burgundian Court," *Studies in the Renaissance* 14 (1967),
33–48. Willard has found that the belief in nobility as virtue existed in the
late Burgundian Court, although I think she may be mistaken in her view
that the main impulse for that belief came from nonnobles below rather than
from the noble courtiers themselves.

[18] Huizinga, *Waning of the Middle Ages*, p. 53. See also Keen, *Chivalry*, especially pp. 156–161.

main fighting force, although that reality was beginning to change. On the other hand, the sources presented in the previous chapter show that people still *saw* nobility as a profession or function, as they apparently had in the eleventh and twelfth centuries. In the meantime, a much greater emphasis upon virtue had been added to that conception during the great period of chivalry.

By the early sixteenth century, the cliché that nobility equals virtue had become standard, especially in noble and pronoble discussions of nobility. Two treatises on the nobility, published in Paris in 1535 and attributed to the Lyonnais physician and writer on occult subjects, Symphorien Champier,[19] show this well. Champier, who apparently was the son of a notary and apothecary, claimed to have received the order of chivalry on the field of Marignano;[20] he also wrote a book on Bayard[21] and knew the military and knightly world well. He was hardly original or perceptive, but the opinions he expressed and his general attitudes do appear to be typical of the time.[22] He believed that the nobility was a fighting class, and *oeuvres chevalereuses* were the means for acquiring *noblesse* and were the way that the ancestors of the present nobles had gained it.[23] At the same time, he uses virtue and nobility almost interchangeably. "Nobility comes from vir-

[19] Symphorien Champier, *Le fondement et origine des tiltres de noblesse . . .* (Paris, 1535), and *Petit dialogue de noblesse . . .* (Paris, 1535). P. Allut, in *Etude biographique et bibliographique sur Symphorien Champier* (Lyon, 1859), p. 59, lists only the *Petit dialogue* as being by Champier, but the later *Catalogue* of the Bibliothèque Nationale lists him as the author of both.

[20] Brian P. Copenhaver, *Symphorien Champier and the Reception of the Occultist Tradition in Renaissance France* (New York, 1978), pp. 45, 59–60.

[21] Symphorien Champier, *Les gestes, ensemble la vie du preulx chevalier Bayard* (Paris, 1525).

[22] Cf. Copenhaver, *Symphorien Champier*, especially p. 96, where he writes: "As 'spokesman of his age,' moreover, he [Champier] is worth more than a glance simply because he has left us a great heap of unoriginal material. He was a successful writer, if only briefly, and usually he wrote what he thought would safely bring him success."

[23] Champier, *Le fondement*, pp. 1–3.

tue [Noblesse vient de vertu]" is a common expression.[24] But if nobility comes from virtue and *oeuvres chevalereuses*, then the implications would be that if one is not virtuous, he should lose his nobility; Champier, in fact, repeats the idea often:

Those *gentilshommes* who at present hold a seigniory, or a fief without restrictions, first received it through the valor and bravery of their forefathers. The greater lords [les supérieurs] had had such lands given to them [bailler] on condition that their successors attempt to resemble their ancestors, and that they not profit too much from the administering of justice nor fail in their duty of defending their country through threat of losing their preeminence and being considered nonnoble persons [viles personnes].[25]

Although Champier argues for *vertu* as the basis of nobility and implies that one would lose his nobility if he were not virtuous, he is still essentially pronoble. He is, for instance, against the old argument, drawn from the story of Adam and Eve, which would negate the nobility by the implication that originally all people were noble.

Some people would sometimes say, in the words of current proverbs, that all of us are nobles born of Adam and Eve, which is a stupid and crazy opinion. For the criminal and the vicious who are descendants of Adam have neither the lineage nor the rank of the virtuous, and if they should have them, they lose them when they do not conform to

---

[24] Ibid., p. 3; see also p. 14 ("de vertu vient noblesse"). In the *Petit dialogue* (p. 6) he writes: "And if anyone asks from where nobility comes originally, my answer is that nobility of ancestors comes first of all from moral and virtuous actions [des meurs et des vertuz]."

[25] Champier, *Le fondement*, pp. 31v–32. Wartburg's *Französisches etymologisches Wörterbuch* does give one of the meanings of *vil* as "nonnoble." See also p. 14 in the *Petit dialogue*: "Nobility is a quality that can be taken away from a person . . . and can be reinstituted, because a noble by his vice can lose his nobility [car celluy qui est noble, pour son vice peut laisser à estre noble]." See also *Le fondement*, p. 14.

the behavior of their forefathers who acquired the prerogatives of nobility by valorous deeds.[26]

This pronoble attitude is also shown in the *Petit dialogue*, where he defends the view that old nobles should be given more respect than recently made ones.[27]

Champier is not explicit, but *armes*, and courage in using them, seem to be the best way of defining what he means by *vertu*. These are the main ways of gaining entrance into the nobility, or of being ennobled. Ennoblement comes about when ". . . the son of a serf or *taillable* who performs a chivalrous deed on the field, so that he deserves to be exempted from *subsides* and to be raised in person to noble rank, becomes in this case a nobleman and his descendants, as well, forever."[28] In this sense, then, attitudes toward ennoblement reflected the basic underlying assumptions concerning virtue. Essentially everyone, noble and nonnoble alike, accepted ennoblement in theory when it was for truly "virtuous" deeds, which were, of course, supposed to be on the battlefield.

Noblesse for Pierre de La Vacherie around 1510 is also a question of virtue, of heart and of courage, and of defense of the weak. "Nobility derives in first instance from those swearing and promising that in them there exists the force, the loyalty, and the strength, the magnanimous heart that from its height sustains the weak and the strong, and the honor that can never be reproached. Men are not ennobled by riches but by the virtues that are in them."[29] He is thus

---

[26] Champier, *Le fondement*, p. 2.

[27] Champier, *Petit dialogue*, p. 15.

[28] Champier, *Le fondement*, pp. 3–4. It is interesting that he associates a *taillable*, or someone who pays the *taille*, as the equivalent of nonnoble. On these *marques de noblesse*, see chap. 7.

[29] Pierre de La Vacherie, "Le gouvernement des trois estatz du temps qui court," in Anatole de Montaiglon and James de Rothschild, eds., *Recueil de poésies françaises des xve et xvie siècles: Morales, facétieuses, historiques* (Paris, 1877), XII, 81–82. Miriam Chrisman pointed out this passage to me. The last sen-

against ennoblement by money, but as with Champier accepts it for *vertu*. The famous anonymous history of Bayard of 1527 reflects similar attitudes as well.[30] In the 1560s, at the outset of the Religious Wars, what we can now call the "feudal-military" view continued to be prevalent with apparently little or no questioning of it. For Pierre de La Place, a nonnoble, writing in 1561 about vocations in general, virtue, and specifically military virtue, is the basis of the noble vocation. He, too, suggests that descendants of the original nobles should remain virtuous in order to keep their privileges.[31] Coming from a nonnoble this could imply an attack on nobles, but it would be difficult to see it as such, since his assumptions are really no different from those found in noble and pronoble writers. We find this view again in 1567 in an anonymous but very strongly pronoble noble writer, who this time, however, is beginning to reflect some of the concerns of the nobles about their problems and difficulties, concerns that were to become very prevalent in the later decades of the sixteenth century. His view of the nobility is the classic one, however:

. . . to fight to maintain the honor of God and a peaceful kingdom, to spread more widely the King's authority against his enemies, and on such occasions not to be afraid of cold nor heat, but to offer one's life courageously, those are the proper qualities of virtue. And that is how Nobility originated and why it is worthy of its privileges [. . . cela est propre à la vertu. Et de là prend la Noblesse sa naissance, et la dignité de ses privilèges].[32]

---

tence reads: "Richesse n'anoblist point l'homme, Mais les vertus qui sont en luy."

[30] Cf. *Tres-joyeuse, plaisante et récréative histoire* . . . in *Nouvelle collection des mémoires pour servir à l'histoire de France*, eds. Michaud et Poujoulat (Paris, 1837), IV, 479–607.

[31] Pierre de La Place, *Traité de la vocation* . . . (Paris, 1561), p. 59v.

[32] *Lettre missive d'un gentilhomme* . . . (n.p., 1567), p. 3.

His specific definition is again virtue, for "under the name of Nobility are designated solely those who feel bound by their dignity to apply their efforts to whatever pertains to *vertu.*"[33] His answer for the troubles of the nobility is that virtue and merit should once again be restored as its basis. The king should reestablish "in his kingdom a government under which upright and virtuous men would be recompensed according to their merits."[34]

NOBLES, then, argued for virtue and merit as the basis of nobility and the grounds for advancement in the first two-thirds of the sixteenth century. They could hold such a view—one that implied loss of their status if they were not virtuous—in part at least because they did not feel themselves to be particularly threatened. Robert Muchembled's analysis of 250 letters written by members of a minor noble family in Artois between 1548 and 1596, for instance, has shown these nobles to be singularly unconcerned with their past, with their race, with their social group, or with their need to defend it.[35] *Sang* and birth are almost never mentioned. The focus seems to be almost entirely on the day-to-day life of the present,[36] as it is in the well-known journal of the Sire de Gouberville, which reflects a similar lack of concern with the past or with race or birth. Gouberville does not seem to feel his status of noble-landlord to be challenged or in need of defense, ex-

[33] Ibid., pp. 2–3.
[34] Ibid., p. 16: "en son Royaume un gouvernement sous lequel les hommes de bien et vertueux soyent honorés et récompensez selon leurs mérites."
[35] Cf. Robert Muchembled, "Famille, amour et mariage: Mentalités et comportements des nobles artésiens à l'époque de Philippe II," *Revue d'histoire moderne et contemporaine* 22 (1975), 233–261, and "Un monde mental clos: étude sémantique et historique du vocabulaire religieux d'un noble artésien à l'époque de Philippe II," *Tijdschrift voor Geschiedenis* 88 (1975), 169–189.
[36] For instance, Muchembled, "Famille, amour et mariage" (p. 236): "This vocabulary leaves little room for the past and focuses very strongly on the present lived by the author and his social group."

cept, to be sure, from overzealous royal officers verifying his right to the privileges of nobility.[37] The general impression one has of Jean-Marie Constant's nobles in the Beauce during the sixteenth century is also one of comfortableness and relative lack of concern for any possible outside threats to their status.[38]

The literature and memoirs of the early and mid-sixteenth centuries also seem to exhibit relatively little need among the nobles to separate themselves from those below them, or to define themselves and their status in relation to those below them. Rabelais' characters, for instance, from a social point of view, are thoroughly mixed and, along with the apparent unconcern with social distinctions, there is almost no attempt made to distinguish or define who is and who is not noble. Marguerite of Navarre in the *Heptaméron* does indeed talk of knights and servants, but she is interested in other questions for the most part and not in relations between one social group and another. The social order is a given in which to fit the love stories she wishes to tell, and there is no sense at all that the upper classes were being attacked or in need of defense. In the *Mémoires* of Claude Haton[39] and the *Commentaires* of Monluc,[40] nobles and nonnobles mix comfortably, without the former seeming to feel any need to set themselves off or define themselves as being different or separate. Claude Paradin, in his book on heraldry in 1557, makes no mention of the separation of the nobility at all;[41] and Henry de Sainct-Didier, in his book on the use of the sword, seems singularly unconcerned with the whole question of nobility,

---

[37] Cf. *Le journal du Sire de Gouberville* and, most recently on Gouberville, Madeleine Foisil, *Le Sire de Gouberville: Un gentilhomme normand au xvie siècle* (Paris, 1981), and the interesting pages (103–119) of Huppert in *Bourgeois Gentilshommes*, who argues that Gouberville is not really noble.

[38] Cf. Constant, *Nobles et paysans*.

[39] Claude Haton, *Mémoires* in *Collection des documents inédits sur l'histoire de France* (Paris, 1857), and, for example, his discussion on p. 21.

[40] Monluc, *Commentaires*, especially vol. I.

[41] Claude Paradin, *Les devises héroïques* (Antwerp, 1567), 1st ed. published in Lyon in 1557.

even though the wearing and the use of the sword were theoretically limited to nobles alone.[42] This is in clear contrast to later works on similar subjects, in which the noble question becomes very important.

For the most part, then, nobles in the first two-thirds of the sixteenth century seemed sure enough of themselves and their *raison d'être* and right to exist not to have to feel the need to differentiate themselves from others, nor to feel the need to change an unrealistic and potentially dangerous view that saw nobility as virtue. People—nobles and others—still believed in the nobles' military function and thus their indispensability to the society; in the relative stability of the early sixteenth century, this belief was barely questioned.

Economically, the nobles as a group—or more precisely, the landholding seigneurs—were not really threatened in this period, nor for that matter—despite vicissitudes and movements up and down in terms of *rente* income and relations with other groups like the peasants and entrepreneurial *fermiers*—during the whole period of the sixteenth and seventeenth centuries.[43] Some noble estates, to be sure, were being bought up by rich nonnobles or recent *anoblis*,[44] but these

[42]Henry de Sainct-Didier, *Traité contenant les secrets du premier livre sur l'espée seule, mère de toutes armes* (Paris, 1573).

[43]This is an enormous and complex subject, but some excellent work has been done on it, and a relatively clear picture is emerging. A few of the major works used here to arrive at the above conclusion include: Immanuel Wallerstein, "Y a-t-il une crise du xviie siècle," *Annales: Economies, sociétés, civilisations* 34 (1979), 126–143; Fernand Braudel and Ernest Labrousse, eds., *Histoire économique et sociale de la France*, I: *De 1450 à 1660*, 2 vols. (Paris, 1977); Emmanuel Le Roy Ladurie, *Les paysans de Languedoc, xvie–xviie siècles*, 2 vols. (Paris, 1966); and Joseph Goy and Emmanuel Le Roy Ladurie, eds., *Les fluctuations du produit de la dîme: Conjoncture décimale et domaniale de la fin du Moyen-Age au xviiie siècle* (Paris, 1972), especially the synthesis by Le Roy Ladurie and Goy on pp. 334–374.

[44]For some well-known examples of these see: Pierre Goubert, *Beauvais et le Beauvaisis de 1600 à 1730: Contribution à l'histoire sociale de France du xviie siècle* (Paris, 1960), especially pp. 206–222; Jean Jacquart, *La crise rurale en Ile-de-France, 1550–1670* (Paris, 1974); Henri Drouot, *Mayenne et la Bourgogne: Etude sur la Ligue, 1587–1596*, 2 vols. (Paris, 1937), especially pp. 30–

nonnobles almost invariably became nobles themselves and took on noble accoutrements and conceptions. Many nobles did very well for themselves in the sixteenth and seventeenth centuries, as has been emphasized in a good deal of recent research.[45] But, in any case, whether used by old nobles or by new nobles or by those soon to become nobles, the economic system, based upon the exploitation of relatively large landed estates and having a system of seigneurial dues, was never in serious trouble.[46] The lower classes may not have liked this situation, and there may be convincing clues in popular culture that reflect a strong critique of the system, as Natalie Davis has shown; but even these critiques tended to recognize the hopelessness of changing the social structure, in general,[47] and, in the countryside, the seigneurial system in particular.

It is thus important to make a clear distinction between nobility and the concept of nobility on the one hand, and the seigneurial system, on the other. Although often juxtaposed, the two were not the same, since nonnobles as well as nobles could be landholding seigneurs. Even if the seigneurial system, and with it a society of landed elites, was not really

43; and Gaston Roupnel, *La ville et la campagne au xviie siècle: Etude sur les populations du pays dijonnais* (Paris, 1955), especially pp. 234–235. See also the discussion at the end of chap. 4.

[45] For instance, J. Russell Major, "Noble Income, Inflation, and the Wars of Religion in France," *American Historical Review* 86 (1981), 21–48. But see also the discussion on this question and the works cited in chap. 9.

[46] For a useful discussion, for instance, of the seigneury and its use and exploitation in a specific context during this earlier period, which reflects indirectly its underlying stability and its use by different segments of the upper classes, see Jonathan Dewald, *The Formation of a Provincial Nobility: The Magistrates of the Parlement of Rouen, 1499–1610* (Princeton, N.J., 1980), especially pp. 162–220.

[47] Natalie Zemon Davis, *Society and Culture in Early Modern France: Eight Essays* (Stanford, Calif., 1975). In an earlier article Elizabeth S. Teall found a somewhat more harmonious relationship between upper and lower classes, but there was still no question of changing the overall structure. Cf. "The Seigneur of Renaissance France: Advocate or Oppressor," *Journal of Modern History* 37 (1965), 131–150.

threatened or under serious attack during this whole period of the sixteenth and seventeenth centuries, nobility could be—and indeed it was. Much of the threat to nobility, which was to come later in the century, may have been imaginary, but because this threat was believed in, it had importance and would help to bring about a change in conceptions.

Meanwhile, many nobles had simply become landholding seigneurs without any military function. Contamine has shown how the military reforms in the fourteenth and fifteenth centuries, resulting in greater specialization within the army and the relative pacification of the nobles, had created the new royal army with some of the nobles, while pushing many others out of the military and into being only seigneurs.[48] The results of this process of "demilitarizing" a large portion of the nobles is clear in our sixteenth-century data. In the Beauce,[49] for instance, in the *élection* of Bayeux,[50] and certainly elsewhere,[51] a very large percentage of nobles were just landholding seigneurs of various economic importance, and had no military function whatsoever.

On the eve of the Religious Wars, then, we have a nobility—many of whose members may never have seen a battlefield or a military camp—that is relatively well defined legally and whose position and privileges are in reality usually determined by birth; and, as landholding seigneurs, it is a group that profits from an economic system whose foundations will remain basically unchanged. On the other hand, we have a medieval view of nobility, based upon virtue and action, that, although less and less relevant to these new conditions still remained the dominant one in society. Such a view of nobility as virtue was able to continue more or less unquestioned because nobles apparently felt comfortable and

[48] Contamine, *Guerre, état et société.*
[49] Constant, *Nobles et paysans*, pp. 158–185.
[50] Wood, *Nobility of Bayeux*, pp. 81–90.
[51] Recently on this, see Manfred Orlea, *La noblesse aux Etats généraux de 1576 et 1588: Etude politique et sociale* (Paris, 1980), especially pp. 56–59. See also the discussion and the works cited in chap. 1, note 28.

unthreatened, satisfied with their military function, and basically unconcerned about defending their status. At the same time, we know that the late fifteenth and first half of the sixteenth century witnessed the introduction of important new ideas into France—especially from the ancients and the Renaissance Italians—and the growth and development of an indigenous humanist movement. How the feudal-military view could remain basically untouched by all these influences in this period before the Wars, as indeed it seems to have been, is a puzzling question, which is addressed in the following chapter.

3

The Ancient and Renaissance Italian
Traditions and the Continued
Predominance of the Medieval View

The feudal-military view of nobility, with its medieval origins emphasizing the military side of nobility, which was perceived essentially as virtuous action, could hardly have lasted as the more modern world took shape in the fifteenth, sixteenth, and seventeenth centuries. And indeed it would change. Surprisingly, the view did not change, at least in France, in the way one might expect. The transformation was not one of the Renaissance, but one of the late sixteenth and early seventeenth centuries, forced along essentially not by the introduction of texts or ideas from outside, but by the pressure of internal social and political events and changes. This is one of the central assumptions of this work. In this chapter I will discuss how French people, almost entirely without exception, could continue, right through the first two-thirds of the century, to believe and accept the feudal-military view and its clichés when so many works from outside of France presenting a basically different view were available to them. This story also offers further evidence for another one of the basic and novel assumptions of this work—that the feudal-military view was not a minority view but was accepted by essentially all the people of the time. In addition, it fills an extremely interesting and important—if complex—chapter in the intellectual history of France during this period.

Another, older view of nobility, basically different from the feudal-military one, had originated and developed among the ancients and was perpetuated among the Italians of the Renaissance; it is a view that is closer to our modern-day conceptions of nobility, that is, that nobility is determined by heredity. This assumption forms the basis for the familiar debate about whether such nobles are really more virtuous than and superior to others in society, or whether, in fact, the "virtuous" nonnoble is the superior one, as the nonnobles would tend to argue. In this framework, virtue and nobility are separate qualities and separate phenomena.

The actual role of this traditional view in sixteenth-century France is not easy to determine. At times it seems to have become grafted onto the feudal-military view. The writings on nobility of the first two-thirds of the century contain many references to the ancients. Most but not all of the ancients emphasized that nobility should be based upon virtue alone, and such an opinion fit well with the sixteenth-century mentality: they could understand, or at least agree with, that much. But nobles and especially nonnobles did not carry on the debate between virtue and birth in the traditional sense, because their reality and their frame of reference were simply too different. However, all did assume and accept the importance of birth in individual family terms, in the sense that being born into a "good" and "virtuous" family with a long and distinguished lineage was considered better than being born into one that had none; one's chances of being virtuous and successful, while not assured, were much enhanced by this good fortune. But the overriding emphasis upon nobility as action overshadowed the idea of nobility as a collective social group determined by birth—an idea and assumption that can indeed be found in many of the foreign works available in France in the period—and the latter simply does not seem to have been part of the *Weltanschauung* of the time. Thus no one could yet argue for or defend nobility as a collective social group justified by birth since the nobles continued to adhere to the feudal-military view.

An apparent result of this dominance of the feudal-military view was that the question of nobility in the first two-thirds of the century had little social significance or relevance to most people. Except in a few instances, it did not form the basis of any group's social program, though the potential was there, to be found in the ancient sources available to sixteenth-century writers, wherein real social debate was often expressed. But the debate did not speak to the people of the time, and they tended to ignore it. Because the question of nobility had not yet become an important one, the relatively small amount of writing on the subject tended to accept the old clichés, and to repeat the views of others without reflection or without applying them to reality; the writing thus is often vague, abstract, inconsistent, or unperceptive. On this subject, people did not question contradictions, nor did they push their thought to its logical extremes as they did in other matters, such as religion, that were much more important to them.

The story of the origins of the traditional view among the ancients is an interesting one, but unfortunately it is not well known yet. It is clear, however, that the views, discussions, and debates concerning nobility, virtue, and birth already existed in inchoate form among the Greeks. Aristotle in the *Politics*, for instance, while he does not attack the problem directly, does reveal opinions indirectly that show a developed concept of nobility. He accepts noble birth as a factor that must be considered, while he thinks of virtue as a quality that may or may not accompany nobility. To Aristotle, the two basic forms of government or constitutions can be summed up in the rule of the few and the rule of the many; and even the former, which includes aristocracy as well as oligarchy, is based upon more than just birth. Virtue and ability form the basis of an aristocracy, property is the foundation of oligarchy, and "freedom" determines democracy.[1] There are thus these three grounds "for claiming equal rights

---

[1] Aristotle, *The Politics*, trans. T. A. Sinclair (Baltimore, 1962), p. 167: "Virtue is the guiding principle of aristocracy, as wealth of oligarchy, freedom of democracy."

in a constitution—'I am a free man,' 'I am a man of property,' and 'I have character and ability.' . . . A fourth claim, that is based upon noble birth, really arises out of the two last of those three—property and virtue. For noble birth is wealth plus virtue going back to one's forebears."[2]

On the one hand, then, Aristotle defines noble birth as wealth plus virtue; on the other hand, he accepts birth as a definite factor, indeed as the basis of nobility: "Nobles regard themselves as well born not only among their own people but everywhere, but to non-Greeks they allow nobility of birth to be valid only in barbarian lands."[3] And virtue and birth are two separate qualities: "The number of people in whom noble birth and virtue is found is very small, but other marks of inequality are present in a larger number, so that while you could not find anywhere a hundred men of good birth and high standards, you could in many places find that number of rich."[4]

Aristotle thus separates virtue and birth, or virtue and nobility—something most Frenchmen did not do consistently until the first half of the seventeenth century; he offers a sense of realism and acceptance of realities that also did not become prevalent until the seventeenth century in France. But there is little suggestion in Aristotle of a debate between virtue and birth, which gives the impression that the question did not have a particularly strong social relevance in his time. The argument for virtue over birth, however, appears in remarkably modern form—and with a good deal of vehemence—in the time of the late Roman Republic in the speech that Marius gives before the people, attacking the Senate, in Sallust's *Jugurthine War*. Marius, the "new" man, the commoner, contrasts his ability and virtue against the nobles who have only their lineage to fall back upon.

You have chosen me to conduct the war against Jugurtha, and this has greatly annoyed the nobility. Now consider

[2]Ibid.
[3]Ibid., p. 36.
[4]Ibid., p. 191.

whether it would be better to alter your decision—I mean, to appoint for this or for any similar work some member of that coterie of noblemen, a man with a long pedigree and a houseful of family portraits, but without a single campaign to his credit, who, faced with a serious task which he does not know the first thing about, will get excited and run about trying to find some commoner to instruct him in his duty. . . . Compare me, the "new" man, with these high and mighty ones. . . . They scorn my lack of illustrious ancestors, I scorn their indolent habits. . . . For my part, I believe that all men are partakers of one and the same nature, and that manly virtue is the only true nobility.[5]

Here we see the sense of outrage of the commoner, being looked down upon and scorned by the "useless" nobleman who has only his birth to fall back upon. These are familiar sentiments that permeated France from the seventeenth century on and became widespread in the nineteenth and twentieth centuries. It does not seem likely, however, that they would have had much relevance to the sixteenth-century French—least of all in the case of the military allusion because of the close relationship between military and nobility. "If these men think they have a right to look down on me," continues Marius,

they ought equally to look down on their own ancestors, who, like me, had no nobility but what they earned by their merits. . . . When they address you in the Senate they spend most of the time in praising their ancestors, because they fondly imagine that by dwelling on their brave exploits they enhance their own glory. . . . Yet surely it is better to have ennobled oneself than to have disgraced a nobility that one has inherited.[6]

Virtue, meanwhile, was a quality separate from nobility:

[5] Sallust, *The Jugurthine War*, trans. S. A. Hardford (Baltimore, 1963), pp. 117–118.
[6] Ibid., pp. 118–119.

Relying on that renown to shed a reflected glory on them, these noblemen, who are so different in character from those ancestors, despise us who emulate their virtues, and expect to receive all posts of honour at your hands, not because they deserve them, but as if they had a peculiar right to them. These proud men make a very big mistake. Their ancestors left them all they could—riches, portrait busts, and their own glorious memory. Virtue, they have not bequeathed to them, nor could they; for it is the only thing that no man can give to another or receive from another.[7]

Virtue thus cannot be passed on by birth. And with this separation of virtue and birth goes the contrast of cultured noble and uncultured nonnoble, again so prevalent in the nineteenth and twentieth centuries:

They call me vulgar and unpolished, because I do not know how to put on an elegant diner and do not have actors at my table or keep a cook who has cost me more than my farm overseer. All this, my fellow citizens, I am proud to admit. . . . Well, then, let them continue to do what pleases them—the lovemaking and drinking that they set such store by; let them spend their old age as they spent their youth, in the pleasures of the table, the slaves of glutony and lust. Let them leave the sweat, the dust, and the rest of it to us, to whom such things are better than a feast. But no: after covering themselves with infamy these rakes contrive to steal the rewards that are the due of honest men. Thus, in defiance of all justice, these foul vices of luxury and sloth are no hindrance to them in their careers; it is the innocent state that suffers ruin.[8]

Clearly the debate between virtue and birth had social relevance in the declining days of the Republic.

Apparently it had less relevance from the end of the Republic onward, probably because, at least under the early

[7] Ibid., p. 120.
[8] Ibid., pp. 120–121.

Empire, aristocratic senators, relying on their heritage, posed less of a threat to the rise of the "new men" than they had before. That nobility should be based upon virtue became more or less of an accepted cliché. Seneca, for instance, in the middle of the first century A.D., talks of virtue in general and of the virtuous qualities that the wise man must have; then he says, almost as if in passing, that virtue is not dependent upon birth.[9] But Seneca's writings exhibit little or no sense of attack upon the nobility. Not until the first third of the second century do we have what is probably the best known and most influential attack on nobility, Juvenal's famous *Eighth Satire*. The base, decadent, and useless nobles are ridiculed in a devastating manner, and Juvenal sounds like Sallust when he writes that "Virtue alone is proof of nobility," and "True nobility lies in more than a name and a title."[10] Even if the *Eighth Satire*, put in the context of Juvenal's other satires and his general pessimism, is read more as part of a general attack on stupid institutions than as a specific social attack on nobility, it would still not necessarily have prevented whose who read him later from seeing it as the latter. In other words, regardless of his real purpose, Juvenal supplies some very useful tools and rhetoric for attacking nobility.

With Aristotle's acceptance of nobility of birth as a given in society and his separation of virtue and birth; with Marius's attack on the nobility in the name of the "new man"; with Seneca's and the Stoics' and most other Roman writers' emphasis upon virtue; and with Juvenal's bitter attack on corrupt and useless nobles, the foundation of what we can call the "traditional view"—nobility determined by birth, with virtue a separate quality—had been laid and would be avail-

[9] For instance, in the forty-fourth letter to Lucilius; see Seneca, *Ad Lucilium Epistulae Morales*, trans. Richard M. Gummere, 3 vols. (Cambridge, Mass., 1961), I, 289.

[10] Juvenal, "Eighth Satire," in *The Satires of Juvenal*, trans. Rolfe Humpries (Bloomington, Ind., 1968), pp. 101–111. The sections cited are from p. 102.

able to anyone in the Renaissance period who had the requisite linguistic knowledge and other tools. In sixteenth-century France these and similar texts were available and seem to have been read at least to some extent.

These ancient texts were also being read in Renaissance Italy, another area that influenced sixteenth-century France, and the subject of nobility was often discussed there. Unfortunately, a systematic history of the concept of nobility in Italy in the fourteenth, fifteenth, and sixteenth centuries—and earlier—has not yet been written,[11] but once it is, it should reveal some very interesting insights. It might well show that the traditional view of the ancients, which was replaced by the quite different feudal-military view in France in the tenth and eleventh centuries (see chapter 2) actually continued more or less unscathed in Italy, at least in the northern and central parts. In any case, the important thing is that the traditional view is prevalent in the literature of the time in Italy, unlike the case in France.

For instance, we find the traditional view in Boccaccio in the fourteenth century (but not in his French contemporary Froissart). It forms the basis for a number of Boccaccio's stories, as, for example, in the story of the daughter of Prince Tancred of Salerno and her lover, who was not noble. The argument is made that the lover is really more noble than the nobles because of his virtue, but in reality little doubt is left that nobility is determined by birth.[12] In that sense the assumptions concerning birth and virtue resemble those in Aristotle and those in the Romans of the first and second centuries A.D., but they have no particular polemical side. The story of the Baronci, the supposedly most ancient family in

---

[11] But for some interesting suggestions, see Paul Oskar Kristeller, *Renaissance Thought II: Papers on Humanism and the Arts* (New York, Evanston, London, 1965), especially pp. 46–49; see also Quentin Skinner, *The Foundations of Modern Political Thought*, vol. I, *The Renaissance*, vol. II, *The Age of Reformation* (New York, 1978), especially I, 81–82.

[12] Giovanni Boccaccio, *Il Decameron*, ed. Giuseppe Petronio, 2 vols. (Turin, 1950), I, 395–404 (Fourth Day, First Story).

Florence, also reflects similar attitudes and assumptions,[13] which seem to take nobility for granted and suggest that the question had relatively little social significance in the period.

In the late fourteenth and early fifteenth centuries, however, the remaining city republics in Italy, especially Florence, became more politically and socially aware.[14] We might expect that the question of nobility had a greater social significance, and indeed it did. In Boccaccio, for instance, the discussion simply forms the groundwork for some interesting and entertaining stories, while in Poggio Bracciolini's *De Nobilitate* of 1440, the debate has once again taken on a polemical tone. Poggio repeats essentially the standard arguments of the ancients,[15] and though he presents both sides, he makes his intentions quite clear: nobility of birth may exist, and seemingly has a right to exist, but real virtue does not necessarily lie there, but is a quality that is in itself more "noble" than nobility.[16] Here he quite obviously reflects the attitudes of the dominant nonnoble patriciate in Florence, in a society in which nobility of birth, if it existed, seems to have had relatively little if any significance in determining and defining the society's elites.[17]

Meanwhile, with the decline of the Florentine republic in the second half of the fifteenth century, the troubles brought

[13]Ibid., II, 22–24 (Sixth Day, Sixth Story).

[14]Cf., for instance, among a large literature, Hans Baron, *The Crisis of the Early Italian Renaissance*, 2nd ed. (Princeton, N.J., 1966), and Gene A. Brucker, *Renaissance Florence* (New York, 1969). Alfred von Martin, in his *Sociology of the Renaissance*, trans. W. L. Luetkens (London, 1944), 1st German ed. 1932, has some penetrating general comments on the subject, which were made, to be sure, without benefit of the rich research carried out on Florence over the past thirty years, but which still suggest some of the conclusions of that research.

[15]For instance, Poggio Bracciolini, *De Nobilitate* in *Opera* (Basel, 1538), pp. 73–74.

[16]For example, ibid., p. 73.

[17]Cf. Brucker, *Renaissance Florence*, and also, for instance, Lauro Martines, *The Social World of the Florentine Humanists* (Princeton, N.J., 1963). The story begins at one level, as is well known, as far back as 1293 when powerful magnate families were excluded from the city's highest offices.

on by the French invasions of the end of the century, and the advent of the more solidly aristocratic society that had essentially lost control of its destiny,[18] the discussion of the nature of nobility seems once again to have taken on less social significance. The question is debated in an urbane and civilized but abstract way, and as if divorced from reality, early in the sixteenth century in a famous section of Castiglione's *Cortegiano*.[19] Later, when the Italians seem to have almost totally lost control of their social and political destinies, there is almost no concern whatsoever·with the question in such lesser-known courtly treatises as those by Della Casa and Guazzo.[20]

The debate in the *Cortegiano*, then, if seemingly quite without passion or heat, does reflect well the assumptions of what I am calling the "traditional view," and it is also interesting in that it is one of the rare cases in humanist writings where birth seems to win. Count Ludovico da Canossa, for instance, states that it is better to be born noble because

. . . noble birth is like a bright lamp that makes manifest and visible deeds both good and bad, kindling and spurring on to virtue as much for fear of dishonor as for hope of praise. And since this luster of nobility does not shine forth in the deeds of the lowly born, they lack that spur, as well as the fear of dishonor, nor do they think themselves obliged to go beyond what was done by their forebears; whereas to the wellborn it seems a reproach not to attain at least to the mark set them by their ancestors.[21]

The other side is argued by Gaspar Pallavicino, who indicates at the beginning that he takes this side simply because he feels it will make the discussion more interesting:

[18] Cf. Brucker, *Renaissance Florence*.

[19] Baldesar Castiglione, *Il Cortegiano*, ed. Vittorio Cian, 3rd ed. (Florence, 1929), pp. 39–43.

[20] Cf. Giovanni Della Casa, *Galateo, Ovvero de' costumi*, ed. P. Pancrazi (Florence, 1947), and Stefano Guazzo, *Le civil conversatione* (Venice, 1551).

[21] Castiglione, *Il Cortegiano*, p. 39. The English translations are by Charles S. Singleton in Baldesar Castiglione, *The Book of the Courtier* (Garden City, N.Y., 1959).

So that our game may have the form prescribed and that we may not appear to esteem little that privilege of opposing which has been allowed us, I say that to me this nobility of birth does not seem so essential. And if I thought I was uttering anything not already known to us all, I would adduce many instances of persons born of the noblest blood who have been ridden by vices; and, on the contrary, many persons of humble birth who, through their virtue, have made their posterity illustrious. . . . Nay, as I said, the greatest gifts of nature are often to be seen in persons of the humblest origin. Hence, since this nobility of birth is not gained either by talents or by force or skill, and is rather due to the merit of one's ancestors than to one's own, I deem it passing strange to hold that if the parents of our courtier be of humble birth, all his good qualities are ruined.[22]

Count Ludovico has the last word, however. He backs up his argument this time with more practical and less theoretical reasons, in particular that noble birth is an advantage, no matter how one feels about it, because public opinion will immediately side with nobility. But what is significant here is not who wins the argument, but the assumptions underlying it—assumptions that are indeed found elsewhere in the book as well.[23] In the *Cortegiano* it is clear that birth—understood as defining collectively a social group—is accepted in a realistic way as the actual determiner of nobility. Virtue is a quality that may or may not go along with nobility: if one favors nobility, one will probably argue that it usually does; if one does not, then one will most likely argue that virtue does not usually lodge itself with nobles. But what is important is that one can be "nonvirtuous" and still remain noble, since nobility is determined in the first instance by birth. Here nobility and virtue are clearly separate, unlike in France

[22] Ibid., pp. 42–43.
[23] As, for instance, in the story of the nonnoble peasant girl who drowned herself because she had been dishonored. See ibid., p. 367.

until late in the sixteenth and early in the seventeenth century (see chapter 6), when, in fact, the *Cortegiano* first actually became popular there as well.

IN a sense there is not just one "traditional view" of nobility and virtue and birth. There are many, as many as the ancient and Renaissance Italian writers I have discussed, all of whom have something different to say on the question. Nevertheless, they all accept similar underlying assumptions concerning nobility and birth, assumptions that are different from those underlying the feudal-military view that sees nobility as action and as something one does. In the previous chapters I presented sources that seemed to indicate that this feudal-military view dominated in France in the sixteenth century. And yet these ancient and Italian Renaissance sources gradually became available to writers in France in the sixteenth century, and are sometimes discussed or cited by them. However, it appears that in most, perhaps even all, cases in the first two-thirds of the century in France, these outside views and assumptions were never fully incorporated into anyone's thinking on the subject. A few writers may have begun by talking about two kinds of nobility, that based upon virtue and that based upon birth; but in the end, as we shall see, they invariably returned to something resembling much more the feudal-military view.

Precise figures on the number of editions and copies of these ancient and Renaissance Italian works available in France are extremely difficult to find. But it is apparent that some copies did exist and were available. In the case of the ancient sources, Latin editions were clearly available throughout the sixteenth century, while translations into French were very rare in the first two-thirds of the century, and a little less rare in the last third. The Bibliothèque Nationale, for instance, has fifty-nine copies in Latin of either Sallust's complete works or of the *Jugurthine War* alone that were published before 1570, and twelve copies that were published between 1570 and 1600; there is only one French edition of 1547, with one in 1577 and two in 1581.[24] For Juvenal the Bibliothèque Nationale has sixty-nine copies of the complete *Satires* in Latin published before 1570, and seven published between 1570 and 1600; there is only one partial edition in French, which includes the *Eighth Satire,* published in 1544, and nothing else appears in French before 1653.[25] It would appear, then, that the non-Latin reading public showed little interest in Sallust and Juvenal before 1570, and a little more afterward, while the interest among the Latin readers was relatively extensive, especially in the first two-thirds of the century.

The one French translation of Sallust's *Jugurthine War,* that of 1547, shows no signs of antinoble feelings, and indeed the translator seems not at all interested in the question of nobility. The work was apparently commissioned by the Connétable Anne de Montmorency, and the translator says that because the Connétable liked it he had decided to have it published.[26] It is unlikely that the Connétable would have commissioned a work that was understood to have dangerous antinoble sentiments.

The author of the French translation of Juvenal's *Eight Satire,* on the other hand, shows himself to be a good deal more interested in the question of nobility. But he presents, in his dedicatory poem, a rather strange amalgam of ideas and as-

[24] B.N., *Catalogue général des livres imprimés,* vol. 161 (Paris, 1941). One of the two 1581 copies is wrongly listed in the *Catalogue* as being published in 1541. It is dated "MDXXXXI" and the other is dated "MDLXXXI," and it became obvious that the "L" had been wrongly replaced by an "X", because the dedication is to the king and it speaks of his return from Poland. This would have to be Henry III after the death of Charles IX in 1574. Also in this dedication, the translator talks of his earlier translation of the *Catiline Conspiracy,* already completed, and that work (included in the same volume at the Bibliothèque Nationale) turns out to be dated 1575. Cf. Salluste, *La Guerre Jugurthine,* trans. Hiérosme de Chomeday (Paris, 15[8]1), B.N., J.13497.

[25] B.N., *Catalogue général des livres imprimés,* vol. 80 (Paris, 1924).

[26] Salluste, *L'histoire de C. Crispe Saluste touchant la coniuration de L. Serge Catelin . . . traduites de latin en françois, par Loys Meigret, Lyonnais* (Paris, 1547), B.N., Rés. J.2770, pp. 3–6.

sumptions that reflects a confusion and lack of clarity on the question, and quite clearly suggests that the discussion of nobility was lacking in any particular social revelance. Oddly enough, the author is a noble[27] and thus could hardly be using Juvenal to attack nobility. He seems to treat the question as one to be debated and judged from different perspectives, somewhat as is done in the *Cortegiano*. He says that yes, of course, we all know that nobility is based upon virtue and courage and good works and good morals ("vertu . . . courage . . . oeuvre très bonne . . . probité des meurs . . . [et] . . . qui de pécher a honte . . . et surmonte"),[28] but if we add to that good parentage then we have an even better nobility. He concludes that, just as a person of inherited nobility cannot be noble without virtue, noble blood can also make a person even more noble, or perhaps really noble. ("Mais des parens le sang noble et subtil, parfaictement rend ung homme gentil, Avecq vertu. Et sans ces deux ensemble [without these two together], Noble parfaict n'est l'homme ce me semble.")[29] He does use the term *sang* here, but what he seems to indicate by it is simply that one should belong to a "good" family and have respectable and virtuous (noble) ancestors in order to be fully noble. The author of this rare sixteenth-century translation of Juvenal's antinoble *Eighth Satire* thus concludes by expressing his relatively pronoble attitude, while still accepting the clichés about virtue and action prevalent in his time. We can assume that he read the work especially carefully because he translated it; yet he still interpreted it in an innocuous and seemingly contradictory way, which suggests that the existence of the relatively few French editions of a potentially dangerous work like the *Eighth Satire* are hardly proof that the question of nobility had so-

[27] He used the title "Escuyer," for instance, which was applied, legally anyway, only to nobles in the sixteenth century.

[28] Juvénal, *Quatre satyres de Juvénal: Translatées de latin en françoys, par Michel d'Amboyse escuyer, seigneur de Chevillon* . . . (Paris, 1544), B.N., Yc. 7223, Dédicace.

[29] Ibid.

cial relevance in the period, or that these sixteenth-century commentators really understood the message of the ancients on the subject of nobility.

Even as late as the 1570s and 1580s (see chapter 4), the ancients do not seem to have been consulted much on the question of nobility, since people turned almost completely to the feudal-military view for answers to their problems and questions concerning nobility. The 1581 edition of Sallust's *Jugurthine War,* for example, was translated by someone who, as he explained in his dedication to Henry III, wanted to publish the work because there were many things to be learned from it (as well as from the *Conspiracy of Catiline,* which he had translated earlier) about the civil wars of their own times. The question of nobility is not mentioned at all except in a note that the translation had been requested by several of the *chevaliers* of the king's order.[30]

As Maurice Magendie has shown, Castiglione's *Cortegiano* also seems to have had relatively little influence in the sixteenth century. It was first translated into French in 1537, but was not read extensively in France, nor used as a model or fully understood until the early seventeenth century,[31] when French views on nobility tended to resemble those found in the *Cortegiano.*

The more numerous Latin editions of the ancients, which were available to substantially fewer people, also do not seem to have been used widely to answer questions on nobility, although Tiraqueau, for instance, who wrote the major work on nobility of the first two-thirds of the century—basically a legal study—makes brief reference to the works we have examined. He cites Aristotle's *Politics* (available in Greek and Latin editions, published in Paris from the early 1540s on but not available in French translation until 1568)[32] for an opin-

---

[30] Salluste, *La guerre jugurthine,* Dédicace.

[31] Maurice Magendie, *La politesse mondaine et les théories de l'honnêteté en France, au xviie siècle, de 1600 à 1660,* 2 vols. (Paris, 1925), I, 305–339.

[32] Werner L. Gundersheimer, *The Life and Works of Louis Le Roy* (Geneva, 1966), pp. 47–56. (The edition of 1568 was Louis Le Roy's.)

ion on how the work of artisans makes them not noble. And he cites Marius's speech in Sallust and Juvenal's *Eighth Satire* together in one paragraph on the question of the relation between *generosus* and *virtus*, and points out that Seneca believed that nobility alone equals virtue.[33] But references to these and other potentially controversial works make up an extremely small percentage of the enormous number of references in this very erudite work. Clearly Tiraqueau's interest lay elsewhere. Other writers who were concerned with nobility (see below and chapter 4), with the exception of Josse Clichtove's few innocuous pages on Juvenal's *Eighth Satire*, refer almost never to the controversial sections of these ancient writers. It appears, then, that if Tiraqueau and his Latin reading contemporaries exhibited enough interest in Sallust and Juvenal to warrant a large number of editions, it was because they were mainly interested in facets of the works of these Roman writers other than their ideas concerning nobility.

DESPITE their relative lack of interest and understanding, some Frenchmen of the first two-thirds of the sixteenth century understood enough to consider nobility of birth as one type of nobility.[34] In doing so, however, they, as did the translator of Juvenal, still continued to accept the dominant clichés of the medieval view, simply adding the ancients' views about virtue to it. The result is often a confusing lack of consistency and an inability to carry ideas on nobility to logical conclusions. Quentin Skinner has found this same disorien-

[33] André Tiraqueau, *De Nobilitate* (Lyon, 1559), 1st ed. 1549, pp. 210, 26, and 54.

[34] Arlette Jouanna has also found some belief in a nobility of birth in approaching the question from the direction of a history of the idea of race (cf. *L'idée de race*, especially pp. 1059–1152). She finds very little emphasis before 1550, however, and as examples of humanists in the first half of the century who accepted the idea of race she uses just Clichtove, who is very ambiguous on the question, as we shall see below, and the Italian Sadoleto (cf. pp. 1105–1122).

tation in the political thought of the humanists on the question of nobility.[35]

Tiraqueau, for instance, lists nobility of birth as a type of nobility; but his overall ideas of nobility, when they can be clarified from the mass of legal opinions he has compiled, reflect a general assumption that nobility is based upon virtue, and that it is, or should be, the prince in the end who determines it.[36] One gets the impression from reading Tiraqueau that it is so obvious to him that nobility is based upon virtue that he does not even need to emphasize the fact.

Bonus de Curtili, an Italian from Brescia, who apparently moved to Lyon where his book on nobility was published in 1528, also recognizes nobility of birth as one type of nobility. He does not share Tiraqueau's idea of the importance of the prince, however, and his work is quite uninspired, though his style is representative of the abstract and literary way that writers approached the question when they consulted and cited the ancients. For instance, he writes:

> Nobility of the soul [and elsewhere he has listed nobility of birth as a type] is nothing else than the quality and elegance which comes from loving, searching after and respecting virtue. On this point Antisthenes wrote that those who to him appeared nobles were those who followed after virtue and attached and submitted themselves to it and those who considered virtue alone as the basis of nobility. And this is where the opinion of the Stoics comes from who would have it that those alone are nobles who are virtuous and wise.[37]

This discussion hardly seems to suggest that the question held a particular social relevance for him, or that his conclusions

---

[35] Cf. Skinner, *Foundations*, I, and especially pp. 255–262, where Thomas More, in his *Utopia*, is treated as an exception to this general rule.

[36] For instance, Tiraqueau, *De Nobilitate*, pp. 63–78, and also p. 44 and p. 56.

[37] Bonus de Curtili, *Tractatus Nobilitatis* (Lyon, 1528), Secunda Pars (48).

were based upon much examination or analysis of the reality around him; reality would have shown far more of a nobility determined by birth than is evident from his book.

Josse Clichtove's treatise on nobility is an example of a different type of work, but in the end it exhibits most of the same traits seen in other writers on the subject. Clichtove's approach is essentially moral and religious. He basically seems to want to make the nobles, whose dominance in society he accepts without question, into better people—more virtuous, more Christian, and more honest—the way a medieval writer might appeal to a powerful prince to be a better prince. But in trying to apply the dominant assumptions of his time about nobility to a society that was in fact quite different, he runs into some understandable problems that result in his lack of consistency and fuzziness of thought. He addresses his work to nobles, talks of nobility of birth and nobility of virtue, seems to imply that he understands that the nobles he is addressing are nobles because of birth, argues strongly that nobility is actually based upon virtue—briefly discussing Juvenal's *Eighth Satire*—and does not face up at all to the question of the person who is noble by birth but has no virtue. In order words, he basically tells the nobles that since everyone knows that nobility is determined by virtue, they should be more virtuous; but he does not attack them.[38]

Other writers of the period, who came to the problem of nobility for different reasons, reflect similar assumptions. Innocent Gentillet, for example, shows a lack of realism and an acceptance of contradictions when he claims that the nobles are responsible for justice in France, when around him the reality was quite different.[39] In one sentence he calls *vertu* the basis of *vraye noblesse*, while in the next sentence he maintains that *noblesse de race* was founded because of virtue; but he does not carry forward the implications of this for *no-*

---

[38] Josse Clichtove, *De Vera Nobilitate Opusculum* (Paris, 1520), 1st ed. 1512.

[39] Innocent Gentillet, *Discours sur les moyens de bien gouverner* . . . (n.p., 1576), p. 633.

bles de race who are not virtuous.[40] Claude de Rubys makes almost exactly the same contradictions in his discussion of virtue and birth, as well as in his demand that all important public offices should be held by nobles.[41] Barthélemy de Chasseneux appears unable to decide just where nobles belong in his general hierarchical scheme and does not seem concerned with trying to work out the problem.[42]

It is clear that the French of the first two-thirds of the sixteenth century simply were not interested enough in the question of nobility to devote much time and serious debate to it.[43] Claude de Seyssel, for instance, who is so original on other questions, devotes only one and one-half pages to the subject of nobility in his famous *Monarchie*. He accepts virtue as its basis but does not emphasize its role especially.[44] The same is true for François Corlieu, who, while clearly assuming that nobles constitute a profession like other groups in society, directly states that because it is so obvious that virtue is the basis of nobility, he will not even bother to discuss the question.[45] And we have already seen the lack of interest in separating and defining the nobility in Claude Paradin's book on heraldry. Paradin accepts the general clichés about

[40] Ibid., pp. 636–637.

[41] Claude de Rubys, *Les privilèges, franchises et immunitez octroyées par les rois très chrestiens . . .* (Lyon, 1573), pp. 69–70. Professor Natalie Davis pointed out this passage to me.

[42] Barthélemy de Chasseneux, *Catalogus Gloriae Mundi . . .* (Geneva, 1617), 1st ed. 1529, and, for instance, p. 308.

[43] A general tendency, in terms of a lack of interest in social questions (as far as social classes are concerned) and social distinctions early in the century that Jouanna has also found. Cf. *L'idée de race*, pp. 1059–60.

[44] Claude de Seyssel, *La monarchie de France et deux autres fragments politiques*, ed. Jacques Poujol (Paris, 1961), 1st ed. 1519. The section on pp. 121–122 is the only one he devotes entirely to the nobility. See pp. 155, 156, and 165 for examples of his seemingly rather automatic acceptance of virtue. On the other hand, his general idea that the upper ranks of society should remain open, specifically to prevent dissatisfaction and possible trouble from those below, is a perceptive and interesting suggestion.

[45] François Corlieu, *Instruction pour tous estats . . .* (Paris, 1559), and see pp. 64–65 for his comment.

virtue, and then goes on to give his description of the coats of arms, without any particular reflection at all on the nature of nobility.[46]

Even Louis Le Roy, so perceptive in many areas,[47] had little to say on the subject, even though he wrote relatively late in the century. Le Roy, not a nobleman, seems to accept noble superiority and dominance in his country without question. He writes that "The king of France is established among persons of ancient nobility and surrounded by princes, counts, barons, and other *gentilshommes*, who have their own subjects and who consider their authority over them as preeminent to that of the king and it would be difficult to take away this authority without their rising in revolt."[48] After declaring that the basis of nobility is *prouesse militaire ou autre vertu* and that its function is to fight (for which historically it received fiefs in return), he goes on to say that gradually some fiefs fell to nonnobles ("such as traders, legal and medical practitioners, and others able to buy them"), that many nobles did not fight, and that the *ban* and *arrière-ban* consequently lost credibility and favor because nonnobles as well as nobles were called.[49] But he stops there, leaving one to puzzle over his contradictions (that is, nobles are nobles because they fight, many nobles do not fight, some nobles do, why should those nobles who do not fight still be nobles).

Le Roy seems to accept nobility the way some people accept the military—as a necessary evil that one must condone for the protection and general good of the state. This is certainly also one of the reasons nonnoble humanists were so willing to accept nobility. Often humanist lawyers would give the impression of attacking nobility in the name of virtue—

[46] Cf. Paradin, *Les devises héroïques*, especially pp. 3–5.

[47] For instance, the assessment by Gundersheimer in *The Life and Works of Louis Le Roy.*

[48] Louis Le Roy, *De la vicissitude ou variété des choses en l'univers* (Paris, 1575), pp. 50–51.

[49] Ibid.

and indeed they did to some extent[50]—but in the end, as, for instance, with Pasquier[51] and Tiraqueau,[52] they simply wanted to emphasize that the legal profession was just as noble, or even more noble, than the military profession.

In this environment of relative lack of concern and interest in the subject, one writer comes close to presenting an actual debate between virtue and birth with social ramifications— Guillaume de La Perrière in his *Miroir politique*. The *Miroir politique* was commissioned by the city fathers of Toulouse in 1539, but was not sent to the publishers until 1553; it was finally published in 1555.[53] La Perrière mixes the feudal-military tradition and the influence of the ancients in an interesting way, and at one point he seems actually to be using the ancients to mount an attack on nobility determined by birth. He argues that virtue is the basis of nobility, and complains about some ancients who feel differently:

. . . but to tell the truth, from a theological point of view, there is no true *Noblesse* but that which proceeds from virtue and good conduct [bonnes meurs]. *Noblesse de race* remains empty and stupid words if not joined to virtue. And one of the great delusions of our time is that some nobles rely solely on their birth and believe that they can be nobles without being virtuous.[54]

[50] See John M. Headley, "Nobles and Magistrates in Franche-Comté, 1508–1518," *The Journal of Medieval and Renaissance Studies* 9 (1979), 49–80.

[51] Cf., for instance, Etienne Pasquier, *Les oeuvres* (Amsterdam, 1723), pp. 229–230.

[52] Cf. Jacques Bréjon, *Un juriconsulte de la Renaissance: A. Tiraqueau* (Paris, 1937).

[53] G. Dexter, "Guillaume de La Perrière," *Bibliothèque d'humanisme et Renaissance* 17 (1955), 70–71.

[54] Guillaume de La Perrière, *Le miroir politique* . . . (Paris, 1567), p. 111. I am indebted to Natalie Davis, who first pointed out this passage to me, a passage that suggests an exception to what I had seen as the general trend of thought in the period. The later part of the original is as follows: "Et l'un des plus grands erreurs que nous voions à présent, est qu'aucuns nobles de

However, when this passage is analyzed in the context of his overall work, it becomes clear that La Perrière did, in fact, share basically the same assumptions about nobility that we have seen in his contemporaries, and the passage is a good deal less threatening than it appears.

Little is known of La Perrière's life, but he apparently was a nonnoble. He had a legal education and training and wrote a good deal of bad poetry; the *Miroir Politique* is his only work of some interest.[55] The work is written in the style of the popular handbooks for princes, emphasizing what one should know and how one should act in order to govern better. The tone is very theological and moral. He writes of the importance of having people with good moral qualities in a well-run state, and derides cruelty, haughtiness, negligence, and the like.[56] Instead, he says, one should act with justice toward one's neighbors and others.[57] "Every Republic falls into ruin," he writes, "if the citizens are not united in friendship."[58] He also has a large section on the "laws" of behavior of the husband toward the wife and the wife toward the husband.[59]

Nobility, meanwhile, plays a very small role in La Perrière's overall work; he devotes only six pages out of a total of over 250 to the subject. He treats the question in two different places, toward the beginning of the work in a general way, and then again toward the end, more specifically, when he discusses groups such as magistrates and priests. In the early part he seems to accept noble dominance without question. He writes:

The decoration of any Republic consists in the nobility, because the normal situation is that the nobles are richer,

---

nostre temps, se confians seulement de leur race pensent estre nobles sans vertu."

[55] Dexter, "Guillaume de La Perrière," especially p. 56.

[56] La Perrière, *Le miroir politique*, especially p. 33.

[57] Ibid., especially pp. 50–70.

[58] Ibid., p. 20v.

[59] Ibid., pp. 87–98v.

of more honest morals and ways of living, and of greater civility and politeness than the lower classes [plébéiens], the artisans and people of low estate; and this is true even more because from their childhood, indeed from the moment they are weaned, they are brought up in and taught the greatest civility, and among honorable people. The normal situation for the people or the masses is that they are badly brought up and neglected in their education, variable, mobile, suspicious, and difficult to lead and (as Virgil and after him Claudien says) always divided, causing dissension, and (to conclude on the imperfections) lacking in all good judgment and civility.[60]

He then goes on to make a rather belabored analogy with milk and butter and cheese, concluding that nobles are on top in society like the cream that rises to the top of the milk, and which produces the best part, the butter; society needs nobles like milk needs cream, for if you remove the cream, the cheese produced from the milk is of very poor quality.[61]

These early statements are vague generalities, and La Pierrière seems more interested in the assumed cleverness of his analogy than in the subject itself. But when he discusses nobility more specifically toward the end of his book, he is even more telling. To begin with, instead of approaching the subject of nobility directly, he treats it under the subject category of *Armes*, that is, nobility is discussed as a profession: "The third thing necessary in any good *République* or *cité* [the first two being religion and thus priests, and justice and thus magistrates] are arms and consequently nobles who have the exercise of these."[62] He then goes on to explain why arms or weapons or the nobility are necessary: to defend the state against exterior enemies, to keep bad citizens in line, to punish criminals, and so on.[63] It is important to note that here

[60] Ibid., pp. 21v–22.
[61] Ibid.
[62] Ibid., p. 110: "La tierce chose nécessaire en toute bonne République et cité, sont les armes, et conséquement les nobles qui ont l'exercice d'icelles."
[63] Ibid., pp. 110–110v.

we have a nonnoble who justifies nobility in terms of its military function: since arms and the military are necessary, nobles are necessary.

As the rest of his discussion on the nobility unfolds, it becomes clear that La Perrière is not attacking the nobles, but rather appealing to them to raise more virtuous and better-educated children, so that they can perform their duties as nobles better and thus create a better state. Still, this is an appeal, not a threat. To make his point more convincing, he delves into the subject of virtue and asks the question, "What makes true nobility?" For answers he turns to the ancients and finds a few, among them Aristotle, who say that nobility is based upon birth.[64] He cites no contemporaries who may have the same opinion. He then goes on to say that even though some ancients may have believed there are several kinds of nobility, theologically and philosophically there is only one true nobility; at this point he makes the reference, cited earlier, about some of the nobles of his own day who seem to think they can be noble without being virtuous. But he inserts this almost as an afterthought, as if he were saying something that everyone, including the nobles, already knew; he quickly returns to the subject that interests him, the view of virtue among the ancients. He cites many of them, including Seneca, Sallust, and Juvenal, who argue that virtue is the basis of nobility.[65]

He closes the section with a story of two greyhounds, brothers born of the same mother. One was well brought up and acted nobly and left the warmth of the *foyer,* or the home, to go and chase the hare; the other, poorly brought up, abandoned his true nature and stayed home, attracted by the comfort and the food. And,

> . . . your children [that is, those of the nobles] will do the same. If from their youth they are well instructed, they will show themselves nobles and of good morals and habits; and

[64] Ibid., p. 111.
[65] Ibid., pp. 111–111v.

on the other hand, if they are poorly instructed and brought up, they will always be nonnoble [vilains], bad and vicious. So, concluding from this discussion, *it is necessary that the nobles and magistrates of any "République" be careful* [il fault que les nobles et magistrats de toute République soient soigneux] that the [noble] children of the *cité* be well brought up and instructed, in the specific or particular as well as in the general or universal, and not less in morals than in letters.[66]

Using the language of morality that went well with an understanding of nobility as action, La Perrière appeals to the nobles to be more virtuous and better brought up so that they will be what by definition they are supposed to be, and all in society can have a more well-managed state.

La Perrière thus belongs with the other writers discussed who show us that despite the existence and availability of texts from the ancients and the Renaissance Italians, which put forward quite different assumptions about nobility, the French in the first two-thirds of the sixteenth century still continued to view nobility essentially from the perspective of the feudal-military view. Old beliefs and old clichés often carry on long after they have seemingly lost their justification in reality. This could be true with the nobility question in part probably because most if not all of the best minds of the time were more concerned with religion than with other things. In any case, that it happened does at least tell us that these minds were *not* particularly concerned about nobility, and that fact in itself tells us a good deal about the period. It should also help us learn what really did matter to people in the first half of the sixteenth century, and what the realities and limits of social and political action of the time really were.

One learns, for instance, that in the first half of the sixteenth century France was a society in which at least the upper classes and the literate people assumed they had no major or overriding social problems. This conclusion helps us in our

[66] Ibid., p. 112. The emphasis is mine.

understanding of the society as a whole and fits well with the general tone of most, if not all, of the major political writings of the time.[67] But of course the situation did not last: the history of the last four decades of the sixteenth century in France is very different from that of the first six. These differences and changes were enough eventually to force a rejection of the medieval view of nobility that had been so persistent. Indeed, this persistence becomes even clearer as we examine the history of the concept of nobility in the 1570s and 1580s.

[67] As, for instance, Seyssel's *La monarchie de France.*

PART TWO

The Beginnings
of Change

4

Troubles of the 1570s and 1580s and the Beginnings of the *Prise de Conscience*

The period of the Wars of Religion in France, beginning in 1559 with the accidental death of Henry II or, if one prefers, in 1562 with the first actual outbreak of serious hostilities, saw the emergence of a series of overwhelming problems that could not be solved with the political and military structures and attitudes of the first half of the century.[1] This period was crucial, as has become clear,[2] for setting the direction of the society of the early seventeenth century, and indeed of the whole ancien régime. Political breakdown, chaos, and confusion, and the intensive debate about the political nature of society, conducted by Bodin and others, laid the intellectual foundations of absolutism and of the absolutist state.[3] Indeed, it is difficult to overestimate the effects of the Wars on almost all aspects of society.[4] No individual seemed immune

[1] Harding, for instance, in *Anatomy of a Power Elite*, in analyzing the changing role and function and actions of the governors over the period, shows this well.

[2] Cf., for instance, the work of J.H.M. Salmon, in particular *Society in Crisis: France in the Sixteenth Century* (New York, 1975).

[3] This story is well known now. William F. Church, *Constitutional Thought in Sixteenth-Century France, A Study in the Evolution of Ideas* (Cambridge, Mass., 1941), remains a good beginning on the subject. For a more recent analysis see Skinner, *Foundations*, II, 284–301; and for some important observations on Bodin in light of the question of the provincial estates, see J. Russell Major, *Representative Government in Early Modern France* (New Haven, Ct., and London, 1980), pp. 253–258.

[4] Including, for example, even the actual slowing of population growth, as Philip Benedict has shown for Rouen in "Catholics and Huguenots in

from the disruption and violence of the time,[5] which often included the collective violence of the mob that we are coming to understand better now, thanks to a series of fascinating studies.[6] The Wars, then, had an enormous effect on people's attitudes and mentalities—Montaigne is only one of innumerable examples—and paved the way to new directions, especially in the intellectual and social spheres. It is little wonder that the long-outdated feudal-military view of nobility did not, in the end, survive the period either.

The complex story of the Religious Wars can be found elsewhere,[7] and we are here primarily concerned with their effects; but a brief outline seems in order. The Wars were hardly constant, by any means. There were many interruptions and truces, and many valiant and honorable attempts to find a moderate solution. A good deal of progress was made

---

Sixteenth-Century Rouen: The Demographic Effects of the Religious Wars," *French Historical Studies* 9 (1975), 209–234; for Nantes and the area around it, see Alain Croix, *Nantes et le pays nantais au xvie siècle: Etude démographique* (Paris, 1974). Benedict has shown the effects of the Wars in many areas also in his important book, *Rouen during the Wars of Religion* (Cambridge et al., 1981). And more recently, James B. Wood addresses this problem, with similar conclusions concerning the widespread impact of the Wars, in "The Impact of the Wars of Religion: A View of France in 1581," *Sixteenth Century Journal* 15, no. 2 (1984), 131–168.

[5] Even a nobleman like Montaigne, for instance, who ostensibly tried to stay out of the fighting, was not safe, and twice he almost came to grief amidst the warring factions of his region, as recounted in two well-known stories in the *Essais*; see Book III, chap. 12, pp. 1059–1062.

[6] Many of these have been brought together in Alfred Soman, ed., *The Massacre of St. Bartholomew: Reappraisals and Documents* (The Hague, 1974); and in the published papers in *Actes du colloque "L'Amiral de Coligny et son temps" (Paris, 23–28 octobre 1972)* (Paris, 1974).

[7] For this, see Salmon, *Society in Crisis*; and for a more recent synthesis, see Mark Greengrass, *France in the Age of Henry IV: The Struggle for Stability* (London and New York, 1984), especially pp. 1–67. Jean-Marie Constant's study of the Guise, *Les Guise* (Paris, 1984), captures well the spirit of the times. For an important work on the political background of the early years, see N. M. Sutherland, *The Massacre of St. Bartholomew and the European Conflict, 1559–1572* (New York, 1973).

administratively,[8] but in the end nothing seemed to work.
The Wars grew more devastating as the years went by, and
the truces became shorter. The famous Massacre of St. Bartholomew in 1572 helped to make moderate accommodation
infinitely more difficult. In 1584 another important turning
point occurred with the death of the Duke of Alençon, the
last surviving son of Catherine de Medici except for King
Henry III himself. Henry of Navarre, a Protestant, became
heir apparent to the throne, which pushed the more radical
Catholics into opposition to the monarch, making the situation even more serious and complicated. This movement
reached its climax in the period of *Ligue* domination in Paris
from 1588 to 1594. In late 1588, after the expulsion of Henry
III from Paris, the Duke of Guise and his brother were mur-
dered at Blois. The following year Henry III himself was as-
sassinated. The gradual reconquering of the kingdom by
Henry IV culminated in his reconversion to Catholicism and
his entrance into Paris in 1594, which restored the peace. The
Edict of Nantes followed in 1598.

The discussions about nobility during this period provide
further evidence for the deep-seated nature of the crisis and
the deep effects of the Religious Wars on all levels of society.
In this environment of growing crisis, discussions about nobility took on a new intensity and the topic became more
significant and relevant to contemporaries. It is interesting,
however, that in the 1570s and 1580s people turned almost
consistently to the feudal-military view for answers to their
problems and questions. In some ways, in fact, only in the
context of this "society in crisis"[9] does the extent of the hold
of the medieval view on people's minds become clear to the
historian. At the same time, however, as the people em-
braced the medieval view and built from it, they also pre-

---

[8]Cf., for instance, N. M. Sutherland, *The French Secretaries of State in the
Age of Catherine de Medici* (London, 1962).

[9]Salmon's designation, used in the title of his book cited in note 2, above.

sented some new ideas on the question. Also, a few even offered a full-fledged new, or what we will call "modern,"
approach on the question of virtue and birth that put them
twenty to thirty years ahead of their contemporaries; however, these more perceptive individuals remained the rare exception.

Nobles, then, began to sense that something was wrong,
that they as a group were threatened in ways that were not
always clear to them. As they began to examine in greater
depth their raison d'être, they employed, almost without exception, the vocabulary of the traditional medieval justification for nobility.[10] Large numbers of nobles and pronoble
apologists called on the noblemen to be virtuous and to live
up to their obligations as nobles, and implied, and sometimes even warned explicitly, that they would lose their status and their privileges if they failed.

The enemy was usually considered to be the rich nonnoble, or recent *anobli,* who used his money instead of his virtue to advance in society and to take advantage of nobles and
often to move beyond them. To counteract this problem,
nobles sometimes called for a return to a society where virtue and good mortality were valued and were the basis for
advancement. But at other times, nobility's problems were
laid directly upon their own shoulders: because they did not
act virtuously, as they were supposed to, they would lose their
position in society. The question was almost always phrased
in moralistic terms, and almost no appeals were made to birth,
though they would come, as André Devyver has shown so
convincingly.[11] The obsession with birth, which would

---

[10] Arthur B. Ferguson, in *The Indian Summer of English Chivalry* (Durham,
North Carolina, 1960), has found some interesting parallels in England of
emphasis on medieval chivalry in the late sixteenth century. In this case,
however, it is seen more as a revival of ideas that were supposedly already
dead in the first half of the century than as a continuation of ideas still very
much alive, as we have seen was the case in France.

[11] Devyver, *Le sang épuré.*

eventually characterize a good number of French nobles, belongs to another period.

Sixteenth-century nobles, then, sound a good deal like their nineteenth-century bourgeois counterparts when they call for ability and merit. If such calls were taken literally and seriously by others in society, they could become dangerous for a social group whose position was in reality essentially a hereditary one. But at least in the 1570s and 1580s, it was the nobles themselves who used these arguments, in this case usually to get themselves moving into a resolution of their problems. Such discussions had not yet become dangerous.

In order to foster and maintain the virtue that was their raison d'être, the nobility often called for the proper education of their youth. It was felt that through good education, nobles could rebuild and restore the high standards of morality and virtue of their ancestors, thus enabling them to confront the threat of those slippery outsiders who were taking away all the good positions in the state. Though these calls were usually phrased in terms of the old view of nobility as virtue, they still reflect an important attempt to begin dealing realistically with the actual problems of a medieval nobility that was adapting to a world that in many areas was becoming very different or more "modern." They offer more examples to add to those found by J. H. Hexter a good number of years ago,[12] and, when joined with calls for a new and better definition, they represent the beginnings of a noble *prise de conscience*—an attempt to understand what their role as a social group should be in the new conditions of the time.[13]

[12] J. H. Hexter, "The Education of the Aristocracy in the Renaissance," in *Reappraisals in History* (London, 1961). Also, see chap. 8.

[13] Lawrence Stone's classic work, *The Crisis of the Aristocracy, 1558–1641* (Oxford, 1965), still remains one of the major groundbreaking studies on this whole general theme of a "medieval" nobility becoming "modern" in the late sixteenth and early seventeenth centuries—in this case, of course, in England.

These attitudes are well illustrated in works such as the dialogue written in 1574 by a nobleman, Eymar de Froydeville.[14] There are three participants in the discussion, the *Gentilhomme* or noble, the *Docteur*, and the *Plébéien*. The most convincing argument is given, not by the *Gentilhomme*, however, but by the *Docteur* who obviously represents the views of Froydeville. The argument for birth is presented by the *Gentilhomme* and is rejected not only by the *Plébéien*, as would be expected, but also by the *Docteur*: both feel that *vertu* forms the basis and justification for nobility. The *Docteur*'s final and concluding opinion is ". . . that to tell the truth there is no true Nobility but the one which proceeds from *vertu* and good morality [parlant au vray, il n'est aucune vraye noblesse, que celle qui procède de vertu, et de bonnes meurs]; nobility of birth is empty and stupid talk if it is not accompanied by virtue."[15] These words almost duplicate the ones used by La Perrière twenty years earlier. But coming from nobility itself, they imply the threat, made from within, that nobles had better be virtuous or they will lose their status. At the same time, education is suggested as a means of saving the nobility and keeping it virtuous. To remain truly noble, children of nobles must be brought up and educated correctly. "Because, if from their youth they are well educated, they will behave as nobles and act morally; and, on the other hand, if they are poorly educated, they will always be villainous or nonnoble, evil, and vicious."[16]

A more developed presentation of a similar view was given by another nobleman, Pierre d'Origny.[17] The overall tone of

[14] Eymar de Froydeville, *Dialogues de l'origine de la noblesse . . .* (Lyon, 1574). The *écuyer* used in his title was supposed to be reserved only for noblemen; while it is no proof that he or his family had been nobles for any particular length of time, it does imply legal status of nobility in the author himself.

[15] Ibid., p. 39.

[16] Ibid., p. 33.

[17] Pierre d'Origny, *Le hérault de la noblesse de France* (Reims, 1578). Origny also uses *écuyer* in his title and argues from a strongly pronoble position throughout.

his work is moral, and Origny preaches to the nobility, pleading with them to be virtuous and to live up to the obligations they owe to their ancestors. Like a good preacher, he knows how to use threats: if the present-day young noblemen of France do not follow in the footsteps of their heroic ancestors they will be "considered as bearing the mark of the most repugnant and low *villenie* which ever debased the reputation of the most repugnant and low *villain* [or nonnoble] of this world."[18] Virtue is the basis of nobility: "The true *point de Noblesse* can thus not be erased except by performing deeds the very opposite to those that give Nobility. For, being truly noble is to hold steadfastly to a virtuous path [estre vrayment noble, est suivre la vertu]."[19] Nobility is thus acquired by virtue ("Noblesse certainement ne procède que d'action de vertu, et s'acquiert par icelle")[20]; and without that virtue and courage it "is almost always lost, and miserably so."[21]

On the surface this appears to be part of an attack of the unprivileged upon the privileged. Origny, however, is certainly a noble[22] and very pronoble. He is, for instance, strongly against the ennobling of *roturiers* who remain *faux Nobles*.[23] In arguing against them, he suggests what it is that seems to be bothering him: nonnobles and undeserving people are taking over noble estates and titles and eventually even use their coats of arms.

But the worst is that powerful, usurious and corpulent *villains* buy noble fiefs that are honored with the coat of arms of the first owners and do not hesitate, and in fact feel perfectly free, to insinuate themselves into the honored status

[18] Ibid., p. 19.
[19] Ibid., p. 20.
[20] Ibid., p. 42.
[21] Ibid.
[22] On Origny being a noble, see also Jean-Marie Constant, "La mobilité sociale dans une province de gentilshommes et de paysans: La Beauce," *Dix-septième siècle* 31 (1979), 11.
[23] Origny, *Le hérault*, pp. 22v–23.

of the family who previously possessed the fief. They not only bear the coat of arms, after they have had it engraved and divided up among several, but also after some time take up the war-cry as well; they thus partake of the splendor of an honor they have not deserved but have acquired thanks to the feats of valor performed by the previous owners of these fiefs.[24]

They are also taking over, he claims, the most important offices and administrative positions in the society. Indeed, this general influx has become so serious for Origny that he can state that

it is the sure sign of the fall and collapse of a Monarchy or Republic when charges, offices, and church dignities [estatz et prélatures] are distributed to people who do not deserve them or sold for money in public sale or auction.[25]

His concern, then, is clear. The old nobility is being swamped with newcomers as well as being outdistanced by wealthy and clever nonnobles. His solution is for the young nobles to work hard and be virtuous in order to counteract this problem.[26] And, like Froydeville, he also feels that the nobility should be educated: "One of the main reasons, thus, for the ruin of the Nobility is that it lacks scholarship and learning and does not consider itself honor-bound to lead a respectable private life."[27] Young *gentilshommes* should learn letters and many modern *(vivantes)* languages as well as the ancient ones. He goes on to suggest that an academy be formed specifically to handle the task of educating the nobility,[28] one of the first appearances of an idea that became increasingly discussed until it was eventually put into effect during the reign of Henry IV.

[24] Ibid., p. 30.
[25] Ibid., p. 33v.
[26] Ibid., pp. 22v–23.
[27] Ibid., p. 38.
[28] Ibid., pp. 39–41.

Many of these same themes are also found in François de L'Alouëte's treatise on the nobility published in 1577. L'Alouëte, a lawyer, was apparently a nonnoble, but wrote the work for the nine-year-old son of a well-known noble family and was extremely pronoble himself. However, he does reject nobility of birth. "For nobility," he writes, "is not related to blood or parentage but to the virtue alone which God inspires and lets flow through the hearts and veins of some men."[29] Like Origny, he feels that the present nobility, unlike its virtuous ancestors, is looked down upon by all others in the society and is losing out everywhere to recent *parvenus* in gaining the honorable positions of the country. The reason for this is that the nobles have lost their virtue and become decadent. He also, therefore, understands the question in moral terms:

That [which he has just described] is the honorable condition of the French nobility of former times and that is the way that today's noblemen should live and would if they were only willing to follow the model of their ancestors. But they are far away from such a way of life, *and the fault lies with them* [il en sont de beaucoup eloingnéz par leur faute], for it is no longer those from the most noble and ancient families that are called to occupy the highest positions of honor and it is no longer the *gentilshommes* who hold the charges and offices of the *maison du Roi* nor those of the judiciary, but it is very often the most infamous and *vils* peasants and other such *roturiers*.[30]

Because of the faults of nobles, then, the king is forced to pick "nonnoble people who do not hold so highly honor nor

---

[29] L'Alouëte, *Traité des nobles*, p. 36: "Car ce n'est au sang ni au parentage que la Noblesse se forme, mais en la seule vertu que Dieu inspire, et fait découler aux coeurs et races d'aucuns hommes." In this case, based upon the context, I have translated "races" as "veins." See also p. 17, where he calls virtue the *vraie mère de Noblesse*.

[30] Ibid., p. 13. The emphasis is mine.

virtue as those who must make a specific profession of following such honor and virtue."[31]

To rectify the situation, the noble must be more virtuous than the most virtuous of the nonnobles.[32] And the situation is serious, for it is a question of the "entire reestablishment of this order."[33] It is the duty of young noblemen such as the boy for whom the book is written to "restore and reestablish the rank of the nobles."[34] One way to do this is to affirm the separateness of the nobility, to make clear outward distinctions between nobles and others,[35] and thus, for instance, to write genealogies as L'Alouëte has done.[36] To these observers, then, the situation did indeed appear to be serious.

The tough soldier Monluc, who actively led the life of a *gentilhomme* and fighter, had much the same advice to give to his fellow nobles in his *Commentaires*, written from 1571 to 1577. He called upon his fellow captains, or nobles, to be courageous and virtuous. During his lifetime he had seen many nobles lose their right to fight or their nobility (the two are used synonymously—"De mon temps il en a esté dégradé des armes et de noblesse . . .");[37] and he had seen others advance from the lowest origins ("fils de pauvres laboureurs") far beyond any nobles by means of their *hardiesse* and *vertu*.[38] In fact, he himself, although born a *gentilhomme*, was poor and one of seven brothers, and it was only by working hard and acting courageously that he rose *degré par degré* to the position where he was and where he was given some of the most difficult and dangerous tasks by the king's lieutenants. Furthermore, he adds, "the writing of this book will

---

[31] Ibid., p. 14: "des gens roturiers, qui n'avaient pas l'honneur et la vertu en telle recommandation que celui qu'en doit faire expresse profession."

[32] Ibid., p. 17.

[33] Ibid., Preface.

[34] Ibid., Dédicace: "faites rétablir le rang des Nobles."

[35] Ibid., pp. 35, 64.

[36] Ibid., p. 73.

[37] Monluc, *Commentaires*, I, 28.

[38] Ibid.

bear witness to these facts."[39] Like a good nineteenth-century liberal, he focuses on performance as the means to rise in the society in the sense of saying "work hard and you will rise *degré par degré* to the top." Included is the same implied threat that if one does not act virtuously, he may lose his noble status. Clearly for Monluc nobility is essentially a question of action.

The noble Pierre de La Primaudaye, a distinctly mediocre writer, in his long and encyclopedic *Académie françoise*, takes the same moral attitude in his section on the nobility. There is much of the tone of the period before the 1570s, with its relative lack of concern and unreflective clichés, as in his argument that a nobility is necessary for the conservation of *toute bonne République*, which, as well as being defended by the nobility, is also "decorated" by it, and in his acceptance of nobility as a given and the statement that "All kings and princes (says Plato) are descended from serfs and all serfs from kings."[40] But at the same time there is a more conscious emphasis upon *vertu* as the basis of nobility and the not-too-veiled threat that loss of noble status would go with decline of virtue. People in the past have spoken of different types of nobility:

> But to speak the truth there is no true Nobility but that which derives from virtue and morality. And since he is a robber who commits robbery and is unrighteous who acts unrighteously, in the same manner he is a *vilain* or a nonnoble or of low social condition who does villainous or nonnoble deeds [faict vilanie]. And it is of no avail to boast of an ancient lineage or to take advantage of or to live from the lustre of one's noble and virtuous ancestors [prévaloir de la Noblesse et vertu de ses ancestres] if you are worth

[39] Ibid., p. 29.

[40] Pierre de La Primaudaye, *Académie françoise*, 3rd ed. (Paris, 1581), 1st ed. 1577, pp. 219v and 222. He calls himself *escuyer* and *gentil-homme ordinaire de la chambre du Roy* and is also considered a noble by Eugène and Emile Haag; cf. *La France protestante, ou vies des protestants français* (Geneva, 1846–1859), the reference under La Primaudaye.

nothing by yourself and if you do not possess the necessary qualities of excellence joined to those of your predecessors.[41]

Others, like Maurice Poncet, in appealing for nobles to become better educated and to know more *bonnes lettres,* argued in a similar manner.[42] Even the strongly pronoble Noël Du Fail, in complaining bitterly against the infiltration of nonnobles into the law courts of Brittany, argued that not just any nobles deserve to control the rendering of justice or to be privileged and set off from the rest of society, but only those who are "virtuous."[43] And finally the goldsmith Jérôme de Bara, writing on heraldry in 1579 with a definite pronoble point of view, makes similar assumptions about virtue. He is, in this case, concerned about the indiscriminate use of coats of arms by those—understood to be nonnobles trying to become nobles—who are undeserving of the honor, and sees this use as a cause and result of a great decline of the noble order in his own day.[44] The coats of arms, used correctly, are a means of pushing the nobles to be what by definition they should be: virtuous.

> It behooves Emperors, Kings, Dukes, Princes and Sovereigns to bestow coats of arms or give the right to enjoy them to whomever they know to be noble and virtuous, and those who deserve it, so that they will stand out and can be spotted out from among the others, *thus encouraging them and urging them to virtue* [les animans et excitans à vertu] in order that they be rewarded and properly honored.[45]

In the 1570s, then, we see the beginnings of a serious interest in the question of nobility. In the decade that fol-

[41] La Primaudaye, *Académie françoise,* p. 222.

[42] Maurice Poncet, *Remonstrance à la noblesse de France . . .* (Paris, 1572), especially pp. 26–27 and 49v.

[43] Noël Du Fail, "Epitre liminaire," in *Oeuvres facétieuses,* ed. J. Assezat, 2 vols (Paris, 1879), 1st ed. 1576, II, 381–383.

[44] Jérôme de Bara, *Le blason des armoiries . . .* (Lyon, 1579), p. 123.

[45] Ibid., p. 6. The emphasis is mine.

lowed, with the increasing chaos and difficulties brought on by the wars and the steadily growing political crisis of the monarchy, people generally became even more concerned with the society around them and the function of their order within it. This increased interest in "social questions" has been found by other historians who have compared the first and second halves of the century,[46] and it is evident in numerous other sources.[47] The discussions of nobility in the 1580s contain an even more marked tone of concern than those of the 1570s, and in this they reflect the times well. But despite some hints here and there of a coming emphasis upon birth, the message in the 1580s still remained basically the same: nobles must become more virtuous in order to save their order.

Louis de Musset, writing in 1582, for instance, reflects this situation well. Musset, not for certain a noble himself, is still quite strongly pronoble. He is especially worried about the attacks being made on the nobility and in particular the "murmurings" against those nobles who do not fulfill their obligations to fight for the king, but instead take advantage of the poorer and weaker members of the society.[48] Consid-

---

[46] For instance, Salmon in *Society in Crisis* and Jouanna in *L'idée de race.* Dewald in *Formation of a Provincial Nobility,* especially pp. 96–101, also found increased harshness in discussion and greater awareness of social distinctions toward the end of the sixteenth century.

[47] An interesting example, for instance, of this increased social concern, and the differences between the middle and the late sixteenth century, is the change between the early and the late Noël Du Fail. In his *Propos rustiques* of 1547 he is simply the storyteller; in his *Contes et discours d'Eutrapel* of 1585 (both available in the above-cited Assezat edition), he is the active reformer making fun of the greedy *gens de justice* and the avarice of the ecclesiastics, and calling for a revitalization and reform of the society with the old nobility leading the way and keeping—or regaining—a dominant position. F. Olivier-Martin in "Noël Du Fail et le rôle social de la noblesse," *Mémoires de la société d'histoire et d'archéologie de Bretagne* 8 (1927), 257–276, has some useful comments on this latter aspect of Du Fail. The *Mémoires* of Claude Haton, meanwhile, reflect a similar change in that the later years show a markedly greater concern with the *gentilshommes* and their lack of performance of their duties as fighters and protectors of the society.

[48] Louis Musset, *Discours sur les remonstrances et réformations de chacun estat* (Paris, 1582), pp. 72v–73v, 162v.

ering the performances of some of these so-called nobles, complains Musset, they should not be surprised that society more and more uses the expression that it is the *noblesse qui nous blesse*.[49] An awareness of a different sort of threat was appearing—the threat from the people. Musset's answer is consistent with his conception of nobility as virtue. Men who act this way, he feels, and who are not virtuous, are simply not real nobles (*vrays nobles*), regardless of what they say. "The true noble is willing to imperil his life for the sake of the people; he does not wish to bring ruin upon the common man." If he does, he is not noble, but *vilain*.[50] The people should learn to make this distinction and thus continue to give respect to the true nobles.

> To which [the nobility] the peasants, laborers, workers, and artisans should be as respectful and obedient as possible; and they should not consider any more that it is nobles who are ruining or harming them, but rather that these are nonnobles or *vilains* who are performing *vilennie* [que ce soit noblesse qui nous blesse, mais vilain qui faict vilennie].[51]

Musset assumes, then, like most of his contemporaries, that a man is judged noble by what he does; and thus those who call themselves nobles but who act in a nonvirtuous way should not be considered noble by the people. He is clearly appealing to people not to let those "bad" nobles give the "good" ones a bad name, because, in any case, since virtue is the basis of nobility, they cannot be true nobles. This may be a strange way to defend an order whose status and legal privileges in society were generally determined by birth; but the argument makes more sense when it is put into the context of the general assumptions about nobility of the time. If such discussion were to change from the moral calls for no-

[49] Ibid., p. 162v: "the nobility which harms or ruins us."
[50] Ibid., pp. 163, 165v–166v.
[51] Ibid., p. 166v.

bles to be virtuous to appeals from below to recognize only those nobles who are virtuous, it could be dangerous. And it did indeed bother the astute Montaigne, as we shall see, but most of Musset's other contemporaries in the 1580s still saw nothing wrong with such talk; they continued to look at the question morally and did not separate virtue from nobility.

Musset's sympathy for the nobles is perfectly clear. He argues, for instance, that a man who comes from a longstanding noble family deserves more credit than the man whose virtuous acts are starting anew a family of nobles or fighting men. It is more difficult, he feels, for someone who has everything already, a rich *gentilhomme*, to give up his comforts and go off to fight courageously in battle than someone who has no such heritage and might be brave and virtuous only for the sake of achieving nobility.[52]

This may be viewed as Musset's defending "old" nobles over "new" nobles. But in arguing in this way, he shows well the limits of the idea of birth within the feudal-military view. He makes the clear implied assumption that one is not automatically noble, regardless of what one does, simply because of one's ancestors. If families have a noble tradition, it is because they have been practicing the profession of fighting and virtue for a long time. Parents certainly are able to pass on to their children an inclination to follow in their footsteps—"volontiers les vaillans naissent des vaillans," as one contemporary put it[53]—or an encouragement to do so. From noble to noble to noble or fighter to fighter to fighter was a logical—but not inevitable—progression to people in the sixteenth century. Musset, who was not looking directly

---

[52] Ibid., p. 164.

[53] Gabriel Chappuys, trans., *Conseils militaires fort utiles* . . . (Paris, 1586), p. ii. Chappuys suggests to the noble to whom he is dedicating his translation that he (the noble) is undoubtedly as illustrious as his ancestors because it is well known that "valiant ones are inclined to be born of valiant ones." Again there is the implied assumption that if son is not to some extent like father, he should not remain noble.

at the reality around him, makes it clear that to be a noble one must continue to practice that profession.

Other writings of the 1580s reflect similar assumptions. Jean Le Masle, for instance, wrote some rather vapid but revealing verse, published in 1586, complaining about the corruption of the nobility and blaming the court, as others did at that time and later, as an evil and corrupting influence.[54] His concern, however, is directed less at the court than at the power and influence of money as a means of gaining status in society and entrance into the nobility. Over and over again, he repeats, above all, that money must not be the basis of nobility. He differs from Musset in stating that it is better and more virtuous to begin a family of nobles than to have taken on the position because of one's ancestors,[55] though he still reflects similar overall views about the role of birth as Musset. For like the latter, he also assumes that virtue is the basis of nobility and that the opposite of nobility is vice. "In short, whoever is given to vice without thought of giving it up, despises the Lord, the King, and Justice and is nonnoble and dishonest even if he had for ancestors Francion or Hector."[56] Thus it is not the title handed down from one's ancestors that makes one noble, he continues, but virtue—that same virtue (defined essentially as wisdom and valor) that had first made those ancestors noble and still makes people noble today.

Again we have the call here to offset the infiltration of the nonnoble rich by recapturing the old virtue of the nobility, with the implication that nobility will be lost if this is not done. There is also the familiar emphasis upon the importance of learning for the nobles, and especially on the study

[54] Jean Le Masle, *Discours traittant de la noblesse, et de son origine* in *Les nouvelles récréations poétiques* (Paris, 1586), pp. 15–15v. Sources concerning the Le Masle family in the genealogical collection of the Bibliothèque Nationale reveal no information about Jean.

[55] Ibid., p. 19.

[56] Ibid: "Bref lequel adonné, et endurcy au vice, Mesprise l'Eternel, le Roy, et la justice: Tel meschant est vilain et deshonneste, encor Qu'il eust pour ses maieurs Francion ou Hector." See also p. 14 for similar views.

of letters: "In short, anyone may, through an education, become a warrior, acting bravely and efficiently in any important circumstance."[57]

Le Masle's general moralistic approach is typical of the time, and it and his sympathy with the nobles become clear in his answer to those who would say, "when Adam delved and Eve span, who was then a Gentleman?" He believed people were simply divided into the *vertueux* and the *vicieux*.

> If all human beings are in general descendants of Adam
>   and Eve,
> Why are some held in high esteem and others not?
> It is because (it seems to me) of virtue and vice,
> Since it was for their great excellence that some were
>   named virtuous [that is, noble].
> While the bad or evil ones were considered slaves.[58]

Perhaps using his knowledge of the origins of the French feudal nobility learned from his historian friends—he dedicated his book to François de Belleforest, whom he admired for being learned and a noble as well—Le Masle becomes less moralistic and more realistic and perceptive, when he continues by stating that it was the stronger ones who, through *force et pouvoir*, became the nobles and kept the poor and weaker people in subjugation.[59]

The nobleman Matthieu Coignet argued in 1584 in a similar vein. Like most of his contemporaries, he put his argument for improved noble education in the context of a view of nobility as a vocation or profession. "It is said that nobility is not complete in its vocation [plusieurs ont estimé la noblesse n'estre accomplie en sa vocation] if it does not employ good letters with arms: learning, discretion and knowledge of histories along with valor and dexterity."[60] Not only

[57] Ibid., p. 13v.
[58] Ibid., p. 11.
[59] Ibid.
[60] Matthieu Coignet, *Instruction aux princes pour garder la foy promise . . .* (Paris, 1584), p. 162. He calls himself "Chevalier, Conseiller du Roy, Maistre des Requestes de son hostel, et n'aguères Ambassadeur aux Ligues des Suisses et Grisons."

is a better-educated nobility good for the nobles, he goes on, but it is also good for France as a whole; he emphasizes "the inconveniences and evils which fell upon France because the nobility is not nourished with *bonnes lettres*."[61] Not surprisingly Coignet, the noble, elsewhere assumes, and indeed argues for, a nobility based upon virtue.[62]

Even Pierre de Dampmartin, who wrote in 1585 and has been presented as someone who believes in a nobility transmitted by blood,[63] actually views nobility essentially as the profession of virtue and valor and believes that a return to these qualities is necessary to save nobility, and indeed society as a whole. He says there is a vocation of letters, a vocation of arms (the nobility), and a vocation of justice.[64] Nobility is courageous action: "The mere, the simple resolution to present oneself in front of death courageously is very beautiful and deserves to be held in high esteem . . . and principally from this *action* have people wished to see created the name of nobility [et a-t-on principalement voulu faire naistre d'une telle action le nom de la noblesse]."[65] Thus nobility is virtue: "Nobility is not a mark of false glory, it is the masculine virtue of a heart that is completely noble [la masle vertu d'un coeur tout généreux]."[66] The dilemma of the times, however, is that few nobles are really virtuous: "But it is certain, and one must admit it with a great deal of regret, that the number of those who can really be called *gentilshommes* [the latter having already been defined by Dampmartin as those having the requisite *vertu* and courage in the face of death] is today very small."[67]

On the surface, however, it could appear that in Damp-

[61] Ibid., p. 379.

[62] Ibid., pp. 118, 119.

[63] Arlette Jouanna, *Ordre social: Mythes et hiérarchies dans la France du xvie siècle* (Paris, 1977), pp. 7–9.

[64] Pierre de Dampmartin, *De la conaissance et merveilles du monde et de l'homme* (Paris, 1585), pp. 37, 37v.

[65] Ibid., p. 38. The emphasis on the word "action" is mine.

[66] Ibid.

[67] Ibid.

martin's view this courage and valor are hereditary, but on closer examination he makes basically the same assumptions as Musset. He writes, for instance:

> But that which is more honorable to our nation is that valor is more natural and hereditary in it than in any other known country, and it comes in the manner of race [this is important because he says *comme de race*, or in the manner of race, or *as if* it came by race] to nobles of importance whose fathers and ancestors have always followed the profession of war. Because children receive by the seed [par la vertu de la semence] this temperament of assurance and courage that their fathers acquired by the habit and practice of arms, it happens that as they emerge from childhood they find themselves thoroughly disposed without other admonition to disdain wounds and even death.[68]

Thus the son of a noble, because he grows up in the "proper" environment and has an inherited inclination to act courageously like his father, has a distinct advantage over the non-noble and is much more likely to be noble than the latter. But still, says Dampmartin—and this is clearly important— without this *hardiesse*, this valor, "one cannot call himself a *gentilhomme* or noble."[69]

Louis Ernaud, meanwhile, in trying to save the nobles by making them more virtuous, pushes the argument of virtue further into another direction. Ernaud, one of the more perceptive and thoughtful writers on the nobility in the 1580s, was apparently a noble,[70] and he certainly resembles the other nobles and noble apologists of his time. On the one hand, he fits a later society's view of the bourgeois by telling the no-

---

[68] Ibid., p. 110v. The first part of the quotation reads as follows: "Mais ce qui est plus honorable à nostre nation, c'est que la valeur y est plus naturelle et héréditaire, qu'en aucun autre pays qui se sçache, et vient comme de race aux gentilshommes de maison, de qui les pères et ancestres ont toujours hanté le mestier de la guerre."

[69] Ibid: "et sans [this valor] ne se peut dire aucun gentilhomme."

[70] His father was ennobled in 1579. See Jouanna, *L'idée de race*, p. 1002.

bles that they must work hard or they will lose their nobility: "The nobility that you aspire to requires someone who is an indomitable worker and who has an active and vigorous spirit [un homme indompté du travail et qui ait l'esprit actif et vigoureux]. It is by these means that it [nobility] is acquired and by the same means it is conserved."[71] On the other hand, he blames the nouveaux riches and ambitious magistrates for the troubles in the kingdom during the previous twenty-five years because these nonnobles and *anoblis* lacked the honor to restrain themselves and to act nobly, as the old nobles did.[72] Virtue remains the basis of nobility,[73] and the nobility is necessary for the "conservation du Royaume."[74]

Indeed—and it is here where his originality lies—in admonishing the nobles to be virtuous, he warns them that perhaps even the whole order, not just some individuals, might be eradicated if no reform occurred. Be virtuous, he writes, so that ". . . they do not act toward us as it is said happened in the past in Switzerland and in other countries where the people grew angry at the misbehavior of the Nobles, ravaged their property and entirely abolished their order."[75] Ernaud thus carries the argument to its obvious conclusion by assuming that since virtue is the basis of nobility, and since the nobles were not being virtuous, people would naturally wish to do away with them since nobility no longer had a raison d'être.

The problem was not usually presented in these terms, however, and most noble writers seemed unaware of the potential danger of seeing nobility as virtue. They continued instead to look at the world in moral terms and to use the

[71] Loys Ernaud, *Discours de la noblesse, et des justes moyens d'y parvenir* (Caen, 1584), p. 36.
[72] Ibid., pp. 21v–22.
[73] Ibid., pp. 24, 25, 27v, 28.
[74] Ibid., pp. 12, 24–28.
[75] Ibid., p. 45. The last part reads: ". . . le peuple irrité par le mauvais déportemens des Nobles du pays, les saccagea et abolit du tout."

old tools and the old terminology to deal with their problems. François de La Noue, for instance, the epitome of the admired and virtuous nobleman of the period, and a writer known well enough today to appear in various literary anthologies, has indeed been treated by some recent scholars as primarily a "moralist."[76] This "moralism," however, at least in La Noue's treatment of the question of nobility, seems perfectly normal and hardly atypical, since he follows the same assumptions as most of his contemporaries. The present nobility, he feels, has lost much of its virtue and is caught up in the general decadence of the times.[77] To remedy this, he proposes, as Origny did before him, the founding of an academy to educate the nobility in the ways of virtue.[78] He reminds the nobles that they can maintain their position only through virtuous actions,[79] and he argues for piety and a happy medium somewhere between extreme avarice and extreme prodigality.[80] Because of the decadence of the times, the important offices in the state are being given to those with money instead of to those with merit, and he argues for a return to merit as a basis for the choosing of officers.[81] He never mentions birth, nor does he argue that a man deserves an important position simply because it is his noble birthright.

THE relative lack of interest on the question of nobility in the first two-thirds of the century, then, was followed by a much

---

[76] Sections of the *Discours politiques et militaires*, for instance, appear in the Classiques Larousses edition, *Historiens et mémorialistes du xvie siècle*, ed. Maxime Roux (Paris, n.d.). The editor, on pp. 28–29, refers to him several times as above all a moralist. Cf. also the title and emphasis in Jean Taboureau's book, *Un moraliste militaire du xvie siècle: François de La Noue* (Paris, 1908).

[77] La Noue, *Discours*, p. 108.

[78] Ibid., pp. 108–133.

[79] Ibid., p. 169: "The nobility makes a mistake to think that a dignity renders the person worthy of honor; this in fact can only be acquired by virtue."

[80] Ibid., pp. 170, 172, 176.

[81] Ibid., p. 122.

greater concern in the 1570s and 1580s. The subject became a favorite topic of discussion. With this increased interest, and with the conditions brought on by the Religious Wars, came the feeling that perhaps something was wrong with the old view, and people were no longer fully satisfied with the old clichés. Still, discussion of the matter took place essentially within the framework of the feudal-military view. Its main thrust was an appeal or demand for a renewed or restored virtue among the nobles, with perhaps a slightly increased interest in birth; but here, too, the discussion was similar to that of the first half of the century and remained within the context of the feudal-military view.

As we have seen, these calls for virtue often included a strong emphasis on the importance of education for the nobles. This appears to be a relatively new and original idea and thus is an important part of what we are calling the noble *prise de conscience*. It differs in a major way from the more general humanist calls for education heard earlier in the century—in the period when there was less concern with the specific social make-up of society—because of its much greater focus upon the importance of education *for the nobles*. In this later period, nobles and noble apologists seem to have applied the more general humanist writings and arguments of the earlier period to their own particular situation. This, and not the emphasis upon education per se, is where their ideas are original.

This increased interest and concern in the question of nobility in the last third of the century has other facets, as well. We know, for instance, that the line between noble and non-noble was actually not at all clear in the early and middle sixteenth century. There was no "fixed frontier" between the two, as J.-R. Bloch has shown,[82] but instead an "ambiguity of noble status," to use Davis Bitton's terminology.[83] Jean-

---

[82] J.-R. Bloch, *L'anoblissement*, especially pp. 213–215.
[83] Bitton, *French Nobility*, pp. 92–117.

Marie Constant's careful research in the Beauce has shown how this relative lack of a fixed frontier actually functioned in reality in the sixteenth century by citing individuals who seemed to move into the nobility without too much difficulty and got there relatively unnoticed.[84] With this apparent lack of clear demarcation, then, it becomes even more understandable why people could continue to believe in this seemingly unrealistic view of nobility as virtue and action. But as nobles began to feel threatened later in the century, and as they and others became interested in the general question of nobility, it is logical that they would become concerned with this ambiguity of status and find it unacceptable. And this was indeed the case.

These reactions, as some scholars have already shown, usually emphasized the need for a better definition of nobility and for a clearer separation between nobles and others.[85] We already saw this emphasis in writers like L'Alouëte and Bara, and the need for better separation is indeed a major theme of L'Alouëte's work. Increased and greater virtue among nobles was suggested as one of the means of separating nobles from nonnobles. But there were other means as well, including the retention of fiefs in the hands of nobles only, since they had originally been given to them and were a sign of nobility; the avoidance of marriages with roturiers; and the writing of family descriptions and genealogies.[86]

Complaints about the mixing of classes, meanwhile, which indicate that the writers were concerned about the need for more separation and better definition, are prevalent among

[84] Cf. Constant, *Nobles et paysans*.

[85] For instance, Bitton, *French Nobility*, especially pp. 92–117, and Devyver, *Le sang épuré*, especially pp. 56–70. Certainly some of this push for separation and better definition should be seen as part of what Philippe Ariès in *L'enfant et la vie familiale sous l'ancien régime* (Paris, 1960) has found as a general movement toward separation and categorization in almost all areas of the viewing of reality.

[86] L'Alouëte, *Traité*, pp. 28–34, 73.

the sources of the time. The *cahiers* of the Estates General, for instance, contain many protests about the mixing of nobles and nonnobles, as well as suggestions for ways to keep nonnobles from flooding their way in.[87] For the anonymous author of the *Harangue pour la noblesse de toute la France*, the attempts of nonnobles to act and live like nobles ". . . have been the cause of a disorder and a *misérable meslange* among the people, and a great loss to the king of his revenue, since everyone wishes to free himself ['s'affranchir,' that is, to be freed from the obligations of the nonnobles] as if they were *gentils-hommes de nom et d'armes*."[88] The *Lettre missive d'un gentilhomme* of 1567 complained, in a very conventional way certainly, that positions in the *campagnie des gendarmes* were given to nonnobles and sons of valets, and that such deeds "corrupt even more the heart of the nobility [le coeur de la Noblesse]."[89] Noël Du Fail complained of the evil influences brought upon society by lawyers and the study of law and how this was leading to a mixing of classes and a destruction of the old order. He used the example of Hungary as a portent of what was taking place in France and what was to be feared, and he wrote that in Hungary these *gens de justice* were introduced ostensibly to preserve the state, but actually they ruined it. For "the *gentilshommes* leaving their fighting, the men of the church their preaching, the merchants their business, and the labourers their tilling of the land, they mixed with each other and mingled so completely [se peslemeslèrent et enveloppèrent si bien l'un l'autre]" that disaster resulted. To this he added demands for an end to the confusion of distinctions and for a clearer separation between nobles and nonnobles.[90] François de La Noue, meanwhile, was also concerned about the *gens de justice*, and even more about the

---

[87] Cf. Lalourcé and Duval, eds., *Recueil des cahiers généraux des trois ordres aux états généraux*, 4 vols. (Paris, 1789), I (1560), 69–275; II (1576), 122–183; III (1588), 91–189.

[88] *Harangue pour la noblesse*, pp. 10–10v.

[89] *Lettre missive d'un gentilhomme* . . . (n.p., 1567), pp. 4–5.

[90] Du Fail, "Epitre liminaire," p. 379, and also p. 383.

financiers (*thrésoriers*) who attempted to outstrip nobles in the building of great châteaux and fancy *bâtiments*.[91]

Even Montaigne believed strongly in the need for better separation and definition of classes. In his "Des loix somptuaires" he speaks of the laws against vain and "insane" expenditures for the table and clothes and the like. These do not work, he says, and should be abandoned, and

> From the example of many nations we may learn enough better ways of distinguishing ourselves and our rank externally (which I truly believe to be very necessary in a state), without for this purpose fostering such manifest corruption and harm.[92]

The complaints about mixing, then, and the demands for better and different separation and distinction of classes are further proof of an awakening noble consciousness in the later sixteenth century.

Another reflection of the changing attitudes in the later part of the century can be seen in the differing attitudes toward heroes early and late in the century. It is almost as if virtue, the quality, became the "hero" in the texts we have examined in this chapter, rather than the great individuals of the first half of the century such as Bayard, Gaston de Foix, or the greatest hero of them all, Francis I.[93] In other words, the virtue of the individual hero had, in a sense, become collectivized in the later period as the nobles began to become conscious of themselves as a social group that had problems and had to confront other social groups. Individual heroes to look up to had been enough in the more relaxed times earlier in the century, but they were no longer adequate at a time when the whole order was under scrutiny and its raison d'être

[91] La Noue, *Discours politiques*, pp. 164–165. See also the complaints of Claude de Bauffremont in his *Proposition de la noblesse de France* (Paris, 1577), p. 7, where he uses expressions such as *mauvais meslange*.

[92] Montaigne, *Essais*, Book I, chap. 43, p. 268.

[93] On the "heroes" of the first half of the century, see William Leon Wiley, *The Gentleman of Renaissance France* (Cambridge, Mass., 1954).

was being questioned. The later sixteenth century has few if any of the kinds of heroes found earlier. The first Duc de Guise was a national hero at Calais in 1559, for instance, but the second was much more a partisan leader when he fell at Blois in 1588; and an admired noble like François de La Noue was still a partisan Protestant leader. What was needed, in noble terminology, was a collective virtue; the whole nobility must become "virtuous" again. That is the message we see continually emphasized in the 1570s and 1580s.[94]

NOBLES, then, began to feel threatened and attacked in the late sixteenth century. We know, as we saw in chapters 1 and 2, that they had slowly been losing their military function and justification for quite some time, but they tended to see the threat not in these terms, but rather as one of social mobility. People were becoming noble for reasons other than military; nonnobles were outstripping nobles in many areas of society, and something had to be done about it. That, as we have seen, is how they saw the problem. The actual dimensions, *in reality*, of the threat of social mobility are, of course, another question.

There was certainly a good deal of movement into the nobility in the first two-thirds of the century.[95] But it is not certain at all that the rate really increased in the last third of

[94] The relationship between the well-known Cornelian hero of another "safer" period in the seventeenth century and this apparently original emphasis in the 1570s and 1580s would, I believe, make an interesting and important study. On heroes in the later period see Alban John Krailsheimer, *Studies in Self-Interest from Descartes to La Bruyère* (Oxford, 1972), especially pp. 1–97, and Paul Bénichou, *Morales du grand siècle* (Paris, 1948), especially pp. 15–120.

[95] For some recent examples of this, see Constant, *Nobles et paysans*, Monique Cubells, "A propos des usurpations de noblesse en Provence sous l'ancien régime," *Provence historique* 20 (1974), 224–301, and the individual cases found by Huppert in *Bourgeois Gentilshommes*. For some important suggestions on the continual movement into the nobility, see the influential article by Edouard Perroy, "Social Mobility Among the French Noblesse in the Later Middle Ages," *Past and Present* 21 (1962), 25–38. For other examples, see the works cited in note 44 of chap. 2.

the century,[96] when nobles became so much more concerned about the question. Conclusions vary, and there is no consensus yet on this. It is probable that the relative collapse of the central government in the later part of the century helped to make it easier to move in; at moments of crisis the rate seems to have increased.[97] But these crises would not necessarily have affected local areas in the same way; the local power—important nobles and clients, or elites in the cities— would largely determine who and how many would enter the nobility, and that local power might not necessarily favor social mobility at all, although it did at least in Paris.[98] On the other hand, we are surer, as we shall see in the coming chapters, that there was a relative cutoff or slowing down

[96] For instance, Wood's conclusions in *Nobility of Bayeux*, especially pp. 43–68; and conclusions drawn from an analysis and charting of ennoblements from 1350 to 1660 that I have made, building from the work of a seventeenth-century scholar and *maître* of the Chambre des Comptes, François de Godet de Soudé. This charting suggests a more or less unabated movement into the nobility without any particular long-term upward or downward trend. See Godet de Soudé, *Dictionnaire des anoblissements: Extrait des registres de la Chambre des Comptes depuis 1345 jusqu'en 1660*, ed. E. de Barthélemy (Paris, 1875), and my article, "Ennoblement in France from 1350 to 1660," *Journal of Social History* 16, no. 2 (1982), 101–110.

[97] J.-R. Bloch, for instance, in *L'anoblissement*, p. 127, sees personal ennoblements going up during wartime and back down during peacetime, while Drouot in *Mayenne et la Bourgogne*, I, 31–32, sees the Religious Wars as giving a temporary push to ennoblements. In Normandy and the *élection* of Bayeux, letters of *anoblissement* issued by the crown seem to have resulted from temporary financial and political difficulties, such as those faced during parts of the Religious Wars; cf. Wood, *Nobility of Bayeux*, pp. 45–68, especially pp. 65–66. At the same time, my long-term charting of ennoblements, discussed in the previous note, shows an upward trend during some "times of trouble" but not during others and suggests that other factors, such as the personality of the king or some unknown causes, could have been responsible for short-term fluctuations.

[98] See chap. 5 and the works cited therein in notes 36–42. On the importance of regional variations, see Jean-Marie Constant, "Les structures sociales et mentales de l'anoblissement: Analyse comparative d'études récentes," paper presented to the Colloque sur la Noblesse (Université de Bordeaux III, November 1982). I am indebted to Professor Constant for a copy of his paper.

of social mobility with the successful implementation of the *"solution Henri IV,"* the *"société de blocage,"* after 1594. Many of the great families that were to dominate affairs in France during the seventeenth and eighteenth centuries, for instance, had their origins in the period just before that date.[99] And for Rouen, Jonathan Dewald has shown how a new elite of the *robe*, itself ready to close ranks, had become discernible and relatively well-defined by the end of the century.[100]

We are sure, then, of the increased awareness of the problem of social mobility in the 1570s and 1580s; we are sure that there was some cutoff after 1594; but we are not sure, despite the increased concern, that there was much of an actual increase of social mobility, or at least of ennoblement,[101] in the late sixteenth century. On the other hand, the long-range problem or threat is obvious. A medieval society was becoming more modern. Factors like money, intelligence, and office were becoming more and more relevant for those below trying to move into the elites of society,[102] while the military justification was changing and declining. The im-

[99] Denis Richet, "Elite et noblesse: La formation des grands serviteurs de l'état (fin xvie-début xviie siècle)," *Acta Poloniae Historica* 36 (1977), 47–63; for a general background on the question, see Richet's earlier work, *La France moderne: L'esprit des institutions* (Paris, 1973), especially pp. 79–93.

[100] Dewald, *Formation of a Provincial Nobility.* Roland Mousnier's classic and groundbreaking work, *La vénalité des offices sous Henri IV et Louis XIII,* 2nd ed. (Paris, 1971), also has some very important information on the closing of ranks of the robe in the late sixteenth and early seventeenth centuries.

[101] Cf. the discussion in my article cited in note 96, above, of the importance of making a distinction, at least sometimes, between "social mobility" and ennoblement.

[102] This is, of course, an enormous, many-sided, and amorphous matter. For some suggestions: on the increasing significance of "money" and "intelligence" in a general context in Italy, see von Martin, *Sociology of the Renaissance*; on their effects in helping the transformation of the aristocracy in England, see Stone, *Crisis of the Aristocracy*; on the growing need for more trained lawyers in an increasingly complex society, see William J. Bouwsma, "Lawyers and Early Modern Culture," *American Historical Review* 78 (1973), 303–327; and on the increasing importance of office, see Dewald, *Formation of a Provincial Nobility,* and Mousnier, *La vénalité.*

mediate culprit, however, seems to have been the relative collapse of society and government during the Religious Wars. The many-sided crisis helped bring on the increased awareness of the problem—an increased awareness that, in the end, was what became basically new in the late sixteenth century. In this period of great stress, people were becoming more socially aware, and the examples of nonnobles entering the nobility and of nonnobles outstripping nobles were becoming more visible.

The noble response to this, as we have seen, included a call for restored virtue in the order as a whole, an emphasis upon the importance of education, and a call for different and better definition and separation. The latter two ideas persisted and helped the nobles redefine themselves in the seventeenth century; but the strong emphasis on virtue was a potentially dangerous means of trying to combat social mobility. As the crisis of society reached its peak in the early 1590s and the threat became even more visible, it was going to become clear at last that the medieval view of nobility would have to be abandoned and that the nobles would have to accept a newer, more modern definition—one that maintained a nobility, but only as part of a newer and enlarged class of elites.

Nobles, then, would continue to exist and would become a relatively well-defined group. The legal and economic foundations of their power, laid in a period when, because of their military importance, their power had been basically unquestioned, would be enough to enable them to change their ideas of themselves to something more modern and more realistic without losing much actual power. But in the end, they had to share a little more of that power with other elites in the society. And "nobility," shed of its military function, would cease to be thought of as virtuous action and instead would take on its more modern meaning as a status or ideal based upon birth, a process in which it lost a good deal of its significance and importance for society.

5

The Crucial Years:
The Early 1590s

Many of the general factors that led to the end of the medieval view of nobility and to the adoption of a much different and more "modern" view had already been at work since the thirteenth century; but the crucial period for this transformation appears to have been the final years of crisis and upheaval in the early 1590s, just before the imposition of the *solution Henri IV* in 1594. We have seen how the feudal-military view remained dominant in people's minds in the first two-thirds of the sixteenth century and how in the 1570s and 1580s, under the stress of the gradual breakdown of society, it was reemphasized. On the other hand, attitudes toward nobility of the first decade of the seventeenth century were, as we shall see, remarkably different, especially in tone but also in content. The "modern" view (as we shall call it) was essentially in place by that time. Using information that we already know about the early 1590s, we can now put together a picture showing how and why the medieval view was finally abandoned. In doing so we offer even further evidence of the importance of these final years of crisis.

During the early 1590s a new threat, or an apparent threat, to the existence of the nobility made its appearance. The emergence of this threat, which came from the people and is evident in some of the more radical political pamphlets and in the social movements at the end of the period, put a certain fear into the upper and established groups in society. This fear, together with a general fear of disorder and an increased awareness of the threat of social mobility, was apparently sufficient to bring about an awareness of contraditions, weaknesses, and dangers in the old view that forced a shift to a new view of nobility. Many but not all of the factors—for instance, the general social disorders and the fear of too much social mobility—were the same as those that led to the success of the royalist-*politique* solution of 1594 and the establishment of the modern absolutist state. To a certain extent the two were born together, emerging out of the same period of chaos, disorder, and breakdown of royal power.

So that we can understand the significance of the period of the early 1590s for the change of conceptions, we need first to look once more at the earlier period. Hints of possible trouble or danger with the medieval view of nobility can be found in a few sources as early as the late 1560s. As we have seen, the nobles' increasing emphasis on virtue as the basis of nobility could have its dangerous sides. All that was needed to cause trouble for the nobles was to have nonnobles use the same argument of virtue against them, to demand that they be virtuous and courageous or cease being nobles and give way to those that were. In the period before the 1590s this argument was indeed made a few times, although it was never pushed to its logical extremes. Already in 1568, for instance, Christophe Cheffontaines, an average uninspired writer, a Catholic from Brittany who called himself a professor of theology, did hint at the argument from a religious point of view. Writing against duels, he argued that one would lose his nobility by not being virtuous, which he defined as the fighting of unnecessary duels.[1] The tone of his work is abstract and theological, however, and not particularly political, and the potential threat it contained could hardly have bothered the nobles very much.

A little later, in 1576, Claude Haton, in his *Mémoires*, complained that the nobility ran instead of fought when called upon by the king, and he shows some nonnoble reflection

---

[1] F. Christophe Cheffontaines, *Confutation du poinct d'honneur* . . . (Paris, 1568), pp. 54–55, 63. One noble, for instance, pardoned another instead of fighting: "That is a true *gentilhomme*," wrote Cheffontaines (pp. 75–76), while those other, nonvirtuous ones, are not.

on the implications of virtue as the basis of nobility. In ancient times nobles had gained their positions through virtuous and courageous actions, he wrote, but now they are vicious and corrupt:

> In the old days the French nobles acquired their Noble status and their privileges from the kings and princes, because of their virtues and because they had been of service to these kings and princes and to their country, France. And these virtues pertained to these nobles and *gentilshommes* in the eyes of the people, and made them glorious.[2]

But now when they are called, he says, they do not go; some send money, others do nothing rather than serve "in the way they were expected to in exchange for the privileges of nobility which their predecessors had acquired for their virtues and shining feats of arms."[3] Haton, however, does not push his argument very far, and in any case did not write for public consumption. He shows simply that some people must have been reflecting on the question.

Jehan de Caumont, the well-known *Ligueur*,[4] on the other hand, takes up the argument a decade later, in 1585, in a more polemical way. He argued not against the duel, as did Cheffontaines, but against Protestantism, and his tone is much more intense, moral, and political. He uses a similar argument however—an argument based upon the assumption that it is impossible for a Protestant, or a non-Catholic, to be a noble. In accepting nobility to be *vertu*, Caumont simply defines that virtue as being Catholic.

[2] Haton, *Mémoires*, pp. 853–855.

[3] Ibid., p. 899: "le service qu'ilz sont tenus à cause de leurs privilèges de noblesse que jadis leurs prédécesseurs leur ont acquise par leurs vertus et beaux faiz d'armes."

[4] Cf., on Caumont, for instance: J.H.M. Salmon, "The Paris Sixteen, 1584–94: The Social Analysis of a Revolutionary Movement," *Journal of Modern History* 44 (1972), 567; Elie Barnavi, *Le parti de Dieu, Etude sociale et politique des chefs de la Ligue parisienne, 1588-1594* (Brussels and Louvain, 1980), pp. 55–57; and Frederic J. Baumgartner, *Radical Reactionaries: The Political Thought of the French Catholic League* (Geneva, 1975), pp. 75–76.

Whoever calls himself noble and does not care for the glory of God [*honneur de Dieu*, which he defines elsewhere as being a good Catholic] is a liar, is a *vilain*, and he has stolen the title of Nobility. This title does not belong to him, he plagiarizes it and indeed acts impiously. For the status of Nobility is a saintly and sacred one; it is the venerable indication that one is honor-bound to respect God; it means indeed that one is standing in the Court of the true temple of God.[5]

Caumont, then, in the middle of the 1580s, seems to use the nobles' view of virtue against them. A similar argument can be found in a milder form, and from the opposite perspective, a few years earlier in a fairly well-known political pamphlet, the *Cabinet du roy*. Herein it is argued that it is impossible for a Catholic to be a true noble, since nobility is virtue and Catholicism is nonvirtue, or the opposite of virtue.[6] These cases suggest that potential problems with the old view were already emerging in the 1580s, though these examples appear to be isolated. Barnavi, for instance, finds no one else among the *Ligueurs* of the period who argued in the same way as Caumont.[7] Arguments such as Caumont's were not pushed very far and apparently were not heeded by most of society. People were still unable to separate nobility and fighting. Nonnobles continued to assume that since the military is necessary, nobility is necessary; and nobles, when pushed, apparently continued to point out that since a military is needed (which had become a good deal less obvious to some, especially since the military no longer seemed to serve the state or the good very much), they as nobles were obviously necessary.

In the midst of the increased emphasis on virtue by nobles

[5] Jehan de Caumont, *De la vertu de noblesse, aux roys et princes très chrestiens* (Paris, 1585), p. 3. The original sounds as strange as the translation.

[6] Cf. *Le cabinet du roy de France* . . . (attributed to Nicolas Barnaud) (n.p., 1581), especially pp. 284–287.

[7] Barnavi, *Le parti de Dieu*, p. 56.

in the 1580s and—despite some arguments against them—the
continued acceptance of the feudal-military view, one ob-
server was astute enough to understand the contradictions and
to warn his contemporaries that they were perhaps making
an error to equate virtue with nobility. With his usual perception and knack of stepping back and surveying the situation from a distance, Montaigne wrote that those people make
a mistake who,

> . . . to favor virtue, hold that nobility is nothing else but
> virtue [pour faire faveur á la vertu, tiennent que la no-
> blesse n'est autre chose que vertu]. These are things that
> have a certain relationship, but there is a great difference
> between them. There is no point in mixing up their names
> and titles; we wrong one or the other by confusing them.
> Nobility is a fine quality, and introduced with reason (that
> is, with justification, it would seem [translator's com-
> ment]). But inasmuch as it is a quality dependent on oth-
> ers, and which can fall to a vicious and worthless man, it
> is well below virtue in esteem. It is a virtue, if indeed it is
> one, that is artificial and visible, dependent upon time and
> fortune, varying in form according to countries, living and
> mortal, with no more source than the River Nile, genea-
> logical and common to many, a matter of succession and
> resemblance, derived by inference, and a very weak infer-
> ence at that. Knowledge, strength, goodness, beauty, riches,
> all other qualities, fall into the range of communication and
> association; this one is self-consuming, of no use in the
> service of others.[8]

All things being equal, Montaigne goes on to say, a noble
should perhaps be preferred over others, but it is stupid to
give an important office, job, or duty to a worthless noble

---

[8] Montaigne, *Essais*, Book III, chap. 5, pp. 850–851. See also his statement (Book II, chap. 35, pp. 745–746) that virtue rarely lodges in men of
high estate, implying obviously the separation of virtue and birth. And in
Book I, chap. 25, pp. 162–163, he agrees that children should be placed in
society according to ability and not birth.

simply because he is noble. On the other hand, there is no implication that one should cease being noble simply because he is worthless; the two factors, virtue and nobility, are separate.

Despite the fact that Montaigne feels called upon in the middle of his discussion to use hesitatingly the old terminology—"it [nobility] is a virtue, if indeed it is one [c'est une vertu, si ce l'est]"—he still presents to all intents and purposes the modern view. Here, in this area, he was a little ahead of his time, which is not surprising for someone as perceptive as he. But by the way he presents the question, he also shows that the discussion of virtue as it related to nobility was an important one in his period and that what he had to say on the subject was indeed different from what others were saying. He thus offers further indirect evidence that almost everyone was continuing to repeat the clichés of the feudal-military view, even as he, on this subject, saw through them.

Only one of Montaigne's French contemporaries, as far as I can determine, was equally clear-sighted. Jean Bacquet, the legal writer, in 1582 showed that he apparently understood that virtue and birth were separate entities and should be thought of as such. In his discussion on the subject he recognized the fact that many nobles did not partake in fighting, and thus he expressed the belief that virtue is not the basis of nobility and that ancestry is far more important.[9] But he makes little of the point. The same was true for Montaigne, who did not discuss anywhere else in his *Essais* the potential dangers of equating virtue with nobility. These isolated and unforceful observations of the 1570s and 1580s, like the trivial cases made for the possible use of the virtue argument against the nobles in the same period, were not enough to bring attitudes into the more modern world; they

---

[9]Jean Bacquet, *Traicté des droits de francs-fiefs* . . . in *Les oeuvres* (Paris, 1644), 1st ed. 1580–1582, pp. 23, 77–78. Although not addressing the problem directly, Bodin also suggests a certain separation between nobility and virtue in the modern way. See Jean Bodin, *Les six livres de la république* (Paris, 1583), pp. 1054–1056.

give us instead yet more evidence of the continued predominance of the feudal-military view during that time. But with the events of the early 1590s that predominance would at last be broken.

THE popular movements of the early 1590s have come under increasing study, in particular those of the *Ligue* in Paris[10] and some of the more important peasant rebellions.[11] Their uniqueness or difference with respect to other rebellions and social movements occurring earlier and later had been suggested by some historians;[12] but now we are beginning to understand these movements better, even if some disagreement remains about how progressive their social programs actually were.[13] It is becoming clearer that these movements were more "social" than those earlier in the century. In this period of extreme openness and lack of central control, with its increased possibilities for social expression—when hopes were higher, in a sense—they tended to lose some of their character of ritual protest doomed to failure[14] and to become

[10] See especially the works cited below in notes 36–40 by Richet ("Aspects socio-culturels"), Descimon, Barnavi, Salmon, and Ascoli).

[11] For instance, Yves-Marie Bercé has studied the rebellions of the *Croquants* of the 1590s, albeit in the larger context of an overall study that focuses on the seventeenth century (see *Histoire des Croquants: Etude des soulèvements populaires au xvii* siècle dans le sud-ouest de la France, 2 vols. [Geneva, 1974], especially I, 257–293), while Salmon has a useful summary of them in *Society in Crisis*, pp. 276–291.

[12] For instance, Gérald Walter, *Histoire des paysans de France* (Paris, 1963), pp. 192, 226, and Corrado Vivanti, *Lotta politica e pace religiosa in Francia fra Cinque e Seicento* (Turin, 1963), especially pp. 28–46.

[13] J.H.M. Salmon has emphasized their modernity, especially in "Paris Sixteen" and "French Satire in the Late Sixteenth Century," *Sixteenth Century Journal* VI, 2 (1975), 57–88; and Peter M. Ascoli has emphasized their lack of modernity in "A Radical Pamphlet of Late Sixteenth Century France: Le Dialogue d'Entre Le Maheustre et Le Manant," *Sixteenth Century Journal* V, 2 (1974), 3–22, and in his "Introduction" to his edition of the *Dialogue*; François Cromé, *Dialogue d'entre le Maheustre et le Manant* (Geneva, 1977), pp. 9–41.

[14] As, for instance, they tended to have in the movements studied by Natalie Davis (see *Society and Culture*), even if Davis does often find, in the

integrated into real social movements with tangible goals.[15] On the other hand, the movements of the early 1590s also differed from the better-known seventeenth-century rebellions[16] because the relative collapse of the central power in the late sixteenth century precluded their having to direct so much energy against an encroaching central state, as seems to be so much the case in the seventeenth century.[17] Thus there was more time to look more closely at class relationships.

The existence of antinoble sentiment within these movements and generally throughout the second half of the sixteenth century, at least until 1594, has become better documented. Bitton found such evidence in some of the works he examined;[18] Myriam Yardeni has shown the importance of the years 1588–1594 for the surfacing of a strong current of popular, *Ligue*-associated antinoble feeling and has ana-

---

lower orders, a serious intent and a real comprehension of what they are doing. Also, the "ritual" aspect still seems to exist among the people of Romans in 1579–1580, as we know from Emmanuel Le Roy Ladurie's *Le carnaval de Romans: De la Chandeleur au mercredi des cendres, 1579–80* (Paris, 1979), and from Liewain Scott Van Doren's "Revolt and Reaction in the City of Romans, Dauphiné, 1579–1580," *The Sixteenth Century Journal* V, 1 (1974), 71–100.

[15] Cf., for instance, in terms of the revolts in the countryside, Salmon's conclusion in *Society in Crisis*, p. 282: ". . . the Croquants laid aside religious differences in the interests of class solidarity and a common stand against their oppressors from the higher orders." Drouot, in *Mayenne et la Bourgogne*, especially pp. 30–72, has found a similar direction.

[16] The large literature on these is well known, but it all tends to suggest a different kind of rebellion than those of the 1590s. This is true both for Boris Porchnev in *Les soulèvements populaires en France de 1623 à 1648* (Paris, 1963), 1st Russian ed. 1948, and for Roland Mousnier, as, for instance, in his "Recherches sur les soulèvements populaires en France avant la Fronde," *Revue d'histoire moderne et contemporaine* 4 (1958), 81–113; also see the more recent studies by Madeleine Foisil, *La révolte des Nu-Pieds et les révoltes normandes de 1639* (Paris, 1970), and René Pillorget, *Les mouvements insurrectionnels de Provence entre 1596 et 1715* (Paris, 1975).

[17] Cf., for an especially strong portrayal of this "evil" state, Bercé, *Histoire des Croquants*.

[18] Bitton, *French Nobility*, pp. 6–26.

lyzed a number of the important pamphlets;[19] Bercé, while emphasizing the local, indigenous, and relatively unified nature of the revolts in the southwest, still finds some antinoble feeling in this period;[20] and Salmon has found it in the Vivarais and elsewhere.[21] Indeed, the antinoble feeling seems to have reached a head in the period of 1593–1594. From the perspective of seeing nobility as a profession, this antinoble feeling seems hardly surprising in a period of civil war during which one was almost constantly reminded of the evils of combat and conflict. In other words, with the close identification of the nobility and military, antiwar feelings could turn easily into antinoble feeling. To some people, especially those in the countryside who were terrorized by the brigandage and looting of the brutalized nobles or those who were taxed to support unwanted local garrisons,[22] it must have seemed obvious that the only way to stop war was to destroy the people who were responsible for making it. This was hardly a very realistic approach, but it must certainly have been a common reaction. The fact that antinoble feeling, as opposed to feelings against the seigneurial system, taxes, or royal officials, disappeared almost totally after the restoration of internal peace in 1594 is evidence that some people must have had such a reaction.

[19] Myriam Yardeni, *La conscience nationale en France pendant les guerres de religion (1559–1598)* (Louvain, 1971), especially pp. 243–261.

[20] For instance, his conclusion (*Histoire des Croquants*, I, 286): "All of these texts leave no doubt that an antinoble sentiment made its appearance, or at least that such sentiments appeared very possible and threatening to many."

[21] Cf. J.H.M. Salmon, "Peasant Revolt in Vivarais, 1575–1580," *French Historical Studies* 9 (1979), 27, and, for instance, in describing the program of the *Croquants* leader La Saigne (*Society in Crisis*, p. 287): "His articles of association required unswerving obedience and the suppression of all religious differences in a united campaign against the *noblesse*."

[22] Cf. Salmon's conclusion in "Peasant Revolt in Vivarais," p. 27: "It seems to have been only as a result of peasant identification of the *gentilshommes* with the military exploiters [that is, those who were taxing the peasants to support the local garrisons] that the popular movement came to refuse payment of dues."

We find the first real examples of the awareness of a serious threat to the nobility, and of the use of the virtue argument against the nobles, in the *Dialogue d'entre le Maheustre et le Manant*, first published in 1593 and revised and republished by royalists the following year, apparently to embarrass the party of the *Ligue* because of the radical statements in it.[23] Much of the pamphlet is devoted to discussions or arguments between pronoble and antinoble sentiments in a way not done before. The *Manant* (a peasant, or villager or man of the people) represents the people, in the broad and popular sense, and more specifically the popular wing of the *Ligue* in Paris, as well as Catholicism and orthodoxy; his views are essentially the views of the author. The *Maheustre* (a soldier of the time) stands for the nobility, the soldiers, Henry IV, and Protestantism (even though the *Maheustre* constantly reminds us that he is a good Catholic). The issue of pronoble versus antinoble emerges particularly vividly.[24] The *Maheustre* is forced to defend himself for carrying on the wars and for following the king, since the pillaging and destruction of the wars were among the main complaints of the people, who, as we have seen, tended to identify war with nobility. The *Maheustre* gives us his three major reasons for fighting:

> Firstly, because we support the one who is rightfully and by nature the King of France, to whom belongs the charge of ruling the State. Secondly, because we are French Catholics *who are standing up against a violent movement of the common people who want to impose their will which is to do away with the nobility and its privileges and create a democracy.* Thirdly, because we want to chase out the Spanish whom

[23] Cf. Salmon, "Paris Sixteen," pp. 575–576. The exact differences between the two editions are listed in Peter Ascoli's excellent edition of the *Dialogue*, cited above in note 13. I used the originals in the Bibliothèque Nationale of both the 1593 and the 1594 editions.

[24] See, for instance, Cromé, *Dialogue* (1593), p. 75, where the nobility is strongly attacked by the *Manant*.

you invited to come into France, and to maintain our-
selves against both you and them.[25]

This quotation indicates without much doubt that the idea
that the popular party wanted to do away with the nobility
was at least "in the air" or floating around (the same words
were kept in the 1594 edition).[26] There is still some disagreement as to the real meaning of the *Dialogue,* but there is little
doubt that a strong tone of antinoble and anti-upper-class
feeling is found in many of the *Manant*'s statements.[27] That
the *Manant*, on the other hand, was not talking of a total an-
nihilation of the nobility,[28] even if accused of this in the above
quotation, also seems quite clear. What is important here,
however, is that it was *understood* in the upper classes that what
was intended was the destruction of the nobility. That Mayenne and the upper-class leaders of the *Ligue* would try to
suppress the pamphlet, and that the royalists would edit and
republish it and spread it around to embarrass the *Ligue,* lends
credence to this view.

On the other hand, the fact that the royalists would actually publish the work with the "dangerous" statements in
it suggests that they could not have been too frightened by
them. In some cases, it seems, as Febvre has described for
the epithet of atheist in the first half of the century,[29] "want-

[25] Cromé, *Dialogue* (1593), p. 17. The emphasis is mine. The emphasized
section reads as follows: "qui résistons à une violence populaire, qui se veut
introduire au préjudice des privilèges de la Noblesse, et pour l'esteindre et
former une Démocratie."

[26] Cromé, *Dialogue* (1594), pp. 8v–9.

[27] As Salmon in "The Paris Sixteen" would argue. For instance, the *Manant* says (Cromé, *Dialogue* [1593], p. 57, left the same in the 1594 edition [p.
26]): "You, *Messieurs les Nobles,* have continued and continue to make war
on Catholics to the ruin of the Catholic religion . . . ," etc.

[28] As argued by Ascoli, "A Radical Pamphlet." The *Manant* does indeed,
for instance (Cromé, *Dialogue* [1593], p. 247), make a distinction between
good and bad nobility (" the *bonne noblesse* will not be bothered by what I
say . . . ," etc.).

[29] Cf. Febvre, *Le problème de l'incroyance,* especially pp. 126–138.

ing a democracy" was thrown at the popular party as the worst possible thing they could advocate, without the accusers really believing that their own accusation was true. Such "slander" could serve as a tool—by making the leaders of the *Ligue* in Paris (the Sixteen) and the other rebels appear to be more radical than they really were—to help make the inevitable repression easier to carry out and justify. But other evidence, including information we have about the popular movements of the time and the reaction to them from above, suggests that some of this fear was still very real.

Two other political pamphlets of these years show similar attitudes. *Le banquet et après disner du Conte d'Arète*, written in 1594 by Louis Dorléans, attacked the nobility from the perspective of the popular party, emphasizing, like the *Dialogue*, the military excesses of the nobles against the poor and unprotected.[30] It provides an additional example beyond the *Dialogue* of the existence of anti-upper-class and antinoble feeling in the popular party, even if this feeling is without a program to replace the nobility with something else. *Le manifeste de la France*, a royalist pamphlet written a few years earlier than the *Banquet*, reflects quite vividly the fear among the upper classes that is also found in the *Dialogue*. The author or authors of the *Manifeste*, for instance, claim that the lower classes led by Mayenne wish to do away with the nobility, and that that is their real intention: "Because there is little doubt that everyone sees clearly that your [that is, the *Ligue*'s] true designs are to create a Democracy and . . . exterminate all the nobility and take over their wealth [exterminer toute la Noblesse et vous emparer de tous leurs biens]."[31] The *Manifeste* thus offers evidence in addition to that in the *Dialogue* to show the other side of the picture: that there was a tendency among the *upper* classes to emphasize that the pop-

[30] Louis Dorléans, *Le banquet et après disner du Conte d'Arète* . . . (Paris, 1594), and see also Yardeni's discussion of the work in *La conscience nationale*, pp. 255–256.

[31] *Le manifeste de la France aux parisiens et à tous les français* (Tours, 1590), p. 27.

ular party wanted to abolish the nobility, an argument that suggests they had some real fears about the situation.

In another passage in the *Dialogue*, the *Manant* goes further than anyone else in actually using the argument of virtue—and thus the feudal-military view—directly against the nobles. "Nobility in general," he says, "is based solely upon the virtue that one acquires oneself and not upon that acquired by others, and the title of nobility should be personal and not hereditary, so much so that whoever is not virtuous cannot be noble."[32] This significant passage, already referred to and cited by two important scholars,[33] is hardly surprising because the *Manant* said nothing that most nobles of the 1570s and 1580s had not at least been implying themselves. Indeed, an analysis of the entire section surrounding the quotation, which is kept the same in the 1594 edition,[34] suggests that both the *Manant* and the *Maheustre* assume that nobility is based upon virtue and action. The only debate between the two is as to whether or not the nobles are in fact virtuous, as both agree they should be. The *Maheustre* argues that it is only a few nonvirtuous nobles who are giving the rest a bad name, and that the others are indeed virtuous, as they are supposed to be, while the *Manant* argues that the order is without virtue now and therefore without justification.[35]

Since both sides accept the old virtue argument, we do not yet have a convincing statement of virtue versus birth. But we do have, for apparently the first time, a strongly stated

[32] Cromé, *Dialogue* (1593), pp. 251–252: "L'espèce générale de la Noblesse est fondée sur le seul subiet de la vertu que l'on acquiert, et non sur celle acquise d'autruy, et le tiltre de Noblesse doit estre personnel, et non héréditaire, tellement que qui n'est vertueux ne peut estre Noble."

[33] Salmon in "Paris Sixteen," p. 571, refers to it and argues that it is a key passage showing the basic antinoble intentions of the Sixteen; and Ascoli, in "A Radical Pamphlet," p. 17, cites it in order to minimize its revolutionary aspects by placing it within the context of the whole pamphlet.

[34] Cf. Cromé *Dialogue* (1594), pp. 106, 106v.

[35] This whole section deserves to be read especially carefully and is more readily available in the Ascoli edition of the *Dialogue*, p. 189.

argument, using the feudal-military view of nobility, made by the lower classes and directed against the nobility. Coming from below, then, the argument had potentially very different implications and could be taken at last as a definite threat to the nobility. In light of this direct argument in the *Dialogue,* of the other antinoble ideas among the lower classes, and of the upper classes' fear of such ideas, the truth must at last have dawned on the nobles—and on those who wanted to see nobility remain—that so much talk about virtue could be a very dangerous pastime.

THE direction taken by the social movements themselves during this period suggests a similar conclusion; they certainly had put some fear into the upper classes. Thanks to the pioneering work of Denis Richet[36] and other scholars working closely with him,[37] the important article on the Sixteen by J.H.M. Salmon,[38] the thesis of Elie Barnavi,[39] and the critical edition of the *Dialogue* done by Peter Ascoli,[40] we know a good deal about the social makeup of the *Ligue* in Paris, especially its leaders, and about its general history. We now know that the main social force for the *Ligue,* for instance, as Drouot suggested,[41] was the jurists and lawyers just below the top of the profession who pushed for upward so-

[36] Carried out over the past twenty years or so, beginning with his unpublished thesis on the Séguier (*Une famille de robe à Paris du 16ᵉ au 18ᵉ siècles: Les Séguier*) and with some of his conclusions on the Paris of the *Ligue* summarized in *La France moderne* and in "Aspects socio-culturels des conflits religieux à Paris dans la seconde moitié du xviᵉ siècle," *Annales: Economies, sociétés, civilisations* 32 (1977), 764–789.

[37] For instance, Robert Descimon, who has published the results of some of his work on Paris during this period in *Qui étaient les Seize? Mythes et réalités de la Ligue parisienne (1585–1594)* (Paris, 1983); see also Denis Crouzet, who has published on other aspects of the *Ligue,* for example, "La représentation du temps à l'époque de la Ligue," *Revue Historique* 270 (1983), 297–388.

[38] Salmon, "Paris Sixteen."

[39] Barnavi, *Le parti de Dieu.*

[40] Ascoli ed., Cromé, *Dialogue.*

[41] Cf. Drouot, *Mayenne et la Bourgogne,* especially I, 160–162 and 334–348.

cial mobility and for a relatively more open society.[42] Many of the aspirations of this "middle" group, a group that apparently had an important social message for the rest of France, were to be silenced to a large extent after 1594 with the imposition of the *solution Henri IV*,[43] the *"société de blocage des notables,"*[44] the society whose mentality Loyseau represents and expresses so well.[45]

One of the indirect results of this study has been the broadening of our understanding of the absolutist state of the seventeenth and eighteenth centuries, for, by examining the *Ligue* itself, we can see how such a really quite different regime, socially and politically, came to be imposed *after* 1594. Such a social analysis of the *Ligue* also suggests that some of the impetus behind the first serious use of the feudal-military view of virtue against nobility, which has just been cited, must have come from this middle group. But in the chaos of the time the threat itself was still often perceived to come from the great mass of the lower classes as well; that conclusion also seems to be supported by the work of the scholars mentioned above. For, thanks to this research on the *Ligue* in Paris,

[42] Cf., for instance, Richet, "Aspects socio-culturels," especially p. 775, and *La France moderne*, pp. 110–112, backed up by Barnavi in *Le parti de Dieu* and in his painstaking tracking down of the profession and social background of the leaders of the Sixteen in 1585, 1591, and 1593. Descimon, meanwhile, expands and completes the job in *Qui étaient les Seize*, while emphasizing less the "social frustration" of this group. Robert Harding has offered some modifications of this scheme for other cities in "Revolution and Reform in the Holy League: Angers, Rennes, Nantes," *Journal of Modern History* 53 (1981), 379–416.

[43] For instance, the conclusion of Barnavi (*Le parti de Dieu*, p. 262): "From then on [after 1594] the *Ligueurs* were destined to fall into the trap that circumstances in society had prepared for them and in which they were nothing but misfits. Their social ideals remained unchanged: offices for those who did not have them, nobility for those who were only officers, honors for everyone. They let venality continue, and participated actively in the race after posts and traditional honors. The rebellion of the Sixteen was indeed a revolution, but it was a misguided one."

[44] Expression used by Robert Descimon in the seminar of Denis Richet at the Ecole des Hautes Etudes en Sciences Sociales in Paris.

[45] As, for instance, in his *Traité des ordres et simples dignitez* of 1610.

it is becoming clearer that a separation between radical, lower-class elements and more established upper-class supporters of the *Ligue* gradually took place. Nobles and other upper-class supporters started to dissociate themselves as the movement took on more and more anti-upper-class overtones.[46] Those in the upper classes who had been willing earlier to use the violence of the masses for their own ends—usually successfully[47]—saw the violence gradually slip out of their control and even be used against them at times. Upper-class supporters of the Sixteen, then, as they lost control of the movement to more radical elements, apparently came to realize that they perhaps had more to fear from the success of the movement than from its failure. This realization would obviously have made them more willing to accept its eventual defeat in 1594.

The work of these scholars shows that some fear of the lower classes existed among some segments of the established orders, and also that this fear was a factor in helping to increase the push for the acceptance of the royalist-*politique* regime. We could therefore also say that this perception of a popular threat was a factor that helped bring about the acceptance of the modern, and less "dangerous," idea of nobility.

In the countryside, meanwhile, the popular rebellions of

[46] For instance, Salmon, "The Paris Sixteen," and Barnavi, *Le parti de Dieu*, especially pp. 199–202, 212–214; and more generally Orlea, *La noblesse aux Etats généraux*, especially p. 165, who has found a definite movement of nobles backing off from the *Ligue* between the Estates General of 1576 and that of 1588. Robert Harding's preliminary work on Rennes, Nantes, and Angers in "Revolution and Reform" and on Marseille in "The Mobilization of Confraternities Against the Reformation in France," *Sixteenth Century Journal* XI, 2 (1980), 92–98, has focused more on the religious side of the *Ligue*, but nothing we know yet—and the same would hold true for Rouen in Benedict's *Rouen during the Wars of Religion* (see, for instance, pp. 226–227)—suggests anything that would contradict that such a separation took place outside of Paris as well. For a focus on Toulouse in the period through 1589, see Mark Greengrass, "The *Sainte Union* in the Provinces: The Case of Toulouse," *Sixteenth Century Journal* XIV, 4 (1983), 469–496.

[47] Cf. Richet, "Aspects socio-culturels," especially pp. 771–778.

1593–1594 seem also to have produced a certain amount of fear in the upper classes in general, and in the nobles in particular. As noted earlier, much of the general antinoble sentiment in the second half of the century blamed the nobles for the wars because of their assumed profession as fighters. This antinoble, and often antiwar, feeling reached a head in the early 1590s and then almost disappeared after the restoration of order and peace. The rebellion of the *Croquants* in Limousin and Périgord in 1593–1594, by far the most widespread and significant of the largely rural uprisings of these years, is the most representative evidence of this antinoble feeling, although there is scanty evidence to suggest similar reactions in other areas.[48]

The *Croquants* rebellion began in Limousin late in 1593 and spread quickly throughout the region. The peasants organized themselves fairly well and had effective leaders, and they were even able to carry on negotiations for a while with the forces of order.[49] No clear program emerged, however. Local issues were often important, and resistance to exploitation by "evil" townsmen was also at times a factor. But dislike of nobles was clearly an important theme in this uprising, even if there was less blind and seemingly irrational hatred of the nobles than is found in the rebellion of the *Jacquerie* in the middle of the fourteenth century. Most of the complaints seemed to be focused not on seigneurial exploitation but on the excesses of the military nobles, the brigandage and general lawlessness that seemed to be brought on by the wars.[50] Because nobles as a group were perceived as the enemy—at

[48] As, for instance, in Brittany as illustrated by the work of J. Baudry, *La Fontenelle le ligueur et le brigandage en Basse-Bretagne pendant la Ligue (1574–1602)* (Nantes, 1920).

[49] For a narration of events, J. Nouaillac's *Les Croquants de Limousin: Une insurrection paysanne* (Tulle, 1906) is still useful when used along with Bercé's and Salmon's analyses (cited in note 11, above).

[50] See, for instance, B.N., Manuscrits Français 23194, fols. 363–376, and Fonds Dupuy, 62, fols. 125, 126, 141; and see especially the famous *Livre noir*, a copy of which can be found in the *Collection Périgord* of the Bibliothèque Nationale, and also Bercé's conclusion cited in note 20, above.

least according to some sources—and because the rebels were relatively well organized and effective, some observers believe it was a class war. Gérard Walter's conclusion about the revolt, for instance, that "for the first time in his history the French peasant appeared, not like a mad dog ripe simply to be struck down, but as a class enemy with whom, should the occasion arise, one would be willing to negotiate,"[51] though perhaps oversimplified and exaggerated, reflects an awareness that something apparently different and new existed in the rebellions.

Among certain segments of the upper classes, this potential threat and antinoble feeling seems to have been quite clearly perceived; one has the impression of the existence of a good deal of fear among the established orders. A group of noble "anti-*Croquants*," for example, was formed in mid-1594, and it specifically accused the rebels at its opening meeting of wanting to "overthrow the monarchy and establish a democracy."[52] Other examples in the sources show this fear in the upper classes that the rebels wanted to create a *démocratie*.[53] We also know that some nobles tended to support the movement at the beginning, and even held leadership positions in it;[54] but by the end they had apparently all dropped out or disappeared from their positions, which suggests they disliked the direction the rebellion had taken. Like the movements in Paris, then, the *Croquants* rebellion clearly helped produce some fear among the nobility and upper classes. In itself, the revolt may not have been that hard to put down and may never have reached national proportions or had a national program. But it still raised the specter of new and potentially more dangerous rebellions—rebellions

[51] Walter, *Histoire des paysans*, p. 226.

[52] Ibid., pp. 215–216, and Salmon, *Society in Crisis*, p. 288.

[53] For instance, B.N., Manuscrits Français 23194, fols. 363–376, and also the sources cited in Vivanti, *Lotta politica*, especially pp. 45, 46; in Nouaillac, *Les Croquants*; and in Walter, *Histoire des paysans*, pp. 208–226. See also Bercé, *Histoire des Croquants*, I, 287.

[54] Bercé, *Histoire des Croquants*.

that, taken at face value, could offer a real threat to nobility and to the general social hierarchy.

THE early 1590's, then, with social movements different in important ways both from those earlier in the century and from those in the period of Richelieu onward, saw the crystallizing of a substantial amount of antinoble and anti-upper-class feeling, and the existence of some real fear about this threat within the upper classes. This antinoble feeling was not especially directed against the *economic* basis of noble predominance, however (as was the case much more in 1789). Instead, the excesses of the military nobles were the main target of the criticism, and nobility was under attack, for the most part, because it was considered to be the profession of the military. Since nobility and the seigneurial regime were separate, nobility could be attacked and threatened without necessarily harming the seigneurial regime. These serious antinoble pressures, then, together with the general effects of the culmination of crisis and the social and political breakdown of the early 1590s, seem to have finally forced the medieval view of nobility—and especially its assumption of nobility as virtue, with its inherent contradictions, potential dangers, and basic lack of looking at reality—to give way at last to something more modern.

PART THREE

The Modern View
Emerges

6

The Separation of Virtue and Nobility
and The Absolutist State in the First Half
of the Seventeenth Century

A comparison of writings on the question of nobility in the first half of the seventeenth century with those sixteenth-century writings we have looked at so far reveals some remarkable differences in tone, in approach, and indeed in basic assumptions. The difference is especially striking when we compare the numerous and very vocal noble writers of the 1570s and 1580s, who strongly emphasized virtue and action, with the upper-class and noble writers of the first decade of the seventeenth century. Indeed, the great distance between the two—a distance that should become clear in the early part of this chapter—becomes in the end one of the most compelling, if indirect, reasons for our accepting the crucial significance of the period of the early 1590s in helping bring on the demise of the medieval view of nobility. This distance reveals yet another difference between the regime imposed or accepted after 1594 (which we know lasted essentially two hundred years) and that before.

These writers of the first decade of the seventeenth century, who accepted in a more realistic fashion the world around them, had a strong tendency not to talk about nobility as virtue in the way earlier writers had done, but instead they separated the two concepts. Nobility for them is simply a group, defined, determined, or justified by birth rather than virtuous deeds. Virtue, on the other hand, is just a quality, certainly excellent but no longer synonymous with nor required for nobility. By separating virtue from nobility, then, these writers accepted for the first time in France the main assumption of what we have called the modern idea of nobility.

With this general shift in thinking came a relative lessening of interest in the question, especially among nobles. Most writers simply accepted that birth was the basis of nobility, and then went on to other subjects that apparently interested them more. For example, Louis Guyon hints at the new orientation and new attitude in a statement he wrote in 1604. His *Diverses leçons* is an example of a relatively new type of literature for France, similar to books such as the *Cortegiano* that tell you how to succeed in the court and in the world. Numerous treatises and handbooks like this one began to appear in the early years of the seventeenth century.[1] Guyon wrote for the nobility, as Musset, L'Alouëte, Le Masle, La Noue and the others had done, but the tone is much less moral than worldly; he concerns himself with describing how to succeed and how to please others *dans le monde*. He makes no calls for *vertu* for its own sake, and the tone of moralism is to a great extent gone.

Guyon gives his advice to an aspiring young courtier. He does not try to define the nobility, but is interested rather in how to get on at court. But in explaining how to do this, he gives away his opinion on the meaning of nobility:

> Whoever wishes to join the Court of Emperors, Kings, Queens, Dukes, Duchesses, Marquis, Marquesses, Counts, Countesses or other illustrious persons must be a noble by birth, and of ancient nobility [faut qu'il soit né gentilhomme, de noble maison d'ancienneté]; for it is less reproachable for a *roturier* not to act virtuously or perform virtuous works than for a nobleman, who, if he does not follow the path his predecessors have taken shames the name

[1] Many of these have been studied by Magendie in *La politesse mondaine*; see especially vol. I, 150–409. He has found a widespread proliferation of this sort of treatise in France in the years 1600–1660.

and the honors of his race [souille le nom et l'honneur de sa race].[2]

This reflects very well what came to be the accepted attitude during the reign of Henry IV. On the one hand, good birth is indispensable, at least for the aspiring young courtier, much as in the discussion of birth in Castiglione's *Courtier* almost a century before. This new French emphasis on the indispensability of good birth became a common cliché in the literature on the subject during the next thirty or forty years. Virtue, at the same time, is separated from the discussion of the social structure. In Guyon, simply being born a noble will push a man to greater virtue. In a sense, the relationship between the two is reversed: it is no longer a question so much of virtue bringing nobility, but instead of nobility (one hopes) bringing virtue.

The more philosophically oriented Pierre Charron also shows this new separation of virtue and birth, and does so in a more conscious way than Guyon. As he does on many subjects, he sounds much like Montaigne, but there is a difference in tone, reflecting both a different personality and ability, a slightly later period, and a different social-class origin (Charron was not a noble and did not pretend to be). For Charron there are two nobilities (*deux noblesses*). One is based upon birth, and in admitting its existence he reflects what we could call the new "realism" of his time. The other is based upon virtue ("the quality of virtue alone, without any consideration of race or ancestors").[3] The first he calls *naturelle*; the second he calls *personnelle et acquise*. Neither one is perfect in itself, but of the two the *personnelle et acquise* is to be preferred. For inherited nobility (and here he echoes Montaigne almost word for word) "can fall upon a vicious and good-for-nothing and lowly born person who is in himself really a *vilain*."[4] But, unlike Montaigne—and like Sal-

[2]Loys Guyon, *Les diverses leçons* (Lyon, 1604), p. 193.
[3]Pierre Charron, *De la sagesse*, 3 vols. (Paris, 1829), 1st ed. 1601, I, 421.
[4]Ibid., pp. 422–423.

lust's Marius and numerous later eighteenth- and nineteenth-century nonnobles—his vanity is hurt by the *mépris* of those who are noble only by birth and have no virtue, but still pretend to be superior to those below them.

> It [the nobles' feeling of superiority] is a totally empty pride, all their glory they get but through paltry means, *ab utero, conceptu, partu,* and it remains buried under the tombstone of the ancestors. Like the criminals who, being chased, resort to the protection of the altar, and the resting-places of the dead and in ancient times to the statues of the emperors, thus these persons, lacking in merit and in any reason for a true honor, resort to the remembrance and coat of arms of their forefathers. What good is it to a blindman that his parents enjoyed good eyesight, and to a stutterer that his grandfather was eloquent.[5]

The other nobility, the *personnelle et acquise,* he feels, is much superior and more worthy of respect. In fact, it is the real nobility: "In a word it is the true nobility, which consists in good and useful effects, and not in dreams and empty and useless fancies; it derives from the mind and not from blood and this former is no different for nobles than for others."[6]

Thus, at a time when an emphasis on birth was becoming more prevalent among nobles, the nonnoble Charron was talking of a different nobility, new in this context—new because in a sense it could not exist without having the more clearly delineated concept of nobility determined by birth as a contrast—a nobility of wit, intelligence, and talent that exists regardless of birth. Charron also accepts nobility of birth, and in this he is similar to Guyon; he simply does not consider it to be of much worth, and indeed dislikes a great deal the "snobbery" of those who would emphasize it. Each of the two, Guyon and Charron, then, reflects a similar accep-

---

[5] Ibid., p. 423.

[6] Ibid., p. 424. The last part reads: "et provient de l'esprit et non du sang, qui n'est point autre aux nobles qu'aux autres."

tance of the reality of the early seventeenth century—that nobility as a social group was indeed determined by birth and not virtue—but Guyon liked the situation while Charron did not. We now have two attitudes toward the nobility—a noble and a nonnoble one, or a positive and a negative one—and therefore a greater separation of views by class or social group because of the new acceptance of birth as a determinant of nobility.

Florentin de Thierriat, who wrote the major treatise on nobility of the first decade of the century, reflects similar assumptions. Apparently employing a more realistic eye than his seemingly less disillusioned predecessors of the 1570s and 1580s, he minimized clearly the importance of virtue as the basis of nobility and simply accepted birth without question, reporting, it would seem, the reality he saw around him.[7]

With Guyon, Charron, and Thierriat, whose views seem to reflect what the average person of the time was thinking, it is clear that the monopoly of the old view had at last been broken. Montaigne had understood to some extent what was wrong with the medieval view of nobility, but in this area he had been an isolated figure. Apparently it took the dramatic and frightening events of the early 1590s to bring other people's conceptions and attitudes out of the Middle Ages and into the modern world.

Nevertheless, a direct connection between this change in conceptions and the apparent threat to the nobility during those important years before the successful implementation of the Henry IV regime is not easy to document specifically. There are a few examples, however, closer in time to the early 1590s, which show that the nobility actually invoked the separation of virtue and nobility, especially in order to defend itself from verbal attack. Guillaume d'Oncieu, for instance, while answering specific charges against the domination of the nobility, stated in 1593 that

[7] Florentin de Thierriat, *Trois traictez sçavoir: 1. De la noblesse de race, 2. De la nobelesse civille, 3. Des immunitez des ignobles* (Paris, 1606), especially pp. 7–11.

It has to be understood that according to our customs, nobility and virtue are very different things: and it does not
follow that he who is virtuous is held to be noble [il y a
grande différence entre noblesse et vertu; et ne s'ensuit que
celuy soit tenu pour noble qui est vertueux]. In place of
such a title he will be qualified as honorable, or honest, or
called master, or other such terms, which express the degree of virtue which is his. As long as no other qualifica-
tion can be pointed at, one's appeal for noble rank cannot
be considered because such a rank implies in itself that one
has precedence over others, that he bears arms and carries
a Coat of Arms, and has other privileges which no one can
arrogate to himself regardless of how virtuous he may be.[8]

Virtue here, then, does not make one a noble.

For the most part, however, the change was more gradual
and the old and new tended to be mixed together and confused. As is true with Guyon, people seemed not especially
conscious that there was a change, or that they were expressing a different attitude than before. Salomon de La Broue,
for instance, writing in the years 1593 to 1599 about horsemanship and the manner in which it should be taught to
young noblemen, resembles those before him in his lack of
discrimination between *vertu* and *noblesse*. He writes that
young noblemen who are sent to the households of important princes and lords to be trained and educated will be at
an advantage over other men because of their more "virtuous" upbringing: "When they become adults there will be
a great difference between their actions and those of numerous other people who would have been educated with less
virtue [moins vertueusement nourris]."[9] Yet, he believes that
good birth is indispensable, just as it is to Guyon and will be

---

[8] Guillaume d'Oncieu, *La précédence de la noblesse . . .* (Lyon, 1593), p. 10.
Bitton has some useful background information on the dispute between nobles and high nonnobles in Dauphiné in *French Nobility*, pp. 18–23.

[9] Salomon de La Broue, *Le cavalerice françois*, 3rd ed. (Paris, 1610), pp. 17–
18.

for Faret and many other writers of courtly treatises in the early seventeenth century. To control and ride a horse well, one must be, among other things, *bien né*. La Broue assumes that good birth is an advantage and will make one better: "But if the rider [Cavalerice] is not good-natured and has no inquiring mind, if he is not patient and well born [bien né], he will never be able to understand and carry out these instructions."[10]

Guillaume de Chevalier, writing in 1598 on the subject of duels and how they are sometimes necessary for the nobility, seems worried about attacks upon the nobility as a whole, and emphasizes the absolute necessity of having a nobility for the preservation and safety of the rest of the people:

> The Institution of Nobility is neither accidental nor tyrannical [L'Institution de la Noblesse n'est casuelle ny tyrannique], as some people would want others to believe; but on the contrary it was found to be so necessary, that at the time it was established everyone thought that it was upon it alone that depended the safety and survival of the rest of the people. The following short dissertation will be on this subject, one which I consider extremely necessary to discuss.[11]

He goes on to draw a close relationship between nobility and birth, and to argue that an hereditary nobility (and he emphasizes the "hereditary" part quite strongly) is necessary.[12] He seems keenly aware that there are others, apparently in the lower classes, who feel that the nobles are tyrannical, and his way of arguing suggests that he feels that a focus on birth would be a good means of dealing with these attacks.

La Béraudière, also writing on the duel a decade later in 1608, sounds much the same as Chevalier. There is still some discussion about virtue as a means of moving into the nobil-

[10] Ibid., p. 178.
[11] Guillaume de Chevalier, *Discours des querelles et de l'honneur* (Paris, 1598), p. 21.
[12] Ibid., pp. 21–32.

ity,[13] but La Béraudière is much more careful to define just what he means by virtue: arms and courage in fighting. Even with this virtue it will still take four generations and careful scrutiny before the *roturier* comes to be accepted as truly noble.[14] On the other hand, he seems quite worried by those who do not respect the significance and superiority of noble birth. The fact that the noble risks his life and his goods fighting for the king and his country

> . . . should be rightly appreciated by everyone, and acknowledged not only by the noble, but also by the *roturier* who should respect and honor it [nobility] because the noble is the issue of an illustrious line and is born of other family and different ancestors [estant sorti d'une race illustre et d'autre parenté que la sienne] whom the *roturier* must not compare to his. Otherwise, if it [such a comparison] was considered we would be all equal and similar one to the other, something which ought not and cannot be.[15]

Again, the fear itself indicates the existence of an antinoble feeling, and the tone of the response, with its emphasis on birth, suggests a direct relationship between the one and the other, between the fear and the response. When one spoke of virtue, one had to be extremely precise, and most of the emphasis had to be placed upon birth.

THIS separation of virtue from nobility, the diminishing role of action in achieving and maintaining nobility, and the accompanying role of birth as its main determiner and justifier fit quite well with what we know about the general thrust of the early absolutist regime under Henry IV. These developments, as was suggested in the previous chapter, were in some ways born together out of the chaos, *and* from the social threat from below, of the preceding period. Exploring

[13] La Béraudière, *Le combat*, p. 91.

[14] Ibid.: "To be held and esteemed as a *gentilhomme*, that quality must have passed from father to son up to four or five generations."

[15] Ibid., pp. 88–89.

some of the interactions or relations of the new view of nobility and the absolutist regime should help us understand
something more about each.

Numerous important and well-known studies over the past
fifteen to twenty years have taught us a good deal about early
absolutism. The monarchy under Henry IV,[16] for instance,
armed with Bodin's concept of sovereignty and similar ideas
of other theorists,[17] started the work of breaking the power
of any too powerful force—such as important nobles and their
clients,[18] Protestants, and independent cities[19]—that threatened its overall authority or that threatened a return to the
disorders of the previous period. Accompanying this partially successful push from the monarchy (which, as is well

[16] The contributions of J. Russell Major help one understand the significance of the period of Henry IV as a turning point in the development of
absolutism; see for example, "The Crown and Aristocracy in Renaissance
France," *American Historical Review* 69 (1964), 631–645; "Henry IV and
Guyenne: A Study Concerning Origins of Royal Absolutism," *French His-
torical Studies* 4 (1966), 363–383; and "Bellièvre, Sully and the Assembly of
Notables of 1596," *Transactions of the American Philosophical Society*, vol. 64,
pt. 2 (1974), which have been especially useful here. Three monographs,
David Buisseret, *Sully and the Growth of Centralized Government in France,
1598–1610* (London, 1968); Raymond F. Kierstead, *Pomponne de Bellièvre: A
Study of the King's Men in the Age of Henry IV* (Evanston, Ill., 1968); and
Edmond H. Dickerman, *Bellièvre and Villeroy: Power in France under Henry
III and Henry IV* (Providence, R.I., 1971), have been particularly helpful in
presenting a detailed description of how the government functioned.

[17] Ernst Hinrichs has examined the role of some of these other theorists
of the time of Henry IV in *Fürstenlehre und politisches Handeln im Frankreich
Heinrichs IV. Untersuchungen über die politischen Denk- und Handlungsformen im
Späthumanismus* (Göttingen, 1969).

[18] Cf., for instance, Salmon, *Society in Crisis*, p. 321: "The king and Sully
correctly perceived that the overmighty subject and his clients remained the
principal danger to royal authority, and for this reason they changed the
institutional structure to undermine the patronage system."

[19] David Parker, for instance, shows well how this new absolutist state—
just after Henry IV, in this case—worked against the Protestants and the
cities in "The Social Fundations of French Absolutism, 1610–1630," *Past and
Present* 53 (1971), 67–89; this analysis is expanded and modified in his *La
Rochelle and the French Monarchy: Conflict and Order in Seventeenth-Century France*
(London, 1980).

known, became even more successful under Richelieu[20]) was a less well-known closing of ranks among the upper classes in the period after the *Ligue* and indeed throughout the first half of the seventeenth century.[21] Some sources from this period concerned with the concept of nobility suggest that an important part of this new regime of political absolutism and relative social *blocage* was in fact the new view of nobility of birth. A medieval view that emphasized the military primacy of a nobility that had virtuous action (and thus a sort of implied independence) as its function could not have been particularly conducive to order, at least in a period of general crisis like that of the Religious Wars. This older view was probably even a factor that prolonged the Religious Wars and the general inability of the monarchy to maintain order, but this is difficult to document. In any case, the modern view of nobility was in the best interests of those forces favoring the imposition of the absolutist state; these forces included many of the upper classes, both noble as well as nonnoble. With it the nobles would lose their old, purely military, function and thus conceivably their independence, putting them under the authority of the monarchy; but, as we shall see, they would also gain in certain ways.

One way of expressing these conceptions of a hereditary nobility placed under the authority of the monarchy was to make a distinction between "good" and "bad" nobles. To defend the nobility as a whole against attack, one had to distinguish between "bad" nobles who used their military function and independence to attack and exploit the people in a lawless way, thus creating antinoble feelings, and "good" nobles who were nobles because of birth but who remained under the authority of the monarch. To save the nobility as a whole, these people were suggesting either to get rid of the few bad ones or to reform them and bring them back into

[20] See the discussion below about the period of Richelieu.

[21] Cf. Richet, "Elite et noblesse," and the works cited in chap. 4, notes 99 and 100. This conclusion certainly needs to be documented further and for more areas of France.

the fold. The two most famous political pamphlets of the time, the *Satyre Ménippée* and the *Dialogue d'entre le Maheustre et le Manant*, show such a view from differing perspectives.

The conflict in the royalist *Satyre*, a pamphlet once but certainly no longer considered bourgeois and thus antinoble, is not at all phrased in terms of noble versus antinoble, and its argument is certainly not antinoble. Rather, it reflects the existence of a struggle between an old kind of nobility and a new kind, or, from the point of view of its authors, between a bad nobility and a good one. The two most revealing sections are the *Harangue* of the Sieur de Rieux, who speaks for the nobles at the mock Estates General satirized in the pamphlet, and the *Harangue* of Monsieur d'Aubray, who speaks for the Third Estate. Monsieur d'Aubray represents essentially the attitude of the authors; the Sieur de Rieux is a stupid and indiscriminately violent noble. Despite the fact that he is a caricature of the brutal noble, so decried by Claude Haton and by many nobles such as Musset, La Noue, Ernaud, and Monluc, he still does not believe in the importance or significance of birth and in fact mocks it:

> I don't care a hoot for all these titles and panels, nor for coats of arms, crested or not: I want to be a *vilain* [still synonymous with *roturier*] with four *vilains* as my ancestors [Je veux être vilain de quatre races], provided that I still receive the *tailles* [taxes] without having to account for them.[22]

He, the typical "bad" noble, does not care about the exploits and honorable actions of the "good" nobles of the past, his ancestors. These exploits and actions should concern him and should inspire him to do great deeds, but they do not.

Monsieur d'Aubray, on the other hand, makes a clear distinction, as has already been hinted at in the *Harangue* of the Sieur de Rieux, between good nobles and bad. In those against

---

[22] *La Satyre Ménippée ou la vertu du catholicon*, ed. Ch. Read (Paris, 1892), 1st ed. 1594, pp. 163–164.

the king and against peace he sees only *étrangers passionnés, femmes ambitieuses et vindicatives, prêtres corrumpus et débauchés*,[23] and the like. In particular, he does not see (in this party against the king)

> . . . any noble worth anything, apart from three or four, whom we cannot keep under control and who will soon abandon us! All those remaining are nothing but wild ones, living off the wealth of the common man and they would not be able to make a living on their own, nor keep on living in the same manner in times of peace! All the *gentilshommes of noble birth and of intelligence and ability* [tous les gentilshommes de noble race et de valeur] have joined the other party and are at the side of their King and for their country.[24]

At least in this case, among the upper-class royalist authors of the *Satyre*—nonnoble or recently ennobled—an emphasis on birth as the basis of nobility, is a good rather than an evil, despite Charron's hesitancy. "Responsible" nobles and nonnobles, and those who would not let religion distort their true interest in this world, seemed to have had a common interest in seeing that birth and not action was indeed considered the basis of nobility.

A comparison of the *Satyre* with the *Dialogue d'entre le Maheustre et le Manant* also suggests a similar conclusion—that is, that the upper classes in general, noble and nonnoble, wanted nobility, with the royalists in particular wanting to base it on birth and under the authority of the monarchy. Any threat to the nobility, then, was perceived as coming in good part from farther down the social ladder, including to some extent the masses, instead of from immediately below. In the *Dialogue* (and especially in the unchanged edition of 1593) the struggle is presented as one between the "good" or popular side represented by the *Manant*, and the "bad" or

---

[23] Ibid., pp. 247–248: "impassioned foreigners," "ambitious and vindictive women," "corrupt and debauched priests."

[24] Ibid. The emphasis is mine.

upper-class side represented by the *Maheustre*. The implication is that the entire nobility is responsible for the fighting, pillaging, and destruction and is therefore bad without exception. In the *Satyre* the struggle is presented differently. The "good" side is that of the *Maheustre* in the *Dialogue*, and the authors defend it by making a distinction between a good and bad nobility. The *Satyre* is almost pronoble, defending all good nobles, or those of *bonne race et valeur*, who are really with the king and for peace; the bad nobles, and those mocking the importance of birth, are those who are really causing the destruction about which the *Manant* complains. The "good" side in the *Satyre*, which is the royalist-*politique* side, wins, of course, but it is also the side of the *Maheustre* and of the nobility in the *Dialogue*.

Along with this emphasis on birth and a de-emphasis on the virtuous and action side of nobility thus came, for some, a sort of separation between what they considered good and bad nobles. Their main point was that nobility should not be attacked as a group because only a few evil ones were giving the rest a bad name. An interesting series of events took place during the rebellion of the *Croquants* of 1593 and 1594, meanwhile, which provides an example of an attempt to separate the "good" nobles from the "bad." The main source for this story is a series of letters addressed to Henry IV from one of his officials in the countryside, the *conseiller d'état* Jean de Thuméry, or Boissize, as he is usually called.[25] Boissize had been charged with restoring order among the rebelling people, and to do this he set out to lay siege to what he felt was the cause of the trouble—the château of a local nobleman from which forays were conducted against the people. The people were complaining about high taxes as well, but he felt they would never return to order and to the paying of those taxes unless something was done about the château and its occupants, who were, "to tell the truth, the cause of

[25] Nouaillac has published these letters from the Fonds Dupuy, no. 62, of the B.N. in *Les Croquants*, pp. 50–53.

all the evil and disorder in this province."[26] An agreement was made with the rebels, stipulating they were to give up their arms and return under the authority of the king (and pay their taxes) just as soon as the offending nobleman, the Sire de Gimel, had been tamed.[27]

It took over three and one-half months, but the château was finally taken. It is interesting to note that the king's officials in the countryside went after the "bad" nobles, just like the ones attacked in the *Satyre*, in order to separate them from the rest and restore the order and authority of the king and the respect for "good" nobles. In this case it seems to have worked; the antinoble and anti-upper-class feeling was successfully directed against individual offending nobles and away from the order as a whole. The Sire de Gimel, when he was finally defeated, was not deprived of his nobility for being "unvirtuous"; he was instead invited to serve the king.[28] He was simply forced by the strength of the king to come to heel and become a "good" noble,[29] one who remained noble by birth but less independent. Clearly this example shows that the modern idea of nobility fit better than did the older one with the aims of the early absolutist state; and the rejection of the old view could even be considered a basic and indispensable part of that state.

OTHER writings on the nobility during the reign of Henry IV confirm the apparently growing prevalence of the new view and show how the new idea of nobility fit well with the aims

---

[26] Nouaillac, *Les Croquants*, p. 50 (letter of August 8, 1594).

[27] Ibid: "To encourage the execution of this enterprise [the siege of the château of Gimel] the rebels have offered nine thousand *écus* and promised to put down their arms, just as soon as the place is in obedience to Your Majesty, and they will then pay the *tailles* that it pleases you to order them to."

[28] Ibid., pp. 51–53 (letter of December 30, 1594).

[29] Cf., also, Bercé in *Histoire des Croquants*, who, approaching his material from the direction of the local community and the ties that bound it together, has found a general tendency among these communities to separate "bad" nobles from "good" ones in order to combat antinoble sentiment.

and directions of the early absolutist state. Among the nobles who supported the king, for instance, were a number of men whose origins are cloudy and who seem to have been recently ennobled. Included in this group is Antoine de Pluvinel, the founder of the first academy for nobility in 1594, and David de Flurance-Rivault, Pelletier, and Alexandre de Pontaymery. Many of these recent nobles wholeheartedly supported Henry IV and the authority of the monarchy, though they emphasized that nobility should be based upon birth and worked for better, clearer, and different means of defining and separating nobles from nonnobles. In this sense they reflect well the *société de blocage* and show the complex nature and variations of the support of early absolutism.

David de Flurance-Rivault, in his treatise on the estates in society published in 1596 and dedicated to Henry IV, expresses partially the attitude of the recent *anobli*. He reflects at the same time a conglomeration of views, emphasizing the separation of the nobility, the acceptance of birth, and the power of the king over the nobility, on one hand,[30] while including some assumptions about nobility as action on the other hand. He says that *honnestie*—and it is significant that he uses this seventeenth-century term instead of the term *vertu*—is the basis of nobility: ". . . for a Noble even loses his rank if he is not *honneste*, since this is his main mark and that which has him stand apart from the manual worker or craftsman, who is just and has to be just whether he likes it or not."[31] He mixes virtue and nobility to some extent, as in the following statement:

> It is more of an honor to be noble through virtue, than, being a noble, to appear to be a *vilain* because of vice: and no one should believe that vice in the ancient noble should be preferred to virtue in the new noble. . . . And it is much better to make a brilliant beginning of Nobility for the

[30] David de Rivault de Flurance, *Les estats* . . . (Lyon, 1596), pp. 257, 276, 296.

[31] Ibid., p. 72.

benefit of those who come after than through *vilenie* and evil actions, to slander and cast a slur upon the praise received by your predecessors.[32]

But there is never a question of allowing an attack on birth or a nobility of birth. "Indeed, I would conclude that all nobility should be honored," he says.[33] He reflects another of his main concerns, finally, when he states that no nonnoble, no matter how virtuous, can ever be considered as having entered the ranks of the *gentilshommes* without the king's approval ("si [il] n'a la marque du Prince").[34]

On the one hand, then, Flurance-Rivault is pronoble and accepts birth and separation of virtue and nobility more readily than the writers of the 1570s and 1580s; on the other hand, he is more consciously and more strongly in favor of the king and against the "people." He, the recent *anobli* in this case, thus seems more aware of the importance of using the king to help block social movement than were the earlier writers. Interestingly enough, his later work of 1612, *Le dessein d'une académie*, shows a further clarification of and emphasis on these views, especially on nobility being based upon birth alone. The hints of 1596 that a noble might lose his rank if he is not *honneste* are totally gone in this later work.[35]

Pelletier's *Nourriture de la noblesse*, published in 1604, also shows some of the differences between writings on nobility in the 1570s and 1580s and those of the period after 1594 and especially during the first decade of the seventeenth century. The work reflects a similar concern with the state and condition of the nobility and indeed has surface resemblances to those many calls for virtue made by the nobles of the 1570s and 1580s. There are subtle differences in tone, however, from the earlier works. There is a greater understanding of, and distinction made between, what is actually true concerning

[32] Ibid., p. 296.
[33] Ibid.
[34] Ibid., p. 76.
[35] Cf. Flurance-Rivault, *Le dessein d'une académie*.

the social makeup of France and what some think it to be; and much of the misguided assurance, confusion, and tension of the 1570s and 1580s is gone. The work instead expresses a tone of relief. It is as if the world was not going to collapse, after all—an attitude prevalent, for instance, in Honoré d'Urfé's *L'Astrée* and other writings of the period.[36] Birth, or *extraction*, for Pelletier, and also to a large extent in *L'Astrée*, is something for nobles to live up to,[37] something to which to add the quality of virtue in order to round things out and become a perfect noble; but still this birth exists and one is automatically noble because of it.

Furthermore, by the time of Pelletier the concerned nobles had something to channel their energies and desires of reforming the nobility into—something they did not have in the 1570s and 1580s—and this helps to explain the changed tone of the discussion. Pluvinel had founded his academy in 1594, and others were founded shortly afterward. As Pelletier specifically pointed out, "virtue" and other qualities a good noble should—but not must—possess could be taught in these academies.[38] Finally, while outlining the duties and privileges of the nobles, Pelletier did not forget to remind them that they are and should remain under the authority of the king. "It is only," he emphasized, "under the authority of the sovereign that the *gentilhomme* has jurisdiction over his subject."[39]

Pelletier's reason for a young nobleman's special training also reflects a different emphasis from that of the sixteenth century, especially the 1570s and 1580s. "The main goal in

[36] A similar sense of relief about the restoration of peace is also found in the work of Honoré's brother Anne d'Urfé in his *Description du Pais de Forez*, written around 1606 and published by Auguste Bernard in *Les d'Urfé: Souvenirs historiques et littéraires du Forez au xvie siècle* (Paris, 1839).

[37] Pelletier, *La nourriture de la noblesse . . .* (Paris, 1604), p. 1. For instance, he writes: "What is the value of glorifying your being the descendant of an illustrious race if you hide yourself in the crowd, without shining by your own proper merit?"

[38] Ibid., p. 96.

[39] Ibid., p. 15.

the education of a young *gentilhomme*," he wrote, "should be teaching him how to converse well in society."[40] This statement would have horrified most of the moralist nobles of the sixteenth century; but it does reflect an attitude that became increasingly widespread as the ideal of the *honnête homme*—a concept that assumes essentially the new idea of nobility—took shape and developed throughout the seventeenth century.[41]

Antoine de Pluvinel, the founder of the first academy for nobility (see Chapter 8) expresses much the same attitude as Pelletier and Flurance-Rivault. Pluvinel's *Maneige royal* or *Instruction du roy en l'exercice de monter à cheval* was first published three years after his death in 1623, but it reflects for the most part the attitudes prevalent during the reign of Henry IV and immediately afterward, when Pluvinel was most active. In it Pluvinel largely describes in dialogue form what was taught at his academy, but he also emphasizes the goals and nature of the new institution. His academy's purpose is to educate only the nobility in virtue (his school is closed to nonnobles); to Pluvinel the nobility is the basis of the state. His academy is an *école de vertu* (a school of virtue),[42] and he believes that educating the young nobles in horsemanship and arms and letters will keep them from falling into vice. But to Pluvinel, virtue is still understood and assumed to be a quality, something that can be taught in a school; and those upon whom this training does not have an effect remain just

[40] Ibid., p. 59v: "La fin principale où doit viser la nourriture d'un jeune Gentilhomme est de bien apprendre comment il faut converser dans le monde."

[41] There is, of course, an enormous literature on the development of the concept of the *honnête homme*, but Magendie's work in *La politesse mondaine* is central, while Carl J. Burckhardt in "Der Honnête Homme: Das Elite Problem im Siebzehnten Jahrhundert," in *Gestalten und Mächte, Reden und Aufsätze* (Zurich, 1941), has some interesting observations and recognizes, as does Magendie, that the concept is the product of quite different historical realities of the seventeenth century.

[42] Antoine de Pluvinel, *L'instruction du roy en l'exercice de monter à cheval* (Amsterdam, 1666), 1st ed. 1625, pp. 154, 148–160.

as noble as those upon whom it does. Thus Pluvinel like his contemporaries, separates nobility and virtue, even if he does talk a good deal about virtue. Like Flurance-Rivault and Pelletier, he also emphasizes his closeness to the king and the importance of the nobles being under the authority of the monarch.

Pluvinel, who was considered fully noble by his contemporaries even though it has been impossible to trace his social origins, suggesting that they may have been covered up,[43] thus founded an academy that was closed to nonnobles or those without "birth." It was also an organ of the state; it therefore reflects very well the mixing of the new, more modern idea of nobility, a closing of social ranks, and an emphasis on the monarch's authority over the nobility. Alexandre de Pontaymery, one of Pluvinel's most enthusiastic backers, expressed similar views. He also separates virtue and nobility and assumes that nobility itself brings virtue,[44] while he considers education a means of rendering the nobles more virtuous. He calls Pluvinel's academy, as Pluvinel himself did, a "vrai oracle et temple de la vertu" (a true oracle and temple of virtue),[45] and, like the others, advises the French nobility to remain loyal to Henry IV.

[43] The sources that I have been able to find on him in the B.N. (Cabinet d'Hozier, 272; Carrés d'Hozier, 499; Manuscrits Français 28790; and Dossiers Bleus, 528) and in the A.N. (P. 74²) say nothing of his ancestors but show him to be fully noble and with a sizable and apparently profitable estate. In 1609, for instance, he was referred to as "Messire Anthoine de Pluvinel Chevalier de l'Ordre du Roy Gentilhomme ordinaire de la chambre de sa Majesté Cappitaine et Gouverneur pour sa ditte Majesté de la Ville et Chasteau de Montfort Laumaury . . . Commandant en sa grande Escurye et Gouverneur de la personne de Monsegneur le Duc de Vendosme. . . ." (B.N., Carrés d'Hozier, 499).

[44] Alexandre de Pontaymery, L'académie ou institution de la noblesse françoise in Les oeuvres (Paris, 1599), p. 17v. For instance, he writes: "All virtue renders illustrious he who employs it, but I would say that the seigneur who is of noble and ancient race, adds to and increases the virtue even, and gives it degrees of perfection that it could not reach in a person of low birth [basse estoffe]."

[45] Ibid., p. 56v.

Although they use some of the old terminology and talk a good deal about virtue, Flurance-Rivault, Pelletier, Pluvinel, and Pontaymery all accept the new idea of nobility. Like other writers of the early seventeenth century, they separate virtue and nobility, assume and sometimes emphasize the primacy of birth, and drop the equation of nobility and action.

IN 1610 in his *Traité des ordres et simples dignitez*, in which he signaled specifically his disagreement with Tiraqueau on the question, Loyseau wrote that nobility was not lost by "non-virtuous" actions: "But as far as nobility of birth [noblesse de race] is concerned, which is as if natural to man, I contend, in opposition to Tiraqueau, that it is not at all lost completely by infamous and ignominious actions [*infamie*]."[46] Loyseau was certainly speaking for the absolutist state and the *société de blocage*, but he was also pointing out what was becoming more and more a standard assumption. Nobility was not something determined by action and could not be lost by *infamie*, as believed in the sixteenth century; it was a status determined simply by birth. Such a conclusion by someone as influential as Loyseau makes it appear that the question had been settled; and indeed a sampling from some of the better-known writers of the next forty to fifty years shows that the modern view underlay their thinking on the question; by the middle of the century nobility as birth, with virtue not being directly relevant to the question, was even more clearly understood and accepted.

Louis de Mayerne Turquet, for instance, one of the more perceptive political and social observers of his time, reflects some interesting attitudes toward nobility in his *La monarchie aristodémocratique*, published in 1611 although it was apparently written earlier.[47] Mayerne Turquet was legally a no-

[46] Charles Loyseau, *Traité des ordres et simples dignitez* in *Les oeuvres* (Paris, 1666), p. 47.

[47] Roland Mousnier in "L'opposition politique bourgeoise à la fin du xvie siècle et au début du xvii siècle: L'oeuvre de Louis Turquet de Mayerne," *Revue historique* 213 (1955), 1, suggests that Mayerne-Turquet actually wrote

ble—he had been one since 1609—though his father had been a merchant from Lyon.[48] He accepts the separation of virtue and birth and assumes that nobility will be based upon birth, but he is definitely not antinoble. Nobility comes from God,[49] for instance, and is as well *le chef-d'oeuvre du souverain*.[50] Nevertheless, he wants to break down distinctions of importance between nobles and nonnobles,[51] by, for instance, opening up all professions to nobles,[52] but also more subtly simply by not having nonnobles *dédaignés* or looked down upon by nobles.[53]

Nobility thus does not play a particularly important part in his scheme, a fact which indeed seems quite understandable since it was accepted by most that nobles no longer had to be virtuous. Thanks in part to the separating of virtue from nobility, then, some social thinkers—and in this case one who was working quite perceptively toward redefining social categories—were able to free themselves more from the old clichés and approach an analysis of the world and how it should be from a more realistic point of view.

Antoine de Montchrestien, author of the famous *Traité de l'économie politique* of 1615, and apparently another recent *anobli*,[54] reflects in his work the same separation of virtue and birth as is found in other writers of his period,[55] while still

---

the work quite a bit earlier, but it seems unlikely that he did not work on and adapt it during the years before he published it in 1611.

[48] B.N., Pièces Originales, 1903, and B.N., Carrés d'Hozier, 423. The latter, the report of an *enquête et vérification* made in 1609, two years before the appearance of the *Monarchie aristodémocratique*, stated that beyond a doubt his two sons were descended from noble blood ("extraits de noble race"). See also Mousnier, "L'opposition politique," pp. 4–5.

[49] Loys de Mayerne Turquet, *La monarchie aristodémocratique* . . . (Paris, 1611), p. 291.

[50] Ibid., p. 146.

[51] Ibid., pp. 79–81, 105.

[52] Ibid., p. 92.

[53] Ibid., pp. 80–81.

[54] Cf. the introduction by Funck-Brentano in Antoine de Montchrestien, *Traicté de l'oeconomie politique*, ed. Th. Funck-Brentano (Paris, n.d), p. iv.

[55] For instance, ibid., pp. 362–363.

at times associating *vertu* and nobility fairly closely. But when he does this he never suggests or even implies that a noble without virtue would ever cease to be noble;[56] he would simply be a nonvirtuous noble (which would have been essentially a contradiction in terms for the minds of the sixteenth century). André Lefèvre d'Ormesson, writing about his father Olivier in 1615, also shows the separation of virtue and nobility. "I know very well," he wrote in reference to his father, "that there are plenty of imprudent men who, through a common error, prefer nobility to virtue and hide the true origin of their father in order to appear as if they came from a better family."[57] Here as well, then—and in this case, like Charron, the writer shows some dislike of the role of birth—nobility and virtue are separated in the modern way.

Mayerne Turquet, Montchrestien, and Lefèvre d'Ormesson all wrote or published in the decade after 1610—that relatively less well-known and seemingly confusing interregnum[58] before the rise to power of Richelieu in 1624; and indeed their

[56] For instance (ibid., p. 361), he associates the two fairly closely when he complains about the importance of money in society, arguing that the king, when choosing his officers, and especially those *de l'espée*, should reward *vertu* (and here he means nobles) instead of money. But he is not suggesting that nobility should be based upon virtue. Instead, in making his appeal against the power of money in society, he simply uses *vertu* as a sort of carry-over term to connote simply being born a noble, but not being rich. A similar plea and use of the term appear as late as 1649 in the *cahiers* of the nobles of Troyes who call for *vertu* over money in the choosing of offices (Mousnier, Labatut, and Durand, eds., *Problèmes de stratification sociale*, p. 141), and also in 1614 in the *cahier* of the nobles of Chaumont-en-Bassigny (B.N., Nouvelles Acquisitions, 2808).

[57] Olivier Lefèvre d'Ormesson, *Journal et extraits des mémoires d'André Lefèvre d'Ormesson*, ed. M. Chéruel, 2 vols. (Paris, 1860–1861), I, iii.

[58] Thanks to a series of research projects under the general direction of Denis Richet, however, which focus on the Estates General of 1614, we are becoming more knowledgeable about this period; and it is clear that by 1614 there had been important shifts in political attitudes and activities from the late sixteenth century even if important differences with what was to come by the middle of the seventeenth century remained. Cf. Roger Chartier and Denis Richet, eds., *Représentation et vouloir politiques: Autour des Etats-Généraux de 1614* (Paris, 1982).

views of nobility were perhaps not as clear-cut as those that followed. For, from the period of Richelieu onward, the separation of virtue and birth appears to have become even more pronounced. It is well known that important breakthroughs in the development of absolutism and of the absolutist state were made under Richelieu,[59] in some ways certainly the decisive ones,[60] and these were continued for the most part under Mazarin.[61] The task of trying to break any force too powerful that threatened the overriding authority of the monarch was continued, and certainly often with increased vigor and greater efficacity.[62] The intellectual justifications for absolutism were pushed beyond Bodin.[63] At the same time recent work has made it even clearer that nobility itself was not threatened,[64] only too independent a nobility.

[59] Recently, for instance, the important work of Richard Bonney, *Political Change in France under Richelieu and Mazarin, 1624–1661* (New York and London, 1978), focusing on the accomplishments of the intendants as seen from the "center"; and also, from an intellectual perspective, the masterful study by William F. Church on the relations between the religious and moral principles of the time and the theories and actions of reason of state, *Richelieu and Reason of State* (Princeton, N.J., 1972).

[60] This is the contention of A.D. Liublinskaia in her useful analysis of the decade of the 1620s in *French Absolutism: The Crucial Phase, 1620–1629*, trans. Brian Pearce (Cambridge, Eng. 1968), 1st Russian ed. 1965, especially chaps. 3–6.

[61] Bonney, in *Political Change in France*, shows this continuity well.

[62] This well-known process, which almost all local historians of seventeenth-century France are well aware of for their particular area, can be understood even better now, thanks to studies such as Bercé's *Histoire des Croquants* and Pillorget's *Les mouvements insurrectionnels*, which show the effects of the encroaching absolutist state on local societies well. William H. Beik, meanwhile, separates "parlementary" resistance to this state from that of the "people" in an interesting way in "Magistrates and Popular Uprisings in France before the Fronde: The Case of Toulouse," *The Journal of Modern History* 46 (1974), 585–608. For some perceptive comments on the role of the royal officers in this process, see Ralph E. Giesey, "State-Building in Early Modern France: The Role of Royal Officialdom," *Journal of Modern History* 55 (1983), 191–207.

[63] See, for instance, Richet, *La France moderne*, pp. 44–57, especially p. 57.

[64] For instance, see Orest Ranum, "Richelieu and the Great Nobility: Some Aspects of Early Modern Political Motives," *French Historical Studies* 3 (1963),

Many nobles continued to support the absolutist state; some resisted it, of course, from time to time, but when they did they were put down, and nobility of birth was never questioned. The separation of virtue and action from the conception of nobility—which, as we have seen, implied the breaking of the independent military power of the nobles—continued clearly to be in the interest of the absolute monarchy and those who supported it. In a sense, then, there could be little serious opposition to nobility determined by birth or an acceptance of birth, beyond mild complaining—for nobles resisting absolutism could hardly oppose it—and all of the articulate upper-class society seems basically to have accepted it.

Charles Sorel's novel, *Histoire comique de Francion*, which was published in 1621, three years before Richelieu's ascent to power, is a mine of information about social habits and mores of the period; the manner in which the story is told and the author's preoccupations and emphases reflect well the changed attitudes toward the nobility. There is a much greater clarity, preciseness, and interest concerning social distinctions than in earlier stories. For example, whereas Rabelais made vague references to *gentilhomme* from time to time, when it is obvious that his interest lay elsewhere, Sorel constantly refers to birth, to *extraction,* and to moving from one class to another. He often uses terms such as *basse condition* and *basses âmes*, and even calls brigands of higher birth *tire-soie* and those of lower birth *tire-laine*.[65] With this increased interest in so-

---

184–204, who shows that despite some apparent antinoble actions, Richelieu was much less antiaristocratic than had been thought; Deyon, "A propos des rapports," who suggests the development of a split in the first half of the seventeenth century between some of the more powerful nobles, who joined with the monarchy and its fiscal policy, and the poorer, weaker nobles; and D.J. Sturdy, "Tax Evasion, the *Faux* Nobles, and State Fiscalism: The Example of the Généralité of Caen, 1634–35," *French Historical Studies* 9 (1976), 549–572, who shows the government's policy of favoring the existing social hierarchy.

[65] Charles Sorel, *Histoire comique de Francion* (Paris, 1965), 1st ed. 1621, p. 59.

cial distinctions, and in particular the realization that birth was an important determiner of these distinctions, came a reflection of that feeling of "social superiority" about birth seen in other writers of the immediately preceding years. Peasants are looked down upon for their *basses âmes*, a noble regrets his contacts with *une telle canaille*, and a financier is looked down upon and considered of no merit because he has only money.[66] Even the decline of law is now blamed on the lawyers because they come from lower classes.[67] This suggests an important shift away from the "battle of professions" view of the sixteenth century. For example, when Noël Du Fail, a noble, attacked the law, he tended to emphasize how the profession of law was harming the nobility—or in his mind the "profession" of nobility—thus causing a general decline, rather than how lack of noble birth supposedly made one almost automatically a bad lawyer. Sorel's book, whether it mocks birth or just describes its role, suggests a society in which the question of birth had become a basic part of people's thinking and assumptions when dealing with social realities and structures.

The separation of virtue from nobility and birth in Nicolas Faret's *L'honneste homme ou l'art de plaire à la cour* of 1630 seems to be even clearer and more pronounced than in other works. Faret in fact discusses the two in completely different places. Early in the book—and essentially like Castiglione in *The Courtier*—he talks of nobility and its advantages, and, except where birth may help bring virtue, he barely mentions *vertu* at all.[68] Later he discusses the quality of *Vertu* (with a capital "V") without once mentioning nobility.[69] *Vertu*, in fact, is the only quality that fortune cannot bring:

> The principal means of acquiring it [virtue] are, in my opinion, good education, diligence and work, good habits

[66] Ibid., pp. 49, 84, 116.
[67] Ibid., p. 111.
[68] Nicolas Faret, *L'honneste homme ou l'art de plaire à la cour*, ed. M. Magendie (Paris, 1925), 1st ed. 1630, pp. 10–11.
[69] Ibid., pp. 23–24.

[bonnes habitudes], the frequenting of good people, the desire for glory, following the example of one's predecessors, and the study of letters.[70]

His discussion of virtue is essentially divorced from social class and politics. Noble or nonnoble has little or nothing to do with the question and indeed is not even mentioned. Similar assumptions about birth are found a little later in M. de Grenaille's *L'honneste garçon* of 1642.[71] In Faret's time, then, people seemed little interested in discussing and philosophizing about the true nature or quality of nobility. Nobility was a given; people accepted it—and this is true even for Sorel— and then addressed questions that apparently interested them more.

Corneille's *Cinna*, first performed in 1640, reflects a gifted writer's understanding of the relationship between the separation of virtue and action from nobility with the concomitant acceptance of noble birth, on the one hand, and the emergence of the early absolutist state, on the other hand. The story is a Roman one. Cinna is a noble of ancient lineage who is driven by honor, by his noble heritage of freedom, and by his mistress, who represents these things, to plan the assassination of Augustus, but the way the situation is presented reflects the problems of Corneille's own time. One of the interesting aspects is that no blood is spilled and that in the end Cinna accepts Augustus as absolute ruler ("I shall obey thee, sire");[72] Augustus pardons Cinna and accepts him as a great noble, after he has first presented himself unarmed before Cinna, telling him that he should kill him if he still wished and that the only reason he acted as absolute ruler was to serve the best interests of the state. Cinna decides not to act and instead accepts Augustus's authority. In the man-

[70] Ibid., p. 75.

[71] Cf. M. de Grenaille, *L'honneste garçon* . . . (Paris, 1642).

[72] Pierre Corneille, *Cinna* in *Théâtre complet*, ed. M. Rat, 3 vols. (Paris, n.d.), act V, scene 1, line 1433. The English translations are by Lacy Lockert in *The Chief Plays of Corneille* (Princeton, N.J. 1957).

ner of Henry IV, and specifically as with the Sire de Gimel, there are pardons in exchange for submission.[73] The story also adds a subtle touch, for Augustus has won this time not by force but by reason: "For thou has learned the way to rule men's hearts [Vous avez trouvé l'art d'être maître des coeurs]," says Livia, his wife, at the end; "Rome with a joy both keen and deep consigns unto thy hands the empire of the world."[74]

It is interesting that in a way the conflict in the play changes from that of liberty versus tyranny—of noble Cinna versus the tyrant Caesar who is destroying the ancient freedoms of the aristocracy—to that of absolutism, or the rule of one man versus disorder and anarchy. It is this change that makes possible the acceptance of Augustus by Cinna and the others. To choose freedom, independence, and virtue—and thus a greater responsibility—over tyranny (a sixteenth-century choice and Cinna's choice at the beginning of the play) is what any noble or honorable person would do; to choose absolutism instead of anarchy (a seventeenth-century choice and Cinna's choice at the end of the play), however, is also perhaps what a noble or honorable person should do. Such a story suggests a change in Corneille's scheme from a view of a nobility that is free, independent, and *vertueuse* to a nobility that is essentially defined by birth, a birth or *rang* that has value only under the authority of the monarch. "You have no influence nor rank except as my favor dispenses it [Tu n'as crédit ni rang qu'autant qu'elle (ma faveur) t'en donne]," says Augustus to Cinna near the end of the play.[75] On the other

[73] This method, to be sure, did not always work for Henry IV. He apparently spent two days talking to the Maréchal Biron, including a nocturnal game of cards, trying to get him to admit his treason and submit, but when he would not the king finally had him arrested and executed. Cf. Irene Mahoney, *Royal Cousin, The Life of Henry IV of France* (Garden City, N.Y., 1970), pp. 387–389.

[74] Corneille, *Cinna*, act V, scene 3, lines 1764–1766.

[75] Ibid., act V, scene 2, line 1530. This translation is mine. The entire passage (lines 1527–1532) shows this relationship between the authority of the monarch and nobility of birth well.

hand, Corneille, like other writers of the period, separates the quality of virtue from social class and politics.[76]

The example of *Cinna* thus suggests that the separation of virtue and nobility was also integrated into some of the great literature of the time. For Corneille, birth is all important, so important that it in itself brings or transmits virtue, and nobles appear to have a monopoly on that quality, though he is able to separate the two in a modern way. Nonnobles, it seems, can almost never be virtuous, but nobles can be nonvirtuous without any serious consequences, especially under the new order at the end of the play. *Généreux* is used often by Corneille, which means essentially *bien né* to him. A revealing passage in *Cinna*, showing Corneille's attitude and the newer view of the seventeenth century, concerns the story of the freed slave, Euphorbus, the only person who ends up acting ignobly in the play. His reason for behaving in this way is that he is lowborn, which of course implies that non-nobles cannot be virtuous and that birth alone brings virtue. He, the lowborn slave, has corrupted the highborn noble Maxime:

> Euphorbus, this is the result of thy / Base counsels, but indeed what else can be / Expected from one such as thou? A Freedman / Is never anything but a vile slave [esclave infâme]. *Though his condition changes, in his soul / He changes not* (Bien qu'il change d'état, il ne change point d'âme). Thine, servile still, with freedom / Hath found no spark of true nobility. / Thou madest me uphold unlawful power; / Thou madest me belie *mine honored birth* [l'honneur de ma naissance].[77]

Polyeucte also reflects similar attitudes, strongly emphasizing and exalting aristocratic virtues that appear to come through noble birth.

Corneille, then, emphasized the virtue brought by birth

---

[76] Virtue is simply a quality, for instance, in Cinna's statement about virtue in act III, scene 4, lines 969–972.

[77] Ibid., act IV, scene 6, lines 1407–1414. The emphasis is mine.

particularly strongly and more consciously than most of his contemporaries, although this emphasis seems understandable in the context of the overall world view he expressed.[78] Most people by the middle of the century, however, held a more moderate view that assumed that virtue could exist both in nonnobles and nobles, but that this question of virtue, since the legal privilege of nobility was determined by birth, was simply not relevant one way or the other to the question of nobility; by that time, everyone had separated virtue from nobility. The perspective Pascal, for instance, reflects in the 1650s this modern view well. Nobility and virtue are completely separate for him, and he unconditionally accepts birth as the basis of nobility. He feels birth does not bring a great advantage, though in terms of personal advancement a nobleman can achieve in eighteen years what another man of equal ability could achieve only after fifty years.[79] For Pascal nobility is not reasonable and noble birth is not superior.[80] He goes on to say that, despite this, it should still be honored, that there is a certain "reason" or wisdom in its unreasonableness: ". . . it is true that we must honor noblemen, but not because noble birth is real superiority."[81] Nobility still fulfilled a need or function, then, but was hardly as significant and indispensable as when it was equated with the military or the military profession; and it hardly restricted or bothered the nonnoble Pascal.

By the time of Pascal, then, the separation of virtue and action from nobility was basically complete. Nobles were essentially defined by their birth. This modern idea of nobility emerged, as we have seen, not because of any one person or persons, and not because of any great influence brought

[78] Cf., for instance, Bénichou, *Morales du grand siècle*, especially pp. 15–120; and Krailsheimer, *Studies in Self-Interest*, especially pp. 47–60.

[79] Blaise Pascal, *Pensées* (Paris, 1960), pp. 157–158.

[80] Ibid., pp. 158–161: (". . . The world again exults in showing how unreasonable this is"). The translations of Pascal are by W.F. Trotter in Blaise Pascal, *Pensées and the Provincial Letters* (New York, 1941).

[81] Ibid., p. 161.

on by ancient and Renaissance texts; but it came about in a sort of hit-or-miss fashion because the old concept, which lacked relevance to new conditions, had become obsolete and even dangerous in the context of the social upheavals of the early 1590s. Furthermore, the new idea fit very well, for the time being at least, with the aims and objectives of the absolutist regime imposed (or accepted) after 1594. Nobility, then, was no longer something you did; it had become what it is usually understood to be today: "une qualité d'exception transmise par le sang."[82] The intellectual groundwork was thus laid for the well-known noble theorists of the late ancien régime and later, such as Boulainvilliers and Saint-Simon, who would put great and almost unique emphasis upon a nobility based on birth and blood.[83] These extremists, however, would usually be on the fringe of the main currents of thought, and the vast majority of people would henceforth simply accept nobility of birth as a normal part of the social and political world. But whether they liked it, disapproved of it, or were indifferent to it, they all erred in common if they believed that their concept of nobility was universal and had existed since the beginnings of nobility.

[82] Philippe Du Puy de Clinchamps, *La noblesse* (Paris, 1968), p. 99: "a quality of superiority transmitted by blood."

[83] Cf., for instance, Devyver, *Le sang épuré*, pp. 243–437.

7

Old and New *Marques de Noblesse* and the Diminished Importance of Nobility in the First Half of the Seventeenth Century

The separation of the concepts of virtue and action from nobility in the first half of the seventeenth century and the new emphasis on birth signalled the downfall of the medieval view of nobility. The key change had taken place. In the sixteenth century, except for some glorification of the ancientness of some individual upper-class families, the only really strong emphasis on birth and blood had been for the families of the kings, in order to separate, for instance, the princes of the blood from the peers.[1] From the early seventeenth century on, then, nobility as a collective social group had joined the monarchy in becoming a hereditary entity. With this change came a series of parallel and sometimes complementary developments and changes in the *marques de noblesse*, or the signs and privileges of nobility that had traditionally helped to define and characterize the nobles. Certain of the old *marques* that grew out of the military origins of the nobility continued, more or less unchanged into the new period; some underwent changes that reflect well the larger change from a medieval to a more modern view of nobility; and several important new ones—or, like birth, essentially new when ap-

---

[1] Cf. Richard A. Jackson, "Peers of France and Princes of the Blood," *French Historical Studies* 7 (1971), 27–46; and Ralph Giesey, *The Juristic Basis of Dynastic Right to the French Throne* in *Proceedings of the American Philosophical Society*, n.s., v. 51, pt. 5 (1961).

plied to the nobility—emerged, such as the duel and special education and culture (see chapter 8).

Most of these changes, developments, and redefinitions reflect the growing awareness of the limitations of the old view and the accompanying desire for a more well-defined and modern view, which had already begun to emerge in the 1570s and 1580s. As mentioned earlier, this growing *prise de conscience* was due at one level to the conditions of general breakdown and crisis of society during the period of the Religious Wars; but in a more general and long-term sense it was a response to the changing social, political, economic, and military realities of the period, and in particular to the declining military function of the nobles. If nobility was going to continue to exist in the more modern world of the seventeenth and eighteenth centuries, and specifically in the context of the new absolutist state, nobles would exist—as they came to realize more and more—with their power diminished or shared with other elites in society. In short, with nobility no longer understood and justified essentially in terms of the military and action, a "noble" would become simply a member of an elite who had the legal privileges of nobility along with usually certain other advantages not peculiar to or limited to nobility (such as wealth, education, office, etc.). The differences in terms of power or influence in society between a nobleman and the person who had the other advantages but not the legal privilege of nobility would usually be small (and sometimes, as with the right to carry on certain forms of commerce, there would even be a disadvantage). That difference would depend on the extent to which the new idea or myth of nobility—that nobles were superior because of birth or culture—was believed by nobility and the rest of society, since it was belief in this idea that theoretically justified the advantages and legal privileges. The history of the *marques de noblesse* in the period reflects well this movement toward a less important function of nobility in later ancien régime society.

The sixteenth-century French already associated a series of

signs and privileges with nobility, and we know most of these if not all their local variations.[2] These inlcude the right to carry a sword and the right to hunt—activities identified with nobility as the fighting profession—and various legal privileges, such as being tried by different courts and being beheaded instead of hanged for most crimes that demanded the death penalty. Nobles apparently also had the right to wear special clothes or other accoutrements, and, according to Montaigne, they had such honorific privileges as being permitted to stand near the king bare-headed.[3] L'Alouëte, as others before and after him, felt that the holding of a fief should be a sign of nobility; along with this and the hunt and the sword, he added the right to have special coats of arms as his fourth distinguishing mark of nobility.[4] Other *marques de noblesse* included exemption from taxation, in particular from the *taille*;[5] a privileged system of inheritance;[6] exemption of the paying of the *franc-fief*;[7] and the limitations on the

[2] For instance, Doucet, *Les institutions*, II, 489–490; Pierre Goubert, *The Ancien Régime, French Society, 1600–1750*, trans. George Weidenfeld (New York, 1973), pp. 162–167; and Mousnier, *The Institutions of France*, pp. 124–126.

[3] Montaigne, *Essais*, Book I, chap. 43, p. 270.

[4] L'Alouëte, *Traité*, p. 35.

[5] Cf., for instance, Edmond Esmonin, *La taille en Normandie au temps de Colbert (1661–1683)* (Paris, 1913), especially pp. 196–199. For an analysis of noble fiscal privilege, put into the larger context of Europe and examined over the long term, see M.L. Bush, *The European Nobility*, vol. I, *Noble Privilege* (New York, 1983), pp. 27–64.

[6] What Tocqueville called the basis of any aristocratic regime; and with the destruction of this privileged system of partition by the French Revolution, the nobility was, he felt, irrevocably weakened. See Alexis de Tocqueville, *Democracy in America*, trans. Henry Reeve, ed. Phillips Bradley, 2 vols. (New York, 1945), I, 47–50. And it is indeed true that among the French nobles two-thirds of the inheritance usually went to the eldest son and the rest was divided among the others, although there were enormous variations throughout France and not all regions followed the two-thirds/one-third system, even if most did. See also the comments on this in Bush, *Noble Privilege*, pp. 192–193, 197–198.

[7] The *franc-fief* was a payment assessed by the king from time to time on nonnobles holding fiefs, or thus what had supposedly once been noble lands.

carrying out of most forms of commerce based on the concept of *dérogeance*.[8]

Probably the best known and most widely accepted sign of nobility in the sixteenth century was the right to carry arms, in particular the sword; this seems to have changed little from the sixteenth to the seventeenth centuries (if there was a change, it was in the question of upon whose authority, the king's or his own, the noble had the right to use his sword). *Homme d'épée*, for instance, was apparently another way of saying *gentilhomme*. This custom was so much a natural part of one's thinking that Montaigne, in telling a story, felt called upon to remark about a particular situation when a noble was *not* carrying a sword. In listing a number of things that might irritate a king, he included ". . . seeing a noble appear, in a place calling for respect, without his sword at his side, all slovenly and untidy, as if he were coming from the toilet."[9] Pelletier was making another point completely when he said, "It is a too voluntary ignorance among certain of the nobility to esteem that they have this privilege to carry a sword at their side only to cause offense to those weaker than they."[10] And Faret in 1630 wrote: "It seems to me, therefore, that the greatest ambition of he who carries a sword is to be considered a man of courage and boldness."[11] From another perspective we see Claude Haton, a nonnoble, who petitioned to the *bailli*, or local official of the king, early in the Religious Wars for the right to carry a sword in his city because of the unrest and disorder, and found it perfectly normal for a nonnoble to make this request.[12]

J.-R. Bloch found, in the first half of the sixteenth century, that the paying of this duty by nonnobles and not by nobles was the only sure distinguishing sign between nobles and nonnobles that was accepted as being valid by everyone. See *L'anoblissement*, especially pp. 213–215.

[8] See below, and notes 43–46.

[9] Montaigne, *Essais*, Book I, chap. 43, pp. 269–270. The translation is from the Donald Frame edition except that I have translated *gentilhomme* as "noble" rather than "gentleman."

[10] Pelletier, *La nourriture*, p. 14.

[11] Faret, *L'honneste homme*, p. 13.

[12] Haton, *Mémoires*, pp. xxv–xxvi.

The carrying of the sword continued to be a sign of nobility into the seventeenth and eighteenth centuries,[13] though it certainly became less and less effective as a distinguishing mark of nobility, partly because of the growing difficulty of preventing nonnobles from wearing one. The sword symbolized the old profession of nobility, but as that profession disappeared and the military developed into a more autonomous institution composed of officers of various social backgrounds, it inevitably become a less effective distinguishing mark.

The hunt as a distinguishing mark of nobility seems to have had a fate similar to that of the sword, at least in the sense that it became more and more difficult to police. The hunt, seen as a right of nobles only, was originally justified because it served two purposes: the nobles killed wild animals and thus theoretically protected the people, and it kept them in good condition and training for fighting.[14] From the sixteenth century on it was associated very closely and almost unconsciously with the nobility. For example, Olivier de Serres in his *Théâtre d'agriculture* is generally unconcerned with social questions or distinctions, and it is therefore revealing that he makes a distinction only in referring to the hunt. When writing about the managing of a country estate, he addresses his comments to the *père de famille* or someone similar; only when he refers to the hunt does he abruptly and without fanfare switch to *gentilhomme* or *noble père de famille*. In moderation the *gentilhomme* will hunt. "The country *gentilhomme* may enjoy such useful amusements . . . he gives to the hunt a few hours of his time." And later he writes: "At such honorable exercises [that is to say hunting] the *noble père de famille* will pass his time."[15] Without any particular emphasis, Serres just assumed that only nobles would be hunting.

There seems little question, then, that hunting was assumed to be a privilege reserved for the nobility. It was le-

[13] For instance, Goubert, *Ancien Régime*, p. 162.
[14] For instance, L'Alouëte, *Traité*, pp. 62–63.
[15] Olivier de Serres, *Le théâtre d'agriculture et mesnage des champs* (Paris, 1804), 1st ed. 1600, pp. 767–770.

galized by the king in various ordinances,[16] and even some
of the *cahiers* of the Third Estate, which opposed the duel,
accepted and indeed argued that the hunt be limited to just
the nobility.[17] But especially from the middle of the seventeenth century onward, nonnoble seigneurs, some of whom
might even have spent some time in the military—as, for instance, the upper-class nonnoble Cléonte in Molière's *Bourgeois gentilhomme*, who spent six years in what was clearly a
top position in the army while remaining nonnoble—would
hunt more or less as they wished on their estates,[18] and certainly often off them as well, and little or nothing could be
done about it.

Different or special clothes such as silks,[19] wigs, and related accoutrements were another traditional *marque de noblesse*, and they have a function in the late sixteenth century
in an amusing story from the *Mémoires* of the wife of Philippe Du Plessis-Mornay. The story concerns a dispute between Mlle. Du Plessis, as she was known, some other noble ladies, and some of the ministers of the Huguenot Church
while she was living in Montauban in 1584. It is clear from
the context of the story that nobles were expected to wear
different clothes from nonnobles, and one of the prerogatives of the ladies of the *noblesse* was to wear wigs on important occasions, such as when they were entertaining or
were at court. Apparently the ministers of the Protestant
church of Montauban complained that it was against God's
word in the Bible to wear false hair, and they could not per-
mit it. Mlle. Du Plessis took the initiative to continue wearing her wig, encouraging the other ladies of the court of Henry

[16] For instance, the ordinance of 1601 published in Isambert, ed., *Recueil
général des anciennes lois françaises*, XV, 248; see also Gustave Fagniez, *L'économie sociale de la France sous Henry IV, 1589–1610* (Paris, 1897), pp. 19–20.

[17] For example, see the *cahier* of the Third Estate of 1614 published in Robert
Mandrou, ed., *Classes et luttes de classes en France au début du xviie siècle* (Florence, 1969), p. 104.

[18] Cf. Goubert, *Ancien Régime*, p. 163.

[19] For instance, A. Racinet, *Le costume historique*, 6 vols. (Paris, 1824–1888),
V, 68.

of Navarre to do so as well. For her pains she was excommunicated along with her husband and the rest of her family. "It was an [added] aggravation," recounts Mlle. Du Plessis,

> that several nobles and people of quality of the other religion were at court at the time. The result was that on Saturday morning when M. Du Plessis went to the King's levée every one began to laugh at him, and some even took it as an occasion to abuse our religion and our ministers which really did annoy him.[20]

The dispute continued. Despite pressure from some of the powerful nobles the ministers refused to give in, and finally the Mornays had to leave Montauban and go to another nearby town, whose less intransigent ministers allowed them to receive communion.

We do not have enough evidence yet to speculate with any certainty what this story might tell us about the history of early Protestantism in terms of its apparent desire to put religion ahead of the social aspirations and needs of the nobility,[21] but it does show us that people seemed to take it for granted for the most part that nobles would or could wear different clothes and the like. At the same time, people were aware that this was hardly an effective way of distinguishing nobles from nonnobles, since many wealthy nonnobles now could buy the clothes they wanted to. As Montaigne remarked when he referred to the period shortly after the death of Henry II, silks, which once were a good *marque de noblesse* had, because of their easy accessibility, "already sunk so low in everyone's opinion that if you saw anyone dressed in them

---

[20] *Mémoires et correspondance de Du Plessis-Mornay*, 12 vols. (Paris, 1824–1825), II, 491. See pp. 487–514 for the entire account of the story. The translation is by Lucy Crump in *A Huguenot Family in the XVI Century* (n.d., n.p.).

[21] It could, for instance, help a little to explain the falling away of nobles from Protestantism in the seventeenth century, the *embourgeoisement* of the Protestant movement, as Emile Léonard has called it; cf. *Le Protestant français* (Paris, 1953), especially p. 58.

you immediately set him down as a bourgeois [homme de ville]."[22] For Claude Haton, special clothes as an indication of rank did not work well, either; he complained that ". . . the bourgeois of the cities have wished to dress, men and women, in the manner of *gentilshommes*, the *gentilshommes* as sumptuously as princes and the people of the villages in the manner of the bourgeois of the cities."[23] The large number of reissuings of sumptuary laws (ten between 1543 and 1639), including especially the edict of 1485 which tried to limit gold cloth and silk to nobles,[24] also suggests, because of the constant need to reissue the laws, the relative lack of success of clothes as a distinguishing mark. Finally, Louise Godard de Donville has shown how nobles made greater and greater efforts in the late sixteenth century and especially in the first three to four decades of the seventeenth century to develop their "mode" and use it as a means of distinguishing themselves, and also how these efforts, at least in terms of stopping nonnobles from imitating them, met with limited success, at best.[25]

With one or two exceptions most other traditional *marques de noblesse* also became less effective as distinguishing signs. One exception was the use of coats of arms, which were already associated with nobility in the sixteenth century. The limiting of special coats of arms to those who "deserved" them had some success; and indeed many efforts were made in this area in the seventeenth and eighteenth centuries and after—in the context of the new idea of nobility, with its emphasis on noble birth—to separate "noble" coats of arms from others. On the other hand, wealthy nonnobles could hardly be

---

[22] Montaigne, *Essais*, Book I, chap. 43, p. 269.

[23] Haton, *Mémoires*, pp. 92–93.

[24] For the edict of 1485, see Isambert, *Recueil*, XI, 155; for listings of the later ones see Isambert, *Recueil*, XII, 30, and XIII, 538; for several other indications, see L.N.H. Chérin, *Abrégé chronologique . . .* (Paris, 1788), pp. 46–47.

[25] Louise Godard de Donville, *Signification de la mode sous Louis XIII* (Aix-en-Provence, 1978).

stopped from purchasing fiefs, and therefore a fief could not be a successful *marque de noblesse*. Another privilege of nobility was being exempted from some taxation, a practice that apparently developed in the late Middle Ages on the grounds that nobles already met their obligations to society by fighting and thus should be free from other assessments.[26] But already in the sixteenth century this had become a privilege bestowed on some nonnobles,[27] and the practice continued into the seventeenth and eighteenth centuries.[28]

LIMITATIONS in the old *marques de noblesse* such as the sword, the hunt, special clothes, the fief, and exemption from taxation—limitations about which people were becoming more aware from the mid-sixteenth century on—helped to spur the search for new *marques* and also encouraged attempts to make the older ones more effective. Meanwhile, certain other important changes in this area can be detected from the sources or are suggested by what we know from other studies. L'Alouëte in the 1570s, for instance, urged the writing of family genealogies as means of glorifying the family and spurring the representatives of that family to greater virtue.[29] It appears that most of the emphasis in his period and before upon genealogies—which were often invented, of course—was phrased in similar terms and was an attempt to enhance the glory of that particular family by showing its descent from ancient heroes and the like. As the seventeenth century progressed, however, genealogies came to serve a different function as well. In a society with a different idea of nobility, one in which the question was much more important,

[26] Most recently on this, see the fine article by John Bell Henneman, "Nobility, Privilege and Fiscal Politics in Late Medieval France," *French Historical Studies* 13 (1983), 1–17, and the wording of the royal fiscal ordinance of 1445 (pp. 16–17) that would exempt from the *taille* nobles "living nobly and pursuing arms."

[27] For instance, J.-R. Bloch, *L'anoblissement*, p. 214.

[28] Goubert, *Ancien Régime*, p. 165.

[29] L'Alouëte, *Traité*, pp. 28–34, 73.

they would serve to determine who was *really* noble and who was not. The first big proliferation of genealogical studies and books on genealogy, framed usually in terms of finding out imposters, seems to have taken place around the middle third of the seventeenth century. The dates of the main collections of genealogies in the Bibliothèque Nationale suggest this, as does the work of Esmonin,[30] the example of a recent noble,[31] and Colbert's actions in weeding out imposters of the 1660s.[32] In other words, there seems to have been a shift in the writing of genealogies from a family orientation, when nobility was assumed much more to be something one did, to a "class" or "social group" or collective orientation, as nobles were forced to become more aware of themselves as a collective group, defined by the accident of birth.

Much more work is needed in this basically unexplored area of the advent of such genealogical studies,[33] but it is true that work now in progress on the *cahiers* of the Estates General of 1614 suggests a similar or parallel direction of change. The *cahiers* show that nobles, building on the advances of the study of history made in the second half of the previous century and the focus on the Germanic conquest, turned more to history and the past to help find a collective identity that would set them off from the rest of society;[34] and thus they contin-

[30] Cf. Esmonin, *La taille en Normandie.*

[31] See Du Puy de Clinchamps, *La noblesse,* p. 42, writing in 1968 about his family's need to prove its nobility through its genealogy, which first became a problem in 1632 and then again in 1668 (and then, of course, throughout the eighteenth century).

[32] On this see, for instance, Jean Meyer, *La noblesse bretonne au xviiiᵉ siècle,* 2 vols. (Paris, 1966), I, 29–61. Cubells' material on Provence in "A propos des usurpations" shows a similar tightening up beginning with the reign of Louis XIV.

[33] On the general desire, however, to determine more accurately who was really noble and who was not during the reign of Louis XIV, see the discussion of the seventeenth-century scholar and *maître* of the Chambre des Comptes, François de Godet de Soudé in my article, "Ennoblement in France."

[34] See the discussion by Roger Chartier in Chartier and Richet, *Représentation et vouloir politiques,* pp. 120–122; and for background on the advances

ued, in this area as well,[35] the process of their *prise de conscience*.

Another area of concern for nobles, as they attempted to come to grips with changing times, was the problem of the fief. In the early days of feudalism, fiefs were awarded in return for military service.[36] Gradually, on the one hand, the ownership of these fiefs (see chapter 2) had become hereditary, as they were often maintained without any military service, while, on the other hand, nonnobles became more and more able to purchase them. Thus by the sixteenth century the fief had, in its strictest sense, become separated from its military origins and from its noble origins. At the same time, a fief was still often considered a *marque de noblesse*, and appeals continued to be made in the sixteenth century to have all fiefs returned to nobles.[37]

However, it gradually became clear, especially in the generally more realistic atmosphere of the early seventeenth century, that it would be unrealistic and totally impossible to keep fiefs only in the hands of the nobles. The attack thus shifted toward attempts to identify and to separate noble holders of fiefs from nonnoble ones. The nobles of Chaumont-en-Bassigny in 1614, for instance, clearly recognized the impossibility of returning the fiefs to their original owners, or even of stopping the process of others passing into nonnoble hands in the future. All that could be done, then, was to identify and to separate: "That it please your majesty to order that all privileged nonnobles, ennobled nobles [nobles ennoblis], and others now possessing any noble lands

---

in the study of history, George Huppert, *The Idea of Perfect History, Historical Erudition and Historical Philosophy in Renaissance France* (Urbana, Chicago, London, 1970); and Donald R. Kelley, *Foundations of Modern Historical Scholarship: Language, Law and History in the French Renaissance* (New York, 1970).

[35] Robert Mandrou, in *Classes et luttes de classes*, also has some useful comments on the concerns of the nobles in this area and on their conceptions of themselves and the distance that separated them from their ideal past.

[36] Cf., for instance, Bloch, *Feudal Society*.

[37] For example, L'Alouëte in *Traité*, p. 35.

[terres des gentils-hommes], or acquiring them in the future, be forbidden to give themselves any other name than that held by their father or other direct ancestor."[38] The new approach to the problem would thus be simply to scrutinize genealogical records and the like more carefully in order to make distinctions between noble and nonnoble fief holders. The holding of a fief alone would not be enough any more to prove one's nobility, and not surprisingly Constant has found in the Beauce a decline in the percentage of ennoblement through the fief from the sixteenth to the seventeenth centuries.[39]

At the same time, certainly, many people continued to believe or came to believe, as so many do today, that a noble must live in the countryside,[40] that this is the true sign of nobility, the *marque de vraie noblesse*.[41] Thus there was a shift in the image of the noble from that of the fief holder who derived income from his lands so he could fight and serve, to that of the country gentleman, the aristocrat farmer himself responsible for the efficient management of his estate, who appears as the typical nobleman in so many works of literature from at least the eighteenth century onward.

We need a thorough study on this question, however, before we can understand or date this change accurately. Such a study might begin with Olivier de Serres and could examine the economic actions and policies of the seigneurs *and* attempt to relate them to the changing concept of nobility.

[38] B.N., Nouvelles Acquisitions, 2808.

[39] Constant, *Nobles et paysans*, especially pp. 45–47.

[40] As they did not believe, according to Marc Bloch, in the Middle Ages. See his remark in *Feudal Society*, II, 302–303, that the ideal of "the 'country gentleman' belongs to quite another age" after, in his opinion, the "economic revolution in the sixteenth century."

[41] Pierre de Vaissière, *Gentilshommes campagnards de l'ancienne France: Etude sur la condition, l'état social et les moeurs de la noblesse de province du xvie siècle* (Paris, 1903), p. 176. And for other older works on the nobility with this assumption see Lucien Romier, *Le royaume de Catherine de Médicis: La France à la veille des guerres de religion*, 2 vols. (Paris, 1922), pp. 160–239 and especially pp. 161–165, and Henri Baudrillart, *Gentilshommes ruraux de la France* (Paris, 1893).

It might well show that the disappearance of the medieval view of nobility and the emergence of the ideal of the country gentleman could have helped to encourage increased efficiency on the estate, as estate management replaced fighting as the prime function of the noble. Such a study might also show a diminishing distance between noble and nonnoble in the later ancien régime, manifesting itself in an enlarged group of elites that had more interests in common than differences[42] and together dominated society. Noble and nonnoble landowners, in short, could look alike, live alike, and function alike in the ancien régime, which suggests a rather small gulf between them; noble and nonnoble holders of fiefs would theoretically have been separated by a much larger gulf—that of fulfilling or not fulfilling the military profession.

The concept of *dérogeance*, or of derogating from noble status when carrying on certain forms of commerce, has fascinated a number of historians, and in this case we do have some very helpful studies of the phenomenon. R. B. Grassby, for instance, in his search to explain why capitalism did not develop to the same extent and at the same rate in France as in England, has tried to explain and understand why the concept seemed to have such a hold on people's minds in the seventeenth century; and he admits his failure.[43] Gaston Zeller traced the idea over a much longer period of time and has shown how the concept—which he also finds strange, illogical, hard to understand or justify, and thus an odd anachronism—gradually became more obsolete as it moved toward extinction in a modernizing world.[44] Zeller does suggest

[42] Cf. the groundbreaking article by Denis Richet, "Autour des origines idéologiques lointaines de la Révolution française: Elites et despotisme," *Annales: Economies, sociétés, civilisations* 24 (1969), 1–23, and the discussion on this in chap. 9.

[43] R.B. Grassby, "Social Status and Commercial Enterprise under Louis XIV," *Economic History Review* (series 2), 13 (1960), 19–38.

[44] Gaston Zeller, "Une notion de caractère historico-sociale: La dérogeance," in *Aspects de la politique française sous l'ancien régime* (Paris, 1964), 337–374. See also the general discussion of the concept by Davis Bitton (*French*

that the idea probably derived from the early Christian era and the Church's attacks on usury, but he does not push this explanation very far, nor does he try to explain why *dérogeance* applied only to nobles.

Thus both historians are perplexed with the apparent illogic and even stupidity of the concept. However, this *marque de noblesse* does in fact make sense so long as nobility is viewed as a profession, as something one does, since a noble cannot fulfill the duties of his profession and carry out commerce as well. As late as 1678, when justifying the concept and the practice, La Roque pointed out what almost everyone in the sixteenth century knew, that "La noblesse est née entre les armes", and that therefore it would be a contradiction in terms for nobles to carry on commerce.[45] By that time, however, many other nobles had forgotten this idea, making it easier to argue the opposite.[46] The matter had simply become one to be debated; because nobility was no longer a profession, *dérogeance* had lost its major justification and was no longer easy to defend or rationalize.

The concept and practice persisted somewhat into the second half of the seventeenth and the eighteenth centuries, and remnants of the attitude can indeed still be found today, probably because this *marque* could be adapted to some extent to the new idea of nobility. It seems, for instance, to have blended into more modern ideas of *noblesse oblige*, with the obligations of birth demanding a certain set of actions or inactions. Such actions would, however, certainly be a good deal more difficult to defend or justify than they were when nobility was in essence the profession of the military, which helps to explain the increasingly successful attack on the concept beginning at the middle of the eighteenth century, as the

---

Nobility, pp. 64–76), who, however, does not seem aware of this important article by Zeller.

[45] Gilles André de La Roque, *Traité de la noblesse et toutes ses différentes espèces* (Rouen, 1734), p. 251, cited also by Zeller in "Une notion," p. 360: "The origin of nobility is in arms."

[46] Zeller, "Une notion," p. 361.

matter of a *noblesse commercante* became a center of attention[47]

The question of the *noblesse de robe*, or the connection between the legal profession and nobility in early modern France, has been treated by many historians. Although "law" was not a traditional *marque de noblesse*, it did become one, in a certain way, and thus deserves some attention here. The question is extremely complex. Much has been written on the matter from various perspectives and is often contradictory. Some historians, for instance, consider the "robe-sword" conflict as one of the basic social struggles of the time,[48] while others feel such a conflict had little significance or was essentially nonexistent.[49] What is certain, however, is that the question of a *noblesse de robe* is closely connected to the general rise in importance of the legal profession,[50] as well as to the emergence of modern ideas of profession in general,[51] and to the changing role and function of offices in the old regime.

Some interesting conclusions emerge when we put our knowledge about this matter into the context of a view of nobility as a profession and the eventual change away from that view. From this perspective, law could indeed be seen as a kind of limited threat to a military nobility during the

[47] See chap. 9.

[48] For example, see Salmon, *Society in Crisis*; Cornelius Sipple, "The *Noblesse de la Robe* in Early Seventeenth-Century France: A Study in Social Mobility*," Ph.D. diss., University of Michigan (1963); and, in terms of his main underlying assumptions, Huppert in *Bourgeois Gentilshommes*.

[49] See the discussion in chap. 9 and the works cited therein in notes 23–27 and 29.

[50] See, for instance, Bouwsma, "Lawyers and Early Modern Culture," pp. 303–327, and his comment on p. 310: "Here [in the Church in this case] as elsewhere law becomes significant in direct proportion to the growth of social and institutional complexity"; and Stone, *Crisis of the Aristocracy*, and his comment on p. 242: "A consequence of the decline of violence was an astonishing growth in litigation. Societies being weaned from habits of private revenge always turn to the law with intemperate enthusiasm, but by any standards the growth of litigation between 1550 and 1625 [in England] was something rather exceptional."

[51] See the beginning section of chap. 9.

Middle Ages and on into the sixteenth century,[52] in the sense that it was based on premises different from military force and power. Conflict was expressed more in terms of a "battle of professions" than a real battle between social groups, or, as Dewald has suggested, as a battle or antagonism between different life styles among the elites, which had emerged because of their different professions, though they often drew their landed income in similar ways.[53] And it is indeed as a battle of professions that such a conflict appears in writers like Du Fail, L'Alouëte, La Noue, and Charles de La Ruelle.[54] To see it as more than that would not make much sense, since there were so many jurists who, although legally noble, seemed still to be attacking the nobility (but were actually attacking the military profession). On the other hand, there were many nobles, like Du Fail and La Ruelle, who appear extremely antilegal, even though many of them were in the legal profession; thus, if this were a social struggle of nobles against others, they would be attacking some of their own— not a particularly logical act. Even Du Fail, who seems so antilegal, was a lawyer, although he thought of himself as a noble first and a lawyer second.

It makes sense, then, to view the expressions of an apparent "robe-sword" conflict in the sixteenth century as not much more than a battle of professions, a difference of views among elites as to what is a good profession, the way that professors and lawyers might debate the matter today in the United States. Law could still be a threat to nobility as a fighting profession, with the implied independence inherent in the view, to the extent that it could suggest that the law apply

[52] For an example of this, see Headley, "Nobles and Magistrates."

[53] Dewald, *Formation of a Provincial Nobility*, especially pp. 16–68.

[54] Du Fail, "Epitre," especially p. 379; L'Alouëte, *Traité*, pp. 26–27; La Noue, *Discours*, p. 165; and Charles de La Ruelle, *Succinctz adversaires contre l'histoire et professeurs d'icelle* (Poitiers, 1574). In this little treatise the nobleman La Ruelle sets up "good" professions, such as the military, against "bad" ones, such as *Jurisprudence* and certain other *sciences* or products of the mind like medicine. See also the discussion of Pasquier and Tiraqueau on this in chap. 3.

equally to noble and nonnoble. At the same time, from the point of view of the robe, law could not present any fundamental threat to the survival of the nobles because of the recognized and accepted need for a military (and thus a nobility) in order for the state to survive. It could also not be a serious threat because of the seemingly contradictory fact that many of the top lawyers in society were already legally noble.

The declining military significance of nobility in the seventeenth century narrowed the gap for possible conflict between robe and sword. Law and the legal profession posed even less of a threat to nobility based upon birth, and its accompanying legal privileges, than to nobility as a fighting profession. The ennobling properties of office became more and more acceptable to the society. Constant, for instance, has found a definite shift in ennoblements from the fief and military in the sixteenth century, to office in the seventeenth century.[55] By the middle of the eighteenth century, Franklin Ford, in his analysis of the ascendency of the high robe within the nobility, has found that significant differences between robe and sword had almost completely disappeared.[56]

From this perspective, the limited amount of antagonism between robe and sword that surfaced during the Estates-General of 1614[57] reflects well that odd mixture of old and new that is characteristic of what we know about the Estates.[58] On the one hand, the Estates were organized in the old way, along the lines of nobility as a profession, as they also would be in 1789, with more portentous consequences (see chapter 9). On the other hand, the actual dominance of the medieval view of nobility had already been broken by

[55] Constant, *Nobles et paysans*, especially pp. 46–47.

[56] Cf. Franklin Ford, *Robe and Sword: The Regrouping of the French Aristocracy after Louis XIV* (Cambridge, Mass., 1953).

[57] Jouanna, for instance, points toward this in *L'idée de race*, especially pp. 1273–1300, as does Salmon in *Society in Crisis*, p. 326.

[58] Cf. Chartier and Richet, *Représentation et vouloir politiques*, and more particularly Chartier's article republished there, "La noblesse et les Etats de 1614: Une réaction aristocratique?" pp. 113–125.

1614. Such a situation certainly helped lead to anomalies, such as men legally noble representing the Third Estate,[59] and it also helped to make much of the "rhetoric" of the Estates seem especially confusing to historians. From the perspective of this study, however, any antagonism in 1614 between robe and sword, when phrased in terms of profession, would be a carry-over from the old; when phrased in other terms, it probably represented a stubborn resistance to accepting the fact that some individuals would be ennobled through law or office—that law would be a sort of *marque de noblesse*—but that law itself would not be a threat to nobles who were noble by birth and were willing to be part of a larger group of elites than they had been before.[60]

BECAUSE we tend to associate the duel with nobility, it may be a surprise to learn that the *direct* association of the two— and of the duel with the honor of the nobility—is a relatively recent phenomenon; it is, in fact, mostly a product of the late sixteenth and early seventeenth centuries. The emergence of the duel at the center of noble preoccupations in this period, especially in the early seventeenth century, reflects well the struggles and realitites of the time of Henry IV and Riche-

[59] For instance, see Mousnier, *Deux cahiers*, p. 35; and J. Michael Hayden, *France and the Estates General of 1614* (Cambridge, Eng., 1974), especially p. 96.

[60] This acceptance of reality was sometimes expressed as "all things being equal you choose a noble" for an important job or some other task, which implies that the noble would have to work as hard as the nonnoble. Such a view was stated quite clearly in the *cahier* of the clergy to the Estates General of 1614 on the subject of the nobility: "Considering that the nobles have some priority rights for the attribution of the highest offices of the Church and of Justice, and all the more when they take greater pains than they used to to render themselves more able to hold such offices by a constant study of the sciences and of the good authors; and in order to urge them even more to such studies, let it be the pleasure of your Majesty to command that a *gentilhomme* will be preferred to other applicants equally able and capable, for the Benefice of the Church that your Majesty confers personally, and whenever there is a vacancy in a judicial office." Cf. Lalourcé and Duval, *Recueil des cahiers généraux*, IV (1614), 97.

lieu. L'Alouëte did not include the duel among the marks of nobles that specifically characterized them, and other, earlier writers on the nobility such as Tiraqueau or Bonus de Curtili did not pay much attention to it.[61] It appears that until the later part of the sixteenth and early seventeenth centuries, dueling, which was still basically judicial in nature, could be carried out by nonnobles as well as nobles—and even between the two—and it was given little or no emphasis as a special prerogative of the nobility. The actual number of "mixed" duels was probably very small, however, if for no other reason than that few nonnobles would have wished to be pitted against someone who had been trained since childhood as a fighter.

To Symphorien Champier in 1535, it seemed normal that nobles and nonnobles would fight judicial duels with each other—judicial duels were the only ones he seemed aware of—and his only concern was whether or not they should be equally armed. "The following statement," he wrote, "could be considered: whether a noble and a nonnoble should have the same arms or not. . . ." And he goes on to explain why it is unfair that they should not be equally armed, concluding, "This proves clearly that the noble should not carry better arms than the nonnoble, reason agrees as well; and that is how the question can be answered."[62] Later, in reference to another question, he says, "This takes place generally in all battles [the reference is to judicial duels] between nobles and nonnobles."[63] Thus he raises the question of who should or should not fight duels only indirectly when discussing possible differences in duels fought between nobles and nonnobles.

It therefore seems entirely possible to him and indeed not

---

[61] L'Alouëte, *Traité*, especially p. 35; and neither Tiraqueau (in *De Nobilitate*), who is essentially interested in legal questions, nor Bonus (in *Tractatus*) connects it directly with nobility.

[62] Champier, *Le fondement* (no pagination), section with heading "Du combat appellé duellum."

[63] Ibid.

unnatural that nonnobles should be fighting judicial duels, even with nobles; his general lack of concern with the question suggests this to be an unchallenged assumption of the time. From this perspective, the major problem for the historian was to determine how and when the judicial duel gave way to the more modern duel based on the *point d'honneur* and generally limited to nobles. We can judge from attitudes toward the duel that the process was a gradual one. Morel has found some impulse for the new duel already in the early sixteenth century,[64] and by the second half of the century the duel was beginning to be referred to as an act only for *gentilshommes*. Cheffontaines, for instance, though he opposed duels for religious reasons, still tended to associate them with nobles and their *point d'honneur* (". . . le poinct d'honneur de la noblesse establ y par les gentils-hommes . . .").[65] But he did assume that others than *gentilshommes* might rely upon the duel to settle their differences.[66] His contemporary, Pasquier, was also against duels and also tended to associate them with the nobility and their *point d'honneur*; however, he did not emphasize this strongly, nor did he make clear distinctions between nobles and nonnobles.[67] Brantôme made similar assumptions, but with a different opinion about their rightness.[68] Other writers, such as Sainct-Didier, continued to mix noble and nonnoble more or less indiscriminately when discussing the duel.[69]

As with the separation of virtue and nobility and the shift toward birth, the crucial period once again appears to have

[64] Henri Morel, "La fin du duel judiciaire en France et la naissance du point d'honneur," *Revue historique du droit français et étranger* 43 (1964), 574–639. Morel found that the judicial duel had almost completely disappeared in the fifteenth century, with a revival of sorts in the early sixteenth century.

[65] Cheffontaines, *Confutation*, p. 51.

[66] Ibid., pp. 68–69.

[67] Pasquier, *Les oeuvres*, p. 52.

[68] See especially Brantôme's "Les discours sur les duels" in *Oeuvres complètes*, ed. L. Lalanne, 10 vols. (Paris, 1864–1882), VI, 233–512.

[69] Cf. Sainct-Didier, *Traité*.

been the late sixteenth and early seventeenth centuries.[70] By the first decades of the seventeenth century the literature is very clear on the matter. The duel and nobility are linked almost without exception in people's minds, and their assumed association had apparently become a common cliché. In writers like Boyssat, Pelletier, and La Béraudière; in literature such as Sorel's *Francion*;[71] in antiduel polemics such as that of Jean Savaron in 1610;[72] in the pages of the *Mercure François*,[73] in ordinances against the duel that concern themselves only with the nobility;[74] and in the *cahiers* of the Third Estate that now direct their complaints against duels toward the nobility,[75] the assumption is clear: duels were for nobles and were associated with nobles.[76]

This emerging view of the duel as being more clearly restricted to nobles—and thus as essentially a new *marque de noblesse*—is to a large extent the product of the general desire, which had already become more important in the 1570s and 1580s, for a better definition of nobility. Since it took two to fight a duel, it was a good deal easier for nobles to shut ambitious nonnobles off by ignoring their challenges than it was to prevent them from carrying a sword, hunting, wearing special clothes, or purchasing a fief. The duel, then,

[70] See as well the fine article by Arlette Jouanna, "Recherches sur la notion d'honneur aux xvième siècle," *Revue d'histoire moderne et contemporaine* 15 (1968), 579–623, who also emphasizes the importance of the period of the late sixteenth and early seventeenth centuries for the development of newer attitudes toward, and purposes for, the duel.

[71] Sorel, *Francion*, p. iv: "Sticking directly to the statutes of nobility, I could if I wished call my adversaries to the combat of the pen the way a *chevalier* calls one to the combat of the sword."

[72] Jean Savaron, *Traicté contre les duels* (Paris, 1610).

[73] See, for instance, *Mercure François* (1617), p. 86.

[74] Isambert, *Recueil général des anciennes lois françaises*, XV, 351–358 (ordinance of 1609).

[75] For instance, the *cahier* of 1614 in Mandrou, *Classes et luttes de classes*, p. 104.

[76] See also Scipion Dupleix, *Les loix militaires touchant le duel* (Paris, 1602), pp. 160–161, and Loyseau, *Traité des ordres*, p. 46.

had definite potential as an effective *marque de noblesse*. As with birth it offered a surer way than the old *marques* of shutting off nonnobles, and much of the well-known emphasis on the duel in the first half of the seventeenth century needs to be understood as a response to this need.

Marc de La Béraudière, in his 1608 treatise on the duel, shows this tendency well. He is particularly interesting because he combines with his defense of a nobility based upon birth (see chapter 6) an emphasis on the duel for nobles only. In this treatise La Béraudière begins by addressing himself to the other *gentilshommes* of the kingdom, assuming that it is they who are concerned with dueling. Although he is against indiscriminate duels and finds it rather foolish that nobles feel called upon to fight to prove themselves valiant,[77] he still devotes most of his book to describing the etiquette surrounding duels and the way that he feels they should be carried out. He obviously favored duels in the right situation and under the right conditions. A particular concern of his was whether nobles should be permitted to fight nonnobles, and here he is especially adamant and clear. To do so for a noble would be committing an *infamie* and sullying his name, and could even, in his opinion, help to undermine all of society—an attitude that indicates how important he felt the question to be. He felt that the noble is superior because he fights for his country—and thus only he should also fight duels—and he wants this fact to be accepted by everyone. It should be "acknowledged not only by the noble, but also by the *roturier* who should respect and honor it [nobility] because the noble is the issue of an illustrious line and is born of other family and different ancestors whom the *roturier* must not compare to his."[78]

In this passage, then, he clearly joins together the emphasis on dueling as an activity only for nobles with the emphasis on birth as an accepted and acknowledged basis for no-

---

[77] La Béraudière, *Le combat*, Dedication.
[78] Ibid., pp. 88–89.

bility. He thus seems particularly concerned with the threat of the hypothetical rich *roturier* who might begin to wear a sword and act like a noble, and then, to prove that he was one, would pick an argument with a noble in order to have a duel. But one must not fight him, says La Béraudière, for nobles should fight only with their equals.[79] Here the apparent advantage of the duel over the sword or the other *marques de noblesse* in defining the nobles effectively is clear, for it is good deal easier to ignore a rich nonnoble than to stop him from carrying a sword.

That the nobles did need to be "educated" on this matter in order to avoid falling into the trap of fighting a nonnoble is suggested by the actions of an ambitious nonnoble of the period who seems to have accomplished what La Béraudière was worried about. Antoine de Montchrestien, already discussed as the author of the *Traité de l'économie politique* of 1615 (see chapter 6), died prematurely in 1621; and, according to the *Mercure François*, he had managed to work his way into the nobility simply by "keeping company with them" until he succeeded in getting one to fight a duel with him. As the *Mercure* put it with some irony after his death:

> . . . he studied, devoted himself to French poetry and succeeded in writing some good verses. [Then] . . . at the age of twenty, he learned with his masters fencing, horseback riding, and *while keeping company with nobles* [en hantant les nobles] he played the noble, the gallant one, the hardy one, the quarrelsome one *so as to fight a duel* [knowing that this would be a sure sign of his being considered noble] and called himself Vatteville, but of land or fief of Vatteville there was none.[80]

Here, then, we see the duel, in its role as a new *marque de noblesse*, doing—by apparently helping a nonnoble into the nobility—what it was originally supposed to help prevent.

[79] Ibid.

[80] *Mercure François* (1621), quoted by Funck-Brentano in Montchrestien, *Traicté*, p. iii. The emphasis is mine.

But at the same time, the story suggests that nonnobles tended to accept the duel and to try to use it as a means of moving into the nobility rather than resisting its status as a privilege limited to nobles. And indeed elsewhere in the sources there is little evidence to show that nonnobles did not want the duel to be considered a mark of nobility. On the other hand, the story also shows how closely associated the duel and nobility had indeed become, and it helps us to understand why there would be such a continued emphasis on the duel for nobles only.

This emphasis is particularly strong in Boyssat, who wrote in 1610. For him the connection of the duel with nobles is of great significance, and indeed it is "imprinted in their hearts":

> . . . The *point d'honneur* [that is, the sense of honor that leads nobles to fight duels] is by nature imprinted in the hearts of the Nobility [est naturellement empreint au coeur de la Noblesse], and it consists in never admitting defeat and considering only victory or death while fighting.[81]

Like his contemporaries, then, he accepts the duel as a *marque de noblesse* and simply assumes that only nobles can fight duels.[82] In general he is against duels, but finds it impossible to oppose them in all instances, which is not surprising since he is a noble himself[83] and duels are now an important mark of nobility. If one must fight, he writes, then

> . . . he should clear his heart of all rancor and bitterness and should become used to the sweet taste of reconciliation and friendship, qualities that pertain much more to the nobility than to the common people.[84]

The end of the passage shows that he also sees the duel as something to help distinguish nobles from nonnobles. Boys-

---

[81] P. Boyssat, *Recherches sur les duels* (Lyon, 1610), p. 31.

[82] Ibid., and, for example, pp. 37 and 57.

[83] He was a recent *anobli*. See his *Remerciement au roy par les anoblis du Dauphiné* (Paris, 1603).

[84] Boyssat, *Recherches*, p. 63.

sat is as well on guard against the Montchrestiens—the non-nobles who might take advantage of the new *marque de noblesse*—when he emphasizes that duels should never be fought with someone of lower rank—that is, a *gentilhomme* must never fight with a nonnoble.[85] He raises yet another important point, the relationship of this emphasis on duels only for nobles to the absolutist state, when he writes in the very next section: "It should be acknowledged that the honor of a *gentilhomme* [l'honneur d'un Gentilhomme (to fight duels, etc.)] is inseparably united with the public honor, the usefulness of his Majesty's service and the good of his State."[86] Here, then, the implication is that duels for nobles only, permitted in the right circumstances, may not necessarily have been in opposition to the authority or the interests of the new absolutism.

The private and often secret nature of duels makes a numerical estimate difficult, but it does seem that the total number of duels increased substantially during the late sixteenth and early seventeenth centuries. That was the opinion of contemporaries, and the many ordinances against the duel[87] bear witness to this proliferation[88] and the problems it was causing for society. Studies have shown that the duel was never effecitvely outlawed during this time,[89] even after Richelieu's famous execution of Bouteville in 1627 for dueling in broad daylight under his window in the Place Royale. A contemporary, Guillaume de Chevalier, well aware of the

---

[85] Ibid., p. 66.

[86] Ibid., p. 68.

[87] Cf. for instance, Isambert, *Recueil général des anciennes lois françaises*, XV, 351–358 (1609); XVI, 175–183 (1626); and XVI, 408 (1634).

[88] The popular, nonscholarly view, as reflected in Robert Baldick, *The Duel: A History of Duelling* (New York, 1965), also assumes a great proliferation of duels at the time of Henry IV and Louis XIII, as does Jouanna in "Recherches sur la notion d'honneur."

[89] See, for instance, Edmund H. Dickerman, "Henry IV of France, the Duel and the Battle Within," *Societas—A Review of Social History* 3 (1973), 207–220, and Richard Herr, "Honor versus Absolutism: Richelieu's Fight Against Dueling," *Journal of Modern History* 27 (1955), 281–285.

increase and trying to explain it, offered an additional explanation: nobles, he felt (with the assumption that duels belonged to them alone), were fighting in fewer wars and battles because of the stronger monarchies and were thus obliged to expend their energy among themselves.[90] This observation certainly makes a lot of sense and has been suggested as an explanation for the apparent increase in noble duels in England during the same period.[91] Some people even argued, according to Chevalier, that duels were a good means of preventing civil wars among the nobles, while others justified them in terms of keeping the nobles fit, sharp, and courageous for the time when they would have to defend the country.[92] But regardless of how people understood them, they were all aware of their increased importance in society. In the context of the evidence presented here, it seems that much of that increase should be seen as a result of the nobles' desire to become better defined as their military justification became less and less applicable.

Agrippa d'Aubigné, one of the more perceptive men of his age, seems to have understood this new role of the duel well. In the *Aventures du Baron de Faeneste*, his satire of court life first published in 1616 and 1617, he mocks this new emphasis on the duel as a separating *marque de noblesse*, because of the innate stupidity and destructiveness of the duel itself. In doing so, he shows how important the duel had in fact become. For example, Faeneste tells his friend Enay, a country gentleman, about life at court. The moment he enters court life, he says, duels and *querelles* seem to be everywhere. One time he meets an *escoulier* but will not fight him: "I replied that I would lose my status of *Gentilhomme* if I fought him."[93]

---

[90] Guillaume de Chevalier, *Discours des querelles et de l'honneur* (Paris, 1598), pp. 29–32.

[91] Stone, *Crisis of the Aristocracy*, pp. 242–250.

[92] Chevalier, *Discours des querelles*, pp. 29–32. See also Boyssat, *Recherches*, p. 2.

[93] Théodore Agrippa d'Aubigné, *Les aventures du Baron de Faeneste* (Paris, 1855), 1st ed. 1616–1617, p. 12.

This seems to have been a common assumption of the time, and is a further indication of the pressure to keep the duel among nobles. Later, he goes off to fight someone else but, again for the familiar reasons, changes his mind: ". . . it has been said that I cannot fight him with honor because he is an *homme de rov[b]e longue.*"[94]

D'Aubigné, the Protestant nobleman, also seems to have understood quite well what drove the nobles to want to fight so many duels, for his supposed remedy for stopping the slaughter was not the complicated schemes of certain "judges and great statesmen," but simply to have them "stripped of their nobility [dégradé de noblesse]." Then you would suddenly see them out preaching the "evil of the duel."[95] He would certainly have been right, even if he did not propose this as a serious remedy: if the nobles were affirming their nobility by fighting duels, they could hardly have wished to lose their nobility for doing just that.

D'Aubigné, then, shows himself more astute than most of his contemporaries in understanding better the reasons for the strong connection between duel and nobility. In another intriguing and interesting passage he shows himself even more astute by suggesting that he is aware that the old *vertu* of the nobles had come to be replaced by new *marques de noblesse* such as the duel. Faeneste relates what the *gentilshommes* of the court talk about and what concerns and excites them the most. Being good nobles, they would be expected to talk of virtue, and this is what Faeneste is told. But actually it is of duels (and women) that they talk all the time.

Faeneste: . . . Once in the hall, you walk up to some gentleman and talk about virtue [vous accoustez quelque galant homme et discourez de la vertu].

Enay: Indeed, Monsieur, I am delighted [to learn of it], and I believe there are few courtiers so learned. But tell me, the virtues which you discuss . . . are these virtues intellectual, or moral?

[94] Ibid., p. 40.
[95] Ibid., p. 47.

171

Faeneste: Yes, I have heard those words. You wish to know of what we talk: we talk about duels, and must be careful not to admire any one's merit or value, but must state calmly: he is or was rather courageous . . . has or had some good fortune with the ladies.[96]

All that seems to interest these nobles at court, adds Faeneste, are duels and the different ways they are fought, the different reasons for fighting them, the different positions taken, and so on.[97] From nobility as virtue, then, to nobility as the right to fight duels; almost unconsciously—and with the intention of satirizing the corrupting influences of the court on the older, more "virtuous" country nobles—d'Aubigné has described one of the basic aspects of the shift away from the old view of nobility and to the modern one.

The big emphasis on the duel in the first half of the seventeenth century thus owes much of its impetus to the fact that the duel seemed to be a good new *marque de noblesse*. Despite the obvious disruptive problems associated with the duel, this emphasis seems not to have been entirely in opposition to the aims of the early absolutist state of the half century after 1594. As we saw, some of the calls for the duel for nobles only were made by apologists for absolutism, who emphasized strongly that nobles should always remain under the authority of the monarch. From this perspective, then, just as the monarchy was willing to accept and even encourage a nobility based upon birth (as long as that nobility was not independent and out of its control), so also it seems to have been willing at times to allow duels, or at least to emphasize that duels were for nobles only, *as long* as they took place with the blessing of the king. Clearly that is the message of Richelieu's *Political Testament*, which puts greater emphasis on the king's authority than on the evil of duels (Richelieu associates duels so directly with nobility that he

[96] Ibid., p. 19.
[97] Ibid.

includes them in a subsection as part of a larger section entitled "De la Noblesse").[98] Even Corneille's *Le Cid* of 1636, where the duel takes on direct political implications as the symbol of the resistance of the nobles against an absolutist king, depicts the real issue in some ways as the unauthorized duel that, in this case, is bad for the state and thus must not take place. Seen in this light, as a question of authority, the apparent ambiguity in Richelieu's and the king's attitudes toward the duel—sometimes accepting them and sometimes not[99]—makes more sense. If the real problem for the monarchy was not nobles fighting duels but nobles fighting unauthorized duels, then its policy toward them becomes much clearer, more consistent, and less ambiguous.

The early absolutist monarchy, which was not antinoble, of course, seemed willing to accept the duel as a *marque de noblesse*, as long as it could be subsumed under the umbrella of the new absolutist state, and as long as it fit satisfactorily with nobility in its more modern form instead of nobility as a military function. As with the history of many of the other *marques de noblesse* in the first half of the seventeenth century, this implies a diminished significance of nobility and a reduced power for the nobles as they fit into a group of larger and differently defined elites, theoretically and often actually under the authority of the monarchy.

[98] Cf. Richelieu, Cardinal de, *Testament politique*, ed. Louis André (Paris, 1947), in particular the section on the nobility (pp. 218–229), especially p. 225.

[99] Cf. Herr, "Honor versus Absolutism" and, for Henry IV, Dickerman, "Henry IV of France." On the other hand, some nobles, those of Chaumont-en-Bassigny who prepared their *cahier* of 1614, for instance, were "officially" at least against most duels. See B.N., Nouvelles Acquisitions, 2808.

8

Education, the Academies,
and the Emergence of the New Image of the Cultured Noble-Aristocrat

If one were to ask people today to designate one *marque de noblesse*, after birth, that most characterizes or belongs with nobility, most would undoubtedly name a certain kind of "culture," a special sort of civilization, an urbanity and savoir-faire, that somehow, they would say, belongs to and with nobles and nobility. We can cite innumerable examples from literature and life of the eighteenth, nineteenth, and indeed twentieth centuries about typical, cultured noble-aristocrats as well as new nobles who, after obtaining the legal privilege or title, would set out to educate themselves and their families and in particular their progeny so that no one could mistake them for boorish nonnobles or imposters. Such has not always been the case, however. Like the duel and, to a large extent, birth, "culture" is basically a new *marque de noblesse* for France, one that was largely absent when nobility was thought of as the military profession. Anyone who would have associated culture with nobility in the middle of the sixteenth century would most certainly have been laughed at, thought stupid or mad, or would simply have been considered the victim of wishful thinking. The view of the typical French noble as courageous but otherwise, at worst, foolhardy, vain, crude, barbarous, and uneducated or, at best, simply disdainful of education—despite the doubts of some historians about such a view's validity[1]—was a deeply en-

---

[1] Cf., for instance, Hexter in "The Education of the Aristocracy" and Lucien Febvre in *Philippe II et la Franche-Comté* (Paris, 1912), pp. 375–377, who,

trenched assumption of the time in France, one that was apparently held about French nobles in other areas of Europe as well.[2] By the second half of the seventeenth century, however, it had almost entirely disappeared in most circles, and the association of noble with culture had instead become a widely held common cliché, one that continues in many ways to the present.

This change, this emergence of "culture" as a new *marque de noblesse*, is a crucial part of the overall story of the emergence of the modern idea of nobility. One important ingredient of the new change involves an almost unknown entity: the new and quite original academies for nobles only founded at the very end of the sixteenth and early in the seventeenth centuries. To help our understanding of the process of the emergence of this new *marque de noblesse*, we shall examine these new academies and attempt to place them within the context of the general question of noble education in the period, while also relating them to the larger theme of the emergence of the modern idea of nobility.

The first really serious push for a better-educated nobility in France had taken place in the 1570s and 1580s and was expressed, interestingly enough, within the framework of the feudal-military view of nobility as virtue. We saw that these demands for education were a major part of the beginning noble *prise de conscience*, as nobles and noble apologists, in the period of breakdown and crisis helped along by the Civil Wars, began to sense that there were serious problems facing the nobility that had to be dealt with. What they proposed for the time being, or until the more realistic years of the very late sixteenth and early seventeenth centuries, was a return to the old virtue upon which nobility was supposedly

---

as early as 1912, finding some carefully educated nobles in *Franche-Comté*, emphasized that one should not exaggerate the brutality, *rudesse*, and ignorance of the nobles.

[2] Cf., for instance, the discussion in Castiglione's *Courtier*, p. 104: ". . . the French recognize only the nobility of arms and reckon all the rest as nought; and thus not only do they not esteem but they abhor letters."

based and justified. Education was to be one important means of retaining this lost virtue. Meanwhile, we saw that these calls for education among writers like Froydeville, Origny, L'Alouëte, Poncet, Coignet, La Noue, and others, while certainly growing in large part out of the general humanist program for education in the first half of the century, differed from that program significantly in their emphasis that education was to be *for* nobles and to save the noble order rather than for deserving people in general.

It was in this context of arguments for a more selective, class-oriented function for education that proposals for a new institution, the academies for nobles, were made in the 1570s and 1580s. Pierre d'Origny, for instance, suggested the founding of such an institution for nobles in 1578,[3] although his proposal, unlike later ones, would not necessarily have excluded deserving or virtuous or "right-acting" nonnobles. His approach to this question is interesting. Origny was strongly pronoble and aimed his proposals directly at young *gentilshommes*. Nevertheless, after describing how the new school would be open to sons of poor nobles who could not pay as well as to the rich, he wrote:

> Still, we cannot speak of the third estate as being excluded and of it not being take care of as by a good father and Prince; for whoever has been rather closely related to the leadership of the affairs of this Kingdom knows how close the estates are one to the other, and how much they keep together [s'entretiennent de si près], so much so that the one has no power but with the two others. The Church is preferred to all the others; nevertheless the Nobility as well as the people can enjoy the very same dignities that the Church enjoys, and the door to the house of the Nobility is open to all those *right-acting members* of the third Estate [à tous les bien faisans du tiers Estat].[4]

[3] Origny, *Le hérault*, pp. 39–41.
[4] Ibid., pp. 40–41. The emphasis is mine.

176

This passage, then, suggests once more that, even as they worked to establish a new institution to meet the new needs of the nobles, people in the 1570s were still not yet able to free themselves from the belief in action as the basis of nobility. And it is indeed further evidence of the dominance of that view during the period.

Others followed Origny in calling for a similar type of academy. La Noue, for example, did so a decade later in a better-known passage: in his academy the training would be more clearly for nobles alone, and, along with military matters, would include letters as well.[5] A few other such appeals can be found sprinkled among the sources.[6] These appeals, although they are sometimes not very clear or precise, also suggest the main purposes and functions of the academy, from the founding of the first one in 1594 by Pluvinel onward. They were to be the nobles' own institutions, a major response to their problems. By helping to educate and polish the nobles they would help improve their "image," and, like birth and the duel, would serve as a means of helping to distinguish and define better and more effectively a nobility that, as it lost its primary military function, was becoming more in need of a new and more-up-to-date raison d'être.

The pleas for educating the nobles continued in the 1590s and early 1600s as the shift to the more modern idea of nobility took place. This need for an expanded definition of nobility based also upon education and letters is expressed even more directly, more clearly, and generally within the context of the newer, nonmedieval view of nobility in a relatively unknown work of the nobleman Du Souhait, published in 1600, called *Le parfaict gentilhomme*. The central theme of Du Souhait's book, indeed, is that the basis of nobility

---

[5] La Noue, *Discours politiques*, pp. 108–132. Roger Chartier, Dominique Julia, and Marie-Madeleine Compère have a good summary of this section in *L'éducation en France du xvie au xviiie siècle* (Paris, 1976), pp. 169–171.

[6] Cf. John David Nordhaus, "*Arma et Litterae*: The Education of the *Noblesse de Race* in Sixteenth-Century France," Ph.D. diss., Columbia University (1974), especially chap. 5.

should be arms and letters instead of just arms. "As nobles," he wrote,

> we have to keep the others faithfully bound to us, and we should become worthy of being considered Nobles in order not to render our opinions and possessions questionable and more worthy of *Roturiers* than of Nobles. I do not wish the study of letters to lead us away from arms; *I wish that they be joined together in order to give birth to the true and genuine Nobility* [je veux qu'elles s'y marient pour enfanter la vraye Noblesse]. If those of our rank have despised letters so greatly and devoted themselves to other activities and exercises, let us, like our forefathers, leave those same exercises and devote ourselves to literary studies [nous jetter à l'estude des lettres].[7]

The book is dull and repetitious; he makes the same point throughout, that there must be this "marriage" of arms and letters in order to form the true nobility. And the argument is often banally put:

> Literature is the foster mother of virtue [Les lettres sont les nourrices de la vertu]; let us drink the same milk so as to become brothers to virtue, by essence and nourishment. Let us choose no other citadel by which to fortify ourselves but letters which fortify the weakest little building. Let us keep from looking at anything else desirable, and let us be wedded to this one demand so as to become virtuous by reading the good authors, and because of this virtue thus become truly great.[8]

[7] Du Souhait, *Le parfaict gentilhomme* (Paris, 1600), pp. 64–64v. The emphasis is mine. Henri Hauser, in discussing a different work of Du Souhait in *Les sources de l'histoire de France: Le xvie siècle (1494–1610)*, 4 vols. (Paris, 1906–1915), IV, 205–206, calls him a *gentilhomme champenois*.

[8] Ibid., pp. 69–69v. It is also interesting the way *vertu* is used at the very end of this statement (of 1600), just as the shift toward the more modern view of nobility was taking place or had taken place. Du Souhait speaks of becoming "truly great" through virtue (par telle vertu [se rendre] vrayment grands), which suggests that this virtue is a sort of addition to nobility, that it is not now a question of really ceasing to be a noble if one is not virtuous.

Despite the book's simplisitc nature and its literary weaknesses, it is an important work because it contains a clear statement of what was a notable shift in thinking about nobility. It was apparently the first book whose major theme was the joining of arms and letters.

Five years later Antoine de Nervèze called for the addition of general education to the training program of young noblemen. He invoked the very practical reason that seems to have been behind many of the appeals for education of the nobility: they must be educated in order to hold the important public, political, and administrative offices and ministries in the state. It is clear to Nervèze that although nobles deserve these posts *because* they are nobles, they simply will not obtain them unless they are properly prepared—what is needed is "a well-rounded intelligence rather than the rank of the person." The king has no choice but to choose nonnobles for the important offices, but that is the fault of the nobles, not the fault of the king, since "they [the nobles] are ignorant because they are not trained for scientific work. They look down upon it, for they are not willing to learn, and this deprives them of those advantages or offices and they are left only with their sword, or arms."[9]

Other writers of the period repeated these calls for education. La Béraudière, for instance, did so in 1608 in general terms;[10] Flurance-Rivault in 1612 stated that by studying, nobles would learn to be ambassadors and hold other important posts;[11] and Pelletier in 1604 emphasized the importance of good letters and traveling for noble development.[12] For Salomon de La Broue in 1610 it was important that the young noble learn letters as well as the usual bodily exercises, but he should also learn to dance,[13] a pastime that was

[9] Antoine de Nervèze, *Le guide des courtisans* in *Les oeuvres morales* (Paris, 1605), pp. 33–33v.

[10] La Béraudière, *Le combat*, pt. IV, pp. 192–271.

[11] Flurance-Rivault, *Le dessein*, p. 14.

[12] Pelletier, *La nourriture*, p. 95v.

[13] La Broue, *Le cavalerice françois*, pp. 19, 21.

to hold, interestingly enough, a certain significance in the new noble educational program. The dance was important for La Broue because "it is an exercise which gives some grace and assurance [grâce et assurance],"[14] two characteristics that would be among the newer attributes of nobles in France.

Subtle changes in the way these pleas for education for the nobles were expressed reflect well how nobles and others let go their belief in the feudal-military view of nobility as action. With birth accepted much more and virtue not emphasized particularly, the writers of the early decades of the seventeenth century no longer implied that *all* nobles must be educated in order to save the order. If nobility is based upon virtuous action, those nobles who did not act virtuously would be a threat to the whole order and the whole order would need to be reformed or brought back to virtue (through education in this case), as emphasized in the 1570s and 1580s. But if one is accepted as being noble by inheritance, instead of by action, then that person would remain a noble even if he was not well educated; but education would make him a better, more effective, more clearly distinguishable, and more powerful noble, and in general would help improve the image of nobility without questioning its existence.

Montchrestien, for instance, talks about competition for a few prizes or openings as being "a spur to nobles to induce them to follow virtuous actions [aiguillon à la noblesse pour l'inciter à suivre les actions de vertu], to urge them to vie with one another in doing the most brilliant and best acts of duty."[15] In making these comments, he was concerned with improving some nobles without ever implying that the unimproved ones would cease to be nobles. And Mayerne Turquet, in suggesting that nobility should not be left alone but rather be "cultivated" and have "arts and sciences" added to it, accepts nobility as determined by birth, but, realizing its limitations, emphasizes that education or training be added to it.[16] It is clear that he assumes that education could only

---

[14] Ibid.

[15] Montchrestien, *Traité de l'économie politique*, pp. 362–363.

[16] Mayerne Turquet, *La monarchie aristodémocratique*, pp. 83, 92.

realistically be applied in some cases, and those without its advantages would not have their nobility questioned.

In the context of these more realistic attitudes of the first half of the seventeenth century, then, two basic reasons were usually given for the importance of educating the nobility, although distinctions between the two were not always clearly made at the time. One was to train nobles for jobs, especially administrative ones, so that they could compete on an equal footing with others. The second was to help redefine them: to add letters and general learning, "grace" and "assurance" and the like, or simply culture, so that they would have a more plausible and appealing "image" and definition. These are very important goals. They reflect a significant shift in thinking about the nobility in France, a shift that was necessary and indispensable before any serious concrete gains and accomplishments in the area of education could be made. For even if nobles had the power and means to educate themselves, they were not going to do it if they did not want to. Here, important changes in mentalities preceded important social and institutional changes. Once this change in thinking had taken place, the new academies reserved for nobility, which turn out to have been more important than they have been considered to be by historians thus far,[17] could actually be founded and have some assurance of success.

THE first academy for nobles only was founded by Antoine de Pluvinel in 1594, and others, often apparently modeled on Pluvinel's, were founded throughout France in the early decades of the new century.[18] These new academies, especially

---

[17] Magendie, for instance, who has studied the *salons* and the books of courtesy in great depth in *La politesse mondaine*, has barely more than one page (p. 57) out of over 900 on the academies. Ariès, on the other hand, in *L'enfant et la vie familiale*, has some brief but important and suggestive pages (pp. 203–208, 217 in the English translation) about them, as do Chartier et al. in *L'éducation en France*, pp. 181–185.

[18] A summary of the scant information available on Pluvinel and the early academies can be found in H. de Terrebasse, *Antoine de Pluvinel* (Lyon, 1911); Commandant de La Roche, *Les académies militaires sous l'ancien régime* (Paris, 1929); and Lucien Hoche, *Contribution à l'histoire de Paris: Paris occidental, xii*ᵉ–

Pluvinel's, recieved a good deal of praise from contemporaries, which included emphasizing the academies' important role in helping to create the new, more modern, and better-educated noble. Pontaymery, for instance, in praising Pluvinel's academy talked of the importance of both intelligence and bravery in nobles.[19] The courageous but vain, empty-headed and foolhardy French noble must go, he felt, and be replaced by a new noble who combined bravery with understanding, judgment, and a general education.[20] And, still using much of the language and focus on *vertu* of the 1580s (he wrote in 1599), he enthusiastically singled out Pluvinel's contribution to the cause:

> All of France feels infinitely indebted to the Sieur de Pluvinel who . . . with devotion offered himself to the Nobility to act as a ladder and a stepping-stone to the highest and most glorious goals that virtue demands of those who search after it.[21]

Much of his treatise is a discussion of various writers, some ancient but the majority modern, and their views about the value of educating young nobles. Later in his work he was even more lavish in his praise of the academy for helping to fashion a different and improved nobility.

> All that is required to be added to arrive at perfection for a *Gentilhomme* is better acquired by practicing the dignified exercise of the *Noblesse*, and is better learned associating

---

xixᵉ siècles; Ses rues, leur passé, leurs passants (Suite des appendices) (Paris, 1912), Appendice XXIII, "Pluvinel et les académies," pp. 873–929. A search of the major Parisian libraries and archives in an attempt to add to this material turned up a little but not very much new on Pluvinel (see the sources cited in chap. 6, note 43), but did turn up some useful material on the other academies, especially in A.N., 0¹ 915–917 (Maison du Roi). The next academy after Pluvinel's seems to have been founded in Toulouse in 1598. See A.N., 0¹ 917, fol. 208.

[19] Pontaymery, *L'académie*, pp. 48–57.

[20] Ibid., pp. 17v–18, 21v, 23v–24v, 48v.

[21] Ibid., p. 2.

with men of honor and merit, than by reading or listening to a course. This is why I send you to the Sieur de Pluvinel, as to a school which is the true oracle and temple of virtue [comme en l'eschole et au vray oracle et temple de la vertu]. A *seigneur* who longs for a rightful glory and a praiseworthy reputation would not find anywhere else to go than in the above-mentioned institution which is as the fresh spring of the graces of heaven, perpetually flowing and distilled.[22]

The tone is banal and exaggerated but the passage is nonetheless the reflection of an important desire that had finally become a reality. That the new academy was to be a *temple de la vertu* (Pluvinel also calls his academy an *école de la vertu*[23]) shows how the terminology of the sixteenth century had been carried over into the actual founding of the new institution. This reflected the fact that much of the impulse for the new schools had grown out of the earlier demands of the 1570s and 1580s for a more "virtuous" nobility. The use of some of the old terminology, however, cannot hide the fact that these new schools, functioning in a different context and in a different political reality, were to teach a number of new and different things that would be very difficult or impossible to associate with any sixteenth-century understanding of *vertu*.

A few years later, Pelletier also praised the academy and the role it would play in the all-around education—including grace and manners and the like—of the nobility. He added another purpose for the academies: they would help keep the nobles from being "corrupted" in Italy and wasting their time and money there.

France is no longer behind Italy in good education of our *Noblesse* in all the exercises that Italy has formerly taken pride in being the sole nation of Europe to offer. The first

[22] Ibid., p. 56v.
[23] Pluvinel *L'instruction*, p. 154.

conception of the *Académie* founded in Paris by the Sieur de Pluvinel as a public service to all this Kingdom happened to become such a pattern for the others, that, following its example, this other school still exists today headed by the Sieur de Benjamin whose merit and abilities fulfill all our wishes, so worthily he acquits himself of his office. Therefore it makes for one less Italian we have to feed. We wish for a French *Gentilhomme*, whose morals, manners, whose grace are genuinely French and not a foreigner's [C'est un Gentilhomme François qu'on désire avoir, les moeurs, la façon, la grâce, vrayment à la Françoise et non à l'estranger]. It is therefore in France alone that he will learn to ride horseback, to race in the tournament ring, to dance and to dress after our fashion, so that the student returning from Italy will not be considered more Italian than French, saving that way time and money as well.[24]

Pelletier's language suggests once more that the French academies should be seen as a direct response to the demands for noble education that were expressed from the 1570s on— a concrete result of the noble *prise de conscience*. It also suggests that some of this need must first have been filled in Italy, at least until the new French institution could begin to fulfill its purpose. We know that the French went to Italian riding academies that were already in existence in the sixteenth century,[25] and could conceivably have served as models, or partial models, for the later French academies. A comparison of the Italian with the French academies is useful in determining what was unique about the latter and the particular function they were fulfilling.

Unfortunately, little is known about the Italian academies. They seem to have had little or no direct connection with the sort of wide general humanistic program of education and

[24] Pelletier, *La nourriture*, p. 96.
[25] Pontaymery also blamed them for corrupting the French nobles, for instance (see *L'académie*, pp. 3–3v, 58v).

training called for in works like Castiglione's *Courtier*, and were instead purely riding schools whose main object was financial profit. Naples and Ferrara appear to have been the centers for the most important academies. Pluvinel himself, for instance, went to Naples for a number of years beginning in 1569 to study horsemanship at the school of the then famous Pignatelli.[26] Bassompierre wrote of going to Naples with his brother almost thirty years later, in 1596, to search out the same Pignatelli; but, after finding the man too old, he moved after a few months to the *manesge* or riding school of another Neapolitan, Cesare Mirabbello.[27] Both Pluvinel and Bassompierre appear to have learned nothing more than riding at these schools. Pluvinel, for example, in his book on his academy, called Pignatelli the best teacher of riding in Italy and stopped there.[28]

Neither Pignatelli nor Mirabbello seems to have left any writings, but Pignatelli's teacher, Cesare Fiaschi, who had a school in Ferrara, did write a treatise on horsemanship, which was published in the middle of the sixteenth century and translated into French in 1564. Fiaschi appears thoroughly uninterested in his institution and concerns himself only with the art of horseback riding—how it is declining in his time and how it can best be taught. There is no indication or emphasis that the institution should have a particular social role such as educating and training noblemen. Fiaschi mentions social classes only when he states that men of all classes, including poor artisans, should be given a chance to learn to ride.[29] From all indications, Fiaschi was only interested in the fact that his riding school, which was almost certainly a pri-

[26] Nicolas Chorier, *L'estat politique de la province de Dauphiné* (Grenoble, 1671), III, 440.

[27] Bassompierre, *Mémoires*, ed. M. de Chanterac, 4 vols. (Paris, 1870–1877), I, 49.

[28] Pluvinel, *L'instruction*, p. 30.

[29] Cesare Fiaschi, *Trattato del modo dell' imbrigliare, maneggiare, e ferrare cavalli* (Venice, 1563), p. 3v.

vate one, should make as much money as possible. The Neapolitan Grisone's treatise on the subject is almost identical, especially in only emphasizing horsemanship.[30]

The originality of the French academies thus lies not in the art of horsemanship, which seems to a large extent to have been copied from the Italians, but elsewhere. First, they were started as a sort of social mission to help "save" and redefine the nobility, and therefore they only catered to nobles. Second, they were products of the state in the sense of being founded through government help and serving a cause the state wished to advance, especially the absolutist regime from 1594 through the first half of the seventeenth century; their primary purpose was not profit. Finally, to help carry out the first goal, the French academies, unlike those in Italy, taught not only horsemanship, but many other subjects as well.

The focus in the academies to "save" the nobility and their association with the new absolutist state are especially clear in Pluvinel. Even the printing history of his own book about his academy illustrates his concern about noble rejuvenation. There were two different editions of his book, published shortly after his death, the first in 1623 and the second in 1625. The edition of 1623 is full of impressive engravings by the fairly well-known Dutch artist Crispan de Pas. The purpose of the book seems essentially to have been to make money, and it was rushed into print without Pluvinel's complete text. The 1625 edition, although it is far less interesting artistically, does contain the full text, and the part that was added concerns itself with the education of the nobility. Here Pluvinel resembles the many other writers of the late sixteenth and early seventeenth centuries who pleaded for special education for nobles. He argues that the academies serve an extremely important function and suggests the formation of four others—in Paris, Lyon, Poitiers, and Tours. Each would be an *ècole de vertu* and would teach many things besides horse-

---

[30] Federigo Grisone, *Gli ordini di cavalcare* (Naples, 1550).

manship, Pluvinel's specialty, including letters. Unlike the first edition, the second edition stresses that these academies exist only to serve the nobility. Apparently these factors did not interest the artist Crispan de Pas, but they must have been important enough to Pluvinel to encourage others closer to him than Crispan to make certain that they appeared in later editions, even if this meant fewer engravings and probably less profit.[31]

The few sources on Pluvinel that do exist suggest that he did well financially and socially and that there was a close relationship between him and the king. We have already seen that his nobility went unquestioned in his own time, even though no traces could be found of his earlier family,[32] suggesting perhaps some collusion with the monarchy. In any case, the two seem to have been serving each other's interests. In a letter of 1594 (the year of the founding of the academy) from Henry IV to Pluvinel, for instance, the king, after expressing much praise of Pluvinel, raises his pension from 400 to 1000 *ècus* annually.[33] And the homage given in 1604 for his lands near Poissy[34] shows, furthermore, a very good sized and profitable estate, suggesting that he must have been doing well as head of the academy.

That there was a close relationship between the monarchy and Pluvinel is also suggested in the text of his book. The work, written as a dialogue, is essentially a description of the type of instruction in horsemanship and in the care of horses given by Pluvinel at his academy. The other participant in the dialogue, besides Pluvinel, is the young King Louis XIII,

[31] Both editions can be found in the Bibliothèque Nationale: cf. Antoine de Pluvinel, *Le maneige royal* (Paris, 1623), and *L'instruction* (1625). The section in the 1625 edition referred to above is found on pp. 148–160. On Crispan de Pas, see Frances Yates, *The French Academies of the Sixteenth Century* (London, 1947), chap. 12. (Yates's book is on the literary, artistic, and musical academies of the sixteenth century and not on the new noble academies under consideration here.)

[32] Cf. chap. 6, note 43.

[33] B.N., Manuscrits Français, 28790.

[34] A.N., P. 74^2.

who, at least according to Pluvinel, was impressed with how good the graduates of his school appeared on horseback. The king says, for instance, that he wants to learn ". . . the manner that Monsieur de Pluvinel uses to train and handle his horses and make them so easy to control and manage, traits that I recognize in all those that are trained in his school."[35]

Beyond this book, however, the source material on Pluvinel's academy is very thin, and we must go to other sources and other academies in order to find out how an academy functioned internally. Fortunately, some detailed records exist for an academy founded at Aix in 1611.[36] Aix is far from Paris, of course, and the founding occurred more than fifteen years after Pluvinel's first venture. But the king's letter establishing the academy states that its formation and institution should be "in the form and manner that is practiced in our city of Paris."[37] By examining the Aix academy, therefore, we should be able to learn substantially what the Parisian academies were like.

The academy at Aix did have a basic difference, however, for theoretically at least it was not exclusively for nobles. The official designation is that the academy is for "la Noblesse et Nosdicts Sujets. . . ."[38] The nobility is named first, probably because those in Paris felt the academies were for them, but there is no question that others could attend as well. The sources give an explanation for this difference for they show that in order to establish and run the academy, a new tax was needed, and the consent of the provincial estates of Provence was required to impose such a tax. These estates continued to be active in some areas of France, as is known, and they were active in Provence.[39] In this case it was the "scindics de la Noblesse et procureurs des gens des trois estats [delegates

---

[35] Pluvinel, *L'instruction*, p. 20.

[36] A.N., 0^1 915, fols. 181–201.

[37] A.N., 0^1 915, fol. 181.

[38] Ibid.

[39] Cf. Major, *Representative Government*, especially pp. 319–324, 431–433, 540–549.

of the Nobility and procurators of the people of all three es-
tates]"[40] who agreed to the necessary salt tax; and if the representatives of the Third Estate had a right to agree to a tax
for a new educational institution, it would not be surprising
that they might try to prevent their children from being ar-
bitrarily excluded from it.

The legal admittance of nonnobles does not seem to have
affected the running of the academy or the idea behind it. A
clear distinction was made between the *collège* at Aix, the old
educational institution, and the academy, the new one,
founded in 1611; they were obviously thought of as two
thoroughly separate institutions.[41] The officially stated purposes for the founding of the academy were several. It is interesting that even the official language promulgated the
combining of arms and letters to make better fighters for the
defense of the country. This was especially important, of
course, for a frontier province like Provence:

> Given the position of this province as a border province,
> there is a need and a necessity for *the practice of arms to be
> joined with the study of letters* [que l'usage des armes soit joint
> avec les sciences des lettres] in the curriculum in order to
> achieve the best education possible in view of the defense
> of this province. This is why it is of considerable interest
> to us that, during the early and most tender years, the youth
> be educated and taught within our very own Kingdom and
> led to the respect and honour and obedience that they owe
> us, and that they do not receive such an education from
> foreigners, who are most often biased in favor of the en-
> emy of the state; and, moreover, avoiding in this way that
> money be spent outside this Kingdon.[42]

The close association of nobility and military is still evident
here, reflecting well the fact that the idea for the academies

---

[40] A.N., 0^1 915, fol. 181.

[41] Ibid., fols. 181–182. See also fol. 184 recounting some of the changes
in personnel at the academy, where the nobles seem completely in control.

[42] Ibid., fol. 181. The emphasis is mine.

grew up originally in the period when nobility was still thought of primarily as the military profession. But we also see a strong emphasis on letters, which became a more and more important part of the curriculum in the academies as the direct association of nobility and military grew fainter. At the same time, the apparent "marriage" of the monarchy and the new noble is also clear: the state encouraged the education of young nobles to ensure their loyalty to the state and to keep them under the authority of the monarchy, to keep them at home to save money,[43] and to keep them out of Italy, where many areas had fallen under the authority of France's main enemy, Spain.

The sources do tell us what was taught at the Aix academy and thus, we can assume, what was taught at the others as well. Riding and horsemanship were indeed the main subjects; the men who taught these were the best paid[44] and always seem to have been nobles.[45] But these subjects, or even training in arms, were not the only ones taught there. Mathematics, writing, and dancing all had their *maîtres*. "The Mathematics master," the regulations stated, "will teach mathematics and drawing [dessin] to the boarders on the day and hours decided by the Head of the [Academy]." The *maître à écrire* would also teach arithmetic, while "the Dancing Master will teach them how to walk, salute and dance, and once a month will organize a ball for them so they can impress and spur each other on [piquer d'émulation] in all three exer-

[43] As is repeated and emphasized in ibid.: the academy will relieve "the nobility and our subjects of having to go to foreign countries to beg the training needed for a good practice in arms, and avoid having money wastefully carried outside this kingdom."

[44] Ibid., fol. 183: 100 livres for these men as opposed to 30 for the others. It seems clear that one of the reasons they were paid more was that they often had to supply horses themselves at their own expense; and the importance and necessity of horses was what made these academies more expensive to run than regular schools. One Baron de Talon was temporarily suspended from the position as director of the academy because he would not supply the horses he had earlier agreed to supply. See fol. 184.

[45] Ibid., fols. 183–184.

cises."[46] Music was added as a main subject five years later in 1616.[47]

Mathematics, the sources suggest, was not in the curriculum to help prepare the nobles for a business life or career, a function it had for some people in the sixteenth century,[48] but rather to help teach the young nobles the art of making fortifications. Thus it essentially had a military purpose, like much of the rest of the curriculum. But dancing, music, and learning how to *marcher* and *saluer* in the right way were factors of a quite different sort, ones that were going to help lead to a different definition of nobility in the coming years.

The academy at Aix apparently grew quickly and was quite successful. Music, as we have seen, was added to the curriculum in 1616, and three more *écuyers* were hired to teach horsemanship between the years 1610 and 1627.[49] Unfortunately, we do not have the same precise information for other academies in the first half of the century,[50] so we cannot confirm that they functioned similarly to the one at Aix, though it seems safe to assume that they did. There is evidence that other academies, such as the one at Angers, were extremely popular with foreign nobles.[51] Also, after the death of Henry IV and during the time of Richelieu, there are sources that suggest what subjects were taught at the acade-

---

[46] Ibid., fol. 183.

[47] Ibid., fol. 184.

[48] See Natalie Zemon Davis, "Sixteenth Century French Arithmetics on the Business Life," *Journal of the History of Ideas* 21 (1960), 18–48.

[49] A.N., 0^1 915, fol. 184.

[50] A search of all of 0^1 915–917 for other information on academies in the first half of the century unfortunately turned up little of substance. One academy was founded in Riom in 1644. But these sources, accumulated probably toward the end of the eighteenth century, are concerned mostly with those academies founded in the 1670s and 1680s, and then later in the eighteenth century. For instance, one was founded in Angers in 1670, in Besançon in 1674, in Rouen in 1677, in Bordeaux and in Montauban in 1680, in Strasbourg and in Saumur in 1681, and in Lille in 1687.

[51] See Willem Frijhoff, "Etudiants étrangers à l'académie d'équitation d'Angers au xviie siècle," *LIAS* 4 (1977), 13–27, and Chartier et al., *L'éducation en France*, pp. 182–183.

mies and that attest to the academies' continued popularity.

Flurance-Rivault, for instance, called in 1612 for yet another academy for nobles only that would teach the young *gentilshommes*—those attached to the court in this case—skills and subjects similar to those they would have learned at Pluvinel's or at Aix, but with greater emphasis on letters and less on military matters. In this academy, for instance, they would be taught "the customs and habits of other peoples, how to conduct themselves in politics and in war, the knowledge of Antiquity, honor, gracious conduct and manners [Gentillesse], and a thousand other important things that will ignite their curiosity to go and search out beauty and perfection."[52] And, showing once again the close connection between the new noble educational program and the absolutist state, Flurance-Rivault emphasized that the overall function of learning all these things would be "in brief to render them capable one day of serving the King and the State."[53]

Richelieu, meanwhile, who had attended Pluvinel's academy as a youth before entering the Church,[54] also seems to have been particularly interested in the academies, for reasons similar to those of Flurance-Rivault. One source, which can be found in manuscript form in at least three Parisian libraries,[55] which suggests it was taken seriously at the time, indicates that in the 1630s he created a number of scholarships for young and poor nobles at one of the academies in Paris, apparently the one originally founded by the Sieur de Benjamin (the location referred to is on the rue Vieille du

[52] Flurance-Rivault, *Le dessein*, p. 3.

[53] Ibid., p. 4. Also, it is very clear in Flurance-Rivault that the academy would be *only* for nobles. Cf., for instance, p. 5v and p. 16.

[54] Gabriel Hanotaux, *Histoire du Cardinal de Richelieu*, vol. I, *La jeunesse de Richelieu (1585–1614), la France en 1614* (Paris, 1893), pp. 73–74.

[55] I found four copies of this document in Paris: Bibliothèque Mazarine, Ms. 2117 (the one quoted from below); Bibliothèque de l'Arsenal, Ms. 4114; B.N., Manuscrits Français 22884; B.N., Manuscrits Français, Nouvelles Acquisitions, 150. There are slight variations from one to the other, but no major differences.

Temple, while Pluvinel's was located on the rue du Faubourg Saint-Honoré). The purpose is plainly and clearly to help nobles ("to nourish, instruct, and educate twenty *gentilzhommes*"),[56] and it is assumed as obvious that the academies were for nobles only.[57] Richelieu explains that he is creating the fellowships because there are many *donations* and *bourses* at *collèges* and *séminaires* for students of "low birth and nonnoble condition [basse Estoffe et condition roturière]," but no one till now had stopped to think of the "support of the poor nobles [entretien de la pauvre Noblesse]."[58]

His language mirrors very closely that of people like La Noue, Du Souhait, the founders of the academy at Aix, and the many others who were calling for the marriage of arms and letters in order to create the perfect *gentilhomme*. "After due consideration," he wrote, for instance, "upon something that is of very great importance, that arms and letters are one to the other like sisters and are an inseparable pair . . . we take the following action. . . ."[59] There is also a substantially greater emphasis on *lettres* here, which again suggests in this later period yet a further moving away from the purely military view of nobility:

> During the two years of their stay, in addition to the usual exercises of the Academy which will be practiced in common with all the other students, such as riding and performing on horseback, fencing, studying Mathematics and fortifications and others, they will also, at regular hours, be taught the principles of Logic, Physics, Metaphysics, briefly the French language but a full course on Ethics [la Morale]; and at another convenient hour after dinner they will also be briefly acquainted with map-reading, or Ge-

[56] Bibliothèque Mazarine, Ms. 2117.

[57] Ibid. These nobles will have the same privileges and duties, etc., as "les autres gentilzhommes [still of course equivalent of 'nobles' at this time]."

[58] Ibid.

[59] Ibid: "Avons faict reflection sur une chose de très grande [importance] considérant que les armes et lettres estant germaines et comme inséparables."

ography, and some ideas about History, the establishment, decline and changing of the Empires of the world, the transmigration of Peoples, the formation and collapse of Cities, and the names and deeds of great men; the students will be also given a brief account of the state of the modern Principalities, and more particularly those of Europe whose interests concern us very much since they are our neighbors. Above all and at full length they will learn Roman History and French History.[60]

Clearly, the "marriage of arms and letters" was not only for the good of the nobles; it also served the interests of the early absolutist state, and, one would suspect, most if not all of the rest of society, which would certainly be better off with a tamed, civilized and "cultured" nobility than with a crude, barbarous, and primarily military one.

Richelieu reflects similar attitudes elsewhere. For instance, in an interesting but unrealistic project for a new academy for one thousand *gentilshommes*, he uses similar language and proposes again a curriculum that would join arms with letters and other subjects. At this proposed new academy, specifically limited to nobles ("Nobles d'extraction"), the young *gentilshommes*

> will learn fencing, dancing, performing on horseback, the use of the Musket and the Pike and all the maneuvers of the Infantry. They will be taught Mathematics from a practical point of view . . . will learn the first four rules of Arithmetic and will read history. [They] will be trained to wrestle, to jump, to throw the bar [jetter la barre], to swim and to do other physical exercises.[61]

This project was certainly never put into effect, but the Cardinal was able eventually to found a new academy, following these principles, in the town of Richelieu, and it appar-

---

[60] Ibid. Chartier et al. in *L'éducation en France*, p. 184, also cite a section of this source.

[61] B.N., Fonds Baluze, 147.

ently met with a good deal of early success, at least until his death.[62]

This concern of the post 1594 and pre-Louis XIV state in encouraging noble education thus suggests clearly that a better educated and more cultured nobility was not really opposed to its interests. What there had been of noble education in the sixteenth century and before had usually been acquired by the young noble at home, by his being farmed out to other private noble families, or by his being in residence at the courts of powerful nobles or the king;[63] and some of the encouragement of the state probably came from its desire to keep a better control over something that was going to happen anyway. But this concern also suggests once again that in the new absolutist state of the seventeenth century there was no room for nobility as a function or as action, with all it suggested in terms of an independent nobility; and that anything that would help build new, less dangerous accoutrements, justifications, and definitions of nobility—perhaps even the use of courtesy as a coercive tool[64]—needed to be encouraged.

The French academies were thus original in that they were limited, or almost always limited, to nobles only; were encouraged by the state; and taught much more than just horsemanship. In this way, they served an important function in France in the first half of the seventeenth century, one that in the differing historical conditions of Italy was appar-

---

[62] Marcel Bataillan, "L'académie de Richelieu, Indre-et-Loire," in *Pédagogues et juristes: Congrès du Centre d'Etudes Supérieures de la Renaissance de Tours, Eté 1960* (Paris, 1963), pp. 255–270.

[63] Nordhaus has a useful discussion, based on individual examples, of how noble education functioned in the sixteenth century in *"Arma et Litterae"*, especially chap. 3.

[64] Cf. Orest Ranum, "Courtesy, Absolutism, and the Rise of the French State, 1630–1660," *Journal of Modern History* 52 (1980), 426–451. Ranum has examined some of the uses made by officials of the monarchy of courtesy as a coercive tool on nobles and other members of the elites, suggesting clearly how a courteous—and thus "civilized" as well, it would seem—nobility was in the interest of the monarchy.

enlty not needed. They did their part, especially in the later years of the first half of the century when the curriculum started to include more and more letters and other nonmilitary subjects, in helping to build a more educated, civilized, and cultured nobility; and, just as important, perhaps, by being the nobles' own institution, they suggested that the nobles were serious about obtaining their new education. The academies must also, in other words, have helped the nobles' "image"—their credibility—in the new times of the first half of the seventeenth century. If they tended to become less discussed and seemingly less important from the middle of the century onward, catering almost as much to foreigners as to Frenchmen,[65] and if they had no lasting significance as forerunners to the *écoles militaires* of the eighteenth century,[66] perhaps they should nevertheless not be written off as failures. The academies had served a significant function at an important turning point in French history and in the fortunes of the nobility, as nobility lost its medieval meaning and justification and as nobles took on new accoutrements and new justifications. Since by the middle of the century that transformation seemed secure and relatively complete, the academies were simply no longer needed to fulfill their original purpose.

THE academies were important, then, because they were the nobles' own institution, for them and limited to them. The wording of the calls for education for nobles from the 1570s on and the specific curriculum of the academies show not only that nobles were trying to educate themselves but also that they wanted that education to be more than just a military one. The academies, meanwhile, were not the only places where nobles picked up their new training and their new polish and culture. The *salons*, such as for instance the famous one of Mme. de Rambouillet—and there were many others in the first half of the century—also did their part, es-

---

[65] Cf. Chartier et al., *L'éducation en France*, pp. 182–183.
[66] Ibid., p. 185.

pecially in terms of polish and culture. Also important were the many books on politeness—*courtoisie*, *honnêteté*, and proper behavior at court—which were usually partly modeled on Castiglione's *Courtier*. These books of courtesy appeared in great numbers in the first half of the century and often were indirectly aimed at nobles. Nicolas Faret, for instance, who wrote one of the better known guides, consciously combined the function of his book with that of the academy. When discussing the training of a *gentilhomme*, for example, he wrote:

> Since you have received all of these gifts from Nature [well formed limbs, etc. . . . .] it is important that they should be used, and that you should study eagerly, not only all that is taught in the *Académies*, but also all the gallantries of address that are customary and befitting for a *Gentilhomme* . . . [which can be learned from his book].[67]

Magendie, who has studied the *salons* and the books of courtesy, has shown how they slowly but relentlessly worked to tame and civilize the uncultured and boorish nobles of the sixteenth century, until, by the middle of the seventeenth century, their focus had tended to shift away from nobles alone and toward serving the needs of the upper classes in general,[68] suggesting that the nobles had been catching up in terms of education and culture with others in these upper classes. It also seems true that an increasing number of nobles attended the public *collèges* as well as the Jesuit schools in the first half of the century, but we still know relatively little about this aspect of noble education.[69]

When we know more about the role of the *collèges* and the Jesuit schools, to supplement the work of Magendie and what has been suggested about the role of the academies in this chapter, we should understand the process of noble educa-

[67] Faret, *L'honneste homme*, p. 16.
[68] Cf. Magendie, *La politesse mondaine*.
[69] Cf. Chartier et al., *L'éducation en France*, pp. 179–181. On the earlier history of the public *collèges*, however, see the useful synthesis by George Huppert, *Public Schools in Renaissance France* (Urbana and Chicago, 1984).

tion, and its actual effect on the nobles, even better. But it is clear that by the 1650s and 1660s, with all of these factors at work, the new and more modern image of the cultured noble-aristocrat had become fairly well entrenched, replacing that of the courageous—but often foolishly courageous—and relatively uncultured and often crude and barbarous noble of the sixteenth century. Indeed, the image had apparently become so fixed that good recent historians of seventeenth-century France, obviously not that familiar with earlier periods, have taken it for granted that culture was a basic noble trait—as indeed it had just become by that time—and that nonnobles, or those trying to move up in society, would attempt to acquire that culture.[70] A famous statement about Pluvinel attributed to Tallement des Réaux a generation later—that Pluvinel "was no more subtle than his horses [n'était pas plus subtil que ses chevaux]"[71]—suggests, ironically in this case, a similar conclusion. The education and culture that Pluvinel and his predecessors and contemporaries had been trying so hard to obtain for the nobles had apparently been successful enough so that these forerunners could be looked back upon as uncultured boors by their more fortunate successors who had profited from the new education.

The new image is depicted humorously, clearly, and in a sense definitively in Molière's *Bourgeois gentilhomme* of 1670. Dorante, the cultured and civilized nobleman, is contrasted with Monsieur Jourdain, the boorish and uncultured "bourgeois." In a sense the roles are reversed from a century earlier, when the typical noble would have been in Monsieur Jourdain's place. What separates the two this time, besides simply not being born a *gentilhomme* or noble, are the very things which Monsieur Jourdain sets out to acquire at the beginning of the play: *bon goût, l'esprit, savoir raisonner,* and

[70] For instance, Carolyn C. Lougee, *Le Paradis des Femmes: Women, Salons, and Social Stratification in Seventeenth-Century France* (Princeton, 1976).

[71] Cited by Mennessier de La Lance in *Essai de bibliographie hippique* (Paris, 1915–17), II, 326.

so on.[72] From the beginning he has hired a *maître de musique*, a *maître à danser*, a *maître d'armes*, and a *maître de philosophie* to teach him to bridge the gap. To do so, however, in this particular play, is portrayed as a hopeless task, and the new *maîtres* know it. They do the job for the money: ". . . he has discernment in his purse, his praises are 'golden' or monied [ses louanges sont monnayées] and this ignorant bourgeois. . . ."[73] Monsieur Jourdain, the audience understands, will never be able to acquire these "skills" and will only appear ridiculous.

What interests us here, however, is not so much the ignorant bourgeois as the cultured aristocrat, as dillettantish as his learning may have been. In the case of the former, it would seem that he was made this way to contrast with Dorante and hardly reflects reality, nor the range of nonnoble characters in Molière's plays as a whole, which contain some quite civilized and cultured nonnobles. On the other hand, the image of a brutal, uncultured noble, typical of the sixteenth century, never seems to appear in his plays, and, as far as one can tell, is absent from most of the other literature of the time. Dorante is the typical nobleman, and this time the nonnoble is *ce bourgeois ignorant* trying to catch up with him. The latter complains to his *maître de philosophie* that he wishes to learn all he can, ". . . for I have the greatest desire in the world to be learned; and it vexes me more than I can tell that my father and mother did not make me learn thoroughly all the sciences when I was young."[74] In the mid-sixteenth century this might well have been the complaint of a noble; now it is the complaint of a nonnoble.

[72] Molière, *Le bourgeois gentilhomme*, in *Oeuvres complètes*, Editions du Seuil (Paris, 1962), act III, scene 3, lines 49–50: "Je veux avoir de l'esprit et savoir raisonner des choses parmi les honnêtes gens [I want to have a good mind and be able to discuss rationally with the decent and respectable and well-bred people]."

[73] Ibid., act I, scene 1, lines 52–53.

[74] Ibid., act II, scene 4, lines 8–11. The translation here is by Charles Heron Wall in *The Dramatic Works of Molière* (London, 1908).

Anyone who has seen the *Bourgeois gentilhomme* performed on the stage has certainly laughed through one of the most amusing scenes of the play, when Monsieur Jourdain appears in the clothes of a *gentilhomme* and the young but clever and common-sensical servant from the country laughs and laughs at the spectacle, unable to stop, while Monsieur Jourdain puts up with it more or less good-naturedly. Knowing that special clothes account for part of the difference between noble and nonnoble, he had hired a *maître tailleur* to see that he was properly outfitted. However, buying and wearing the clothes of nobles in order to look like them was no longer enough, as it had been for some in the sixteenth century. It is not the clothes themselves—foolish as they may seem to modern spectators—that make Nicole laugh; it is Monsieur Jourdain in the clothes.[75] Without the other accoutrements that contribute to the outward characteristics of the noble—the *bon goût*, the grace, the wit, and the rest—the clothes are ridiculous and look like a costume. And, indeed, it is a measure of the successful actor and a successful performance to give this effect.

The things that separate Monsieur Jourdain from Dorante are clearly things that have little or nothing to do with one's profession, as they would have had a century before. The would-be noble of the middle of the sixteenth century would have had to have a professional military career. (A parallel story to the *Bourgeois gentilhomme* for that time would probably have found the nonnoble buying a suit of armor and, looking ridiculous, trying unsuccessfully to handle a difficult horse.) The stereotypical would-be noble of the middle of the seventeenth century, on the other hand, after an earlier stint at trying to fight a duel would have had to acquire the sorts of things that Monsieur Jourdain set out to acquire—things

---

[75] The tailor did, perhaps, arrange some of the clothes in a somewhat odd manner on Monsieur Jourdain (see act II, scene 5), but the main point is that Monsieur Jourdain does not know whether they are right or wrong and does not know how to wear them. The scene referred to above is act III, scene 2.

that could now be associated with nobles, thanks to their change in attitude toward education, which helped lead to the new academies and to the whole general process of noble education in the first half of the seventeenth century. This transformation, with the emergence of a substantially less "dangerous" image, suggests once again, as with most of the other changes in the *marques de noblesse* that we have studied, the diminished importance of the distinction between noble and nonnoble in the more modern world that emerged on the other side of the crisis years of the late sixteenth century.

9

Conclusions
and Perspectives

The End of Nobility As a Profession

At the beginning of this study we saw that nobility in the sixteenth century was understood quite differently than is normally assumed, that it was still thought of in essentially medieval terms as a profession or function, a métier, or as something one does. We then saw that at the heart of this view, in terms of what people were actually supposed to do to be noble, lay the concept of *vertu*, or of virtuous action. We saw that this view not only persisted throughout much of the sixteenth century, but actually dominated people's thinking on the question almost without exception. We saw its eventual abandonment, especially the concept of *vertu*, under the pressure of events at the very end of the sixteenth and early in the seventeenth centuries; and we have watched the emergence of new *marques de noblesse* and changes in the old ones, both influenced by the repudiation of the old view, especially the key part of that process, the separation of virtue from nobility. With the declining emphasis on virtue, came also a corresponding emergence of more modern ideas of profession as they related to nobility. Profession, like virtue, became separated from nobility. The military became simply a profession like others, which one could choose to follow or not to follow, as one wished. With the acceptance of nobility as a hereditary status, the nobleman became free to choose professions such as arms, the church, or law, without the choice affecting his noble status.

This change apparently did not take place as abruptly as

202

the separation of virtue and nobility. For example, two of the texts cited in chapter 1 to illustrate the old view, La Béraudière's *Combat* and Flurance-Rivault's *Dessein*, are from the early 1600s (1608 and 1612).[1] But this period already gave rise to some apparent misgivings and confusion about the view. In 1604 Louis Guyon, for example, looked at the nobiltiy of the past with some historical perspective, and wrote as if he were describing things as they had once been but no longer were:

> The second estate of the Republic of Gaul was that of the nobility, or knights [les gens nobles, ou chevaliers], and their duty was to go to war and to fight: the nobles would pay no taxes and were not permitted any craft, nor trade, under penalty of loss of their noble rank: and if a noble was found not carrying any arms, he was condemned to carry none for one year and declared dishonored for that time since he was no longer able to perform his duty like the others.[2]

Guillaume de Chevalier, meanwhile, called in 1598 for nobles to stick to their *vraye vocation*,[3] which suggests clearly an awareness that some were not doing so. And Pelletier, showing a practical as well as theoretical interest in the education of young nobles, shows, however unwillingly, a more conscious adjustment to reality:

> From this diversity of study and training [which the young noble should receive during his educational upbringing] one becomes a theologian, another a lawyer. But the proper, the true, the inseparable virtue of a *Gentilhomme* seems to me to be valor alone [Mais la propre, la vraye, et inséparable vertu d'un Gentilhomme me semble estre la seule valeur].[4]

[1] Cf. chap. 1, notes 17 and 18.
[2] Guyon, *Diverses leçons*, p. 864.
[3] Chevalier, *Discours des querelles*, p. 26.
[4] Pelletier, *La nourriture*, p. 66v.

Here the new and old appear both to coexist and to conflict. A profession is, on the one hand, something one chooses, such as *théologien* or *jurisconsulte*, without affecting one's position as noble or nonnoble; on the other hand, it is the old *vertu* of the *gentilhomme*—obviously implying valor in arms— a nobility that *derives* from the profession itself, rather than nobility being brought to the profession.

With the growing sophistication of the age of Richelieu,[5] this confusion and mixing of views seem to have gradually disappeared. Certainly the growth of more modern ideas of profession in general, about which we still have much to learn,[6] helped a good deal, as did, more specifically, the development of the military into a better organized and more clearly definable institution. The spreading, in some circles at least, of antiwar and antimilitary attitudes must also have done its part. Pierre Charron, for instance, expressed such attitudes well, even if he was following to a large extent humanists like Erasmus and More. "We can state," he wrote in 1601, that the

> art and experience of vanquishing and killing each other, of causing the downfall and destruction of our own species, seems a perverted act and a product of a distracted judgment. . . . Indeed . . . what is this craze to put oneself in danger of losing one's limbs and of undergoing what is a thousand times worse than death, that is the fire and sword, trepanning, being tortured with red-hot pincers, being cut up by a pinking iron, being torn to pieces, your body being exhausted to the last drop, a prisoner and a galley slave forever? All this to oblige someone else's passion, for a cause which one does not know to be just, and which is usually not; for wars are unjust most of the time.[7]

[5] Magendie, in *La politesse mondaine*, has examined in great detail this process of "sophistication."

[6] This is a very complicated question. For a recent article that raises some of the important issues, see Donald R. Kelley, "Johann Sleidan and the Origins of History as a Profession," *Journal of Modern History* 52 (1980), 573–598.

[7] Charron, *De la sagesse*, I, 415–416.

The diffusion of such sentiments could certainly have en-couraged some nobles, who would obviously want to re-main noble, to separate themselves from military matters—to be noble without being military.

By the 1630s, then, a more modern and familiar view of the relation between nobility and profession had become prevalent. For Nicolas Faret, for instance, in his *L'honneste homme ou l'art de plaire à la cour*, arms is one profession among many, certainly preferable for a nobleman, but not obliga-tory since a nobleman is no longer defined by his actions. He advises the young nobleman:

> But, *since there is no man who does not choose a profession in order to employ himself* [comme il n'y a point d'hommes qui ne choississent une profession pour s'employer], I feel that there is none to be found more appropriate or honest and more essential for a *gentilhomme* than the profession of arms.[8]

This is a quite thorough reversal from the attitudes prevalent in the sixteenth century and one that, of course, is familiar today. Arms is something, for Faret, that the nobleman *chooses*; he should fight—that is the most *honnête* profession—but still he is nobleman first and fighter second instead of vice versa. The assumption thus is that one is born into the nobility and remains a noble no matter what one does, rather than being considered noble by one's actions. When, in the *Histoire co-mique de Francion*, Sorel's young *gentilhomme* hero speaks of arms as a "very nasty profession" (très méchant métier), a similar attitude—that arms is one profession among others that a noble might choose—is being expressed.[9] Later, in Molière's *Bourgeois gentilhomme*, Cléonte, an upper-class nonnoble, spends six years *dans les armes*, clearly in an im-portant position; but there is no assumption that this would make him a noble,[10] as would have been assumed earlier.

---

[8] Faret, *L'honneste homme*, p. 12. The emphasis is mine.

[9] Sorel, *Francion*, p. 119. Francion says: "My father, seeing that my nat-ural inclination was toward letters, did not wish to discourage me because he knew that arms, the profession he had followed, was a very nasty one."

[10] Molière, *Le bourgeois gentilhomme*, act III, scene 12.

Interestingly enough, this change has been inadvertently documented in Wartburg's great *Französisches etymologisches Wörterbuch*, for his analysis of the term "profession" implies a similar narrowing down in meaning and a working toward a greater precision in the use of the word. Wartburg gives one of the older definitions of the term, for example, as being *état, condition, métier* all joined together; but after 1637 the meaning of the word is narrowed down simply to *embrasser un emploi, un métier.*[11] He apparently also discovered that the term *profession* meant more in the sixteenth century than it does today, and in trying to explain that meaning he fell upon the very social-status-oriented words *état* and *condition.* If nobility in the sixteenth century had been a profession, it had ceased to be so by 1637, by the time of Faret and Sorel and by the time of Molière's *Bourgeois gentilhomme,* and had become simply a series of legal privileges, explained and justified by birth instead of by one's actions.

Some Suggested Implications

This study consists of two basic parts. The first, covered in chapters 1–3 and parts of chapters 4 and 5, focused on almost the entire sixteenth century and has argued that nobility was viewed in that period in ways quite different than what has normally been assumed. The second, including parts of chapters 4 and 5 and the remainder of the book, has told the story of the change from that view to what we have called the modern idea of nobility, a change that took place essentially in the late sixteenth and early seventeenth centuries. It seems appropriate now to draw together and briefly summarize some of the larger implications that have emerged in these two parts.

To begin with, the fact that nobility was conceived of essentially as the military profession in the sixteenth century has potentially important implications for the way we look

---

[11] Wartburg, *Wörterbuch,* IX, 429, and also the reference to the same definition in chap. 1, note 3, above.

at social classes and groups and their interaction in the period. Also, the fact that these medieval ideas about an issue as important as nobility continued throughout most of the sixteenth century suggests that, in this area at least, the Middle Ages may not have ended as soon as we have thought. The early part of the study suggests as well the great importance of military questions for helping our understanding of much more than just military matters, at least for the sixteenth century, and one suspects for other periods as well. It also gives us perspcetives on how a whole society could continue to believe—seemingly without exception, at least for most of the century—in an idea whose time, by almost all factual indications, had come and gone. This information may also lead us to ask some new questions about sixteenth-century nobility elsewhere in Europe.

Despite the fact that the sixteenth-century view did change in fundamental ways, there were still some carry-overs of the old view into later times, and we need to watch for these. We know, for instance, that many nobles in France and other European countries continued to feel strongly obliged to follow a military career long after nobility ceased to be thought of as a profession.[12] This is an obvious vestige from the feudal-military origins of the nobility and seems to separate a good deal the nobility of the later ancien régime from that of the ancient period. These military origins also seem undoubtedly to have had an important effect on ennoblement. Possibilities for ennoblement and the belief therein (for the "right" reasons, of course) were basic ingredients of the understanding of nobility as a profession and as action, and we know that ennoblement continued to be a reality (even as the concept of nobility came to be based much more upon birth) throughout the later ancien régime.[13] The connection be-

---

[12] Corvisier in *Armées et sociétés*, especially pp. 100–122, and Labatut in *Les noblesses européennes*, especially pp. 85–101, have some useful comparative comments on this question.

[13] This well-known fact is especially well documented in François Bluche and Pierre Durye, *L'anoblissement par charge avant 1789* in *Les cahiers nobles*, nos. 23–24 (1962), and Cubells, "A propos des usurpations."

tween the earlier view and the later reality seems quite obvious here; and the continued existence of ennoblement was of great importance in helping to minimize the distinction between noble and nonnoble in the later period. It also seems to offer another important difference between the ancient view and the "modern" view, or that which took shape from the early seventeenth century on. In short, the long feudal-military interlude has helped to make modern views of nobility different from ancient views, even though they resemble each other in their fundamental assumptions.

The change to the modern idea of nobility also has important implications. As we have seen, it is a complex story that needs to be connected to the social, political, and military realities of the time. We have already suggested that without this change—without the nobility abandoning its medieval function—the new absolutist state in France could not have taken form the way it did. Nobility as the military profession implied too much independence for the nobles and thus was in direct opposition to the tendency and need of the new state to insist that all authority must in the end emanate from it. On the other hand, it became clear that there was no inherent contradiction between this absolutist state and nobility in its more modern form as a legal status represented by a series of legal privileges, determined by birth, and defined by culture (and even defined partially by the duel as long as all duels were fought only with the permission of the central authority). These ideas, along with the realization that nobility as virtue had potential dangers for the nobles and for those who favored nobility, were accepted by much of the upper classes during the social and political upheavals of the late sixteenth century and the half century that followed them.

We have seen that, concurrent with this change in the view of nobility in the late sixteenth and early seventeenth centuries, came what we have called a noble *prise de conscience*, which expressed itself first in the 1570s and 1580s in terms of the old ideas of virtue and the old way of looking at things. It began with an awareness that there were problems, though it was not very clear to contemporaries what some of these problems were; as a solution, demands were made simply for a return to or a restoration of the old virtue that defined nobility. But within this context other demands were made as well: for more and better education, for instance, and for new and better means of defining and differentiating nobles from nonnobles. When the nobles dropped their demands for virtue in the late sixteenth and early seventeenth centuries, they continued with their other demands and pursued them to help shape their new image.

This description of a *prise de conscience*, then, suggests an adaptation and a transformation by the nobility in response to changing circumstances during that period, rather than a decline, a conclusion that agrees with most recent research. William Weary, for instance, has discovered a strong and successful La Trémoille family in the sixteenth century,[14] and J. Russell Major has found an equally healthy Foix-Navarre-Albret family becoming even more prosperous in the second half of the century.[15] Continuity and adaptation characterize the findings of Wood,[16] Constant,[17] and to some extent Labatut,[18] and these in turn suggest continued noble health

[14] William A. Weary, "Royal Policy and Patronage in Renaissance France: The Monarchy and the House of La Trémoille," Ph.D. diss., Yale University, 1972.

[15] Major, "Noble Income."

[16] Wood, *Nobility of Bayeux*.

[17] Constant, *Nobles et paysans*.

[18] Jean-Pierre Labatut, *Les ducs et pairs de France au xviie siècle* (Paris, 1972), and see also William A. Weary, "The House of La Trémoille, Fifteenth through Eighteenth Centuries: Change and Adaptation in a French Noble Family," *Journal of Modern History* 49 (March 1977), On-Demand Supplement. Further evidence for these conclusions can be found in Mack P. Holt, "Patterns of *Clientèle* and Economic Opportunity at Court during the Wars of Religion: The Household of François, Duke of Anjou," *French Historical Studies* 13 (1984), 305–322. In terms of the vitality of the lesser nobility in the middle of the sixteenth century, see Kristen Brooke Neuschel, "The Prince of Condé and the Nobility of Picardy: A Study of the Structure of Noble Relationships in Sixteenth-Century France," Ph. D. diss., Brown University, 1982.

through the eighteenth century when merged with the conclusions of, for instance, Robert Forster,[19] Jean Meyer,[20] and Guy Chaussinand-Nogaret.[21] As François Billacois summed up for the period from 1550 to 1650, "The nobility does not decline but transforms itself into aristocrats";[22] and in this sense the material presented in this study adds further evidence for this conclusion.

This story of transformation and continued strength for the nobility, joined with the decline of the medieval view and the fact that nobility was becoming less important as a dividing factor in society, leads us to see enlarged elites, who have more similarities than differences, as the main key to understanding the relations between the upper classes from the late sixteenth century onward. This also fits well with recent research. James Wood, for instance, has found relatively little difference between old nobles and new ones in the *élection* of Bayeux.[23] Jonathan Dewald has found little difference, especially economically and in terms of sources of wealth, between the high magistrature and other nobles in and around Rouen.[24] Robert Harding has also found relatively little robe-sword conflict, as the relations between the older governors and the newer intendants changed and developed from the sixteenth into the seventeenth century.[25] And Denis Crouzet has found, for the second half of the sixteenth century, im-

[19] Robert Forster, *The Nobility of Toulouse in the Eighteenth Century: A Social and Economic Study* (Baltimore, 1960); "The Provincial Noble: A Reappraisal," *American Historical Review* 68 (1963), 681–691; and *The House of Saulx-Tavannes, Versailles and Burgundy 1700–1830* (Baltimore and London, 1971).

[20] Meyer, *La noblesse bretonne* and "La noblesse française au xviiiᵉ siècle; Aperçu des problèmes," *Acta Polonia Historica* 36 (1977), 7–45.

[21] Guy Chaussinand-Nogaret, *La noblesse au xviiiᵉ siècle, De la féodalité aux lumières* (Paris, 1976).

[22] François Billacois, "La crise de la noblesse européenne (1550–1650)," *Revue d'histoire moderne et contemporaine* 23 (1976), 277.

[23] Wood, *Nobility of Bayeux*.

[24] Dewald, *Formation of a Provincial Nobility*.

[25] Harding, *Anatomy of a Power Elite*.

portant financial ties, which suggest closer political connections than might have been expected, between a well-known and influential noble family (the Nevers) and members of the robe.[26] A similar picture of a lack of important distinctions between robe and sword emerges from work done on the later ancien régime as well;[27] thus all this research tends to confirm—though some differences between noble and nonnoble remain[28]—the conclusions put forward by Denis Richet in a very important article about elites some time ago.[29]

From this perspective, then, France of the late ancien régime, from 1594 on, was dominated by a series of elites of which nobles were only one. More accurately, it was dominated by an upper class or group for which "nobility" was a relatively easy-to-obtain legal status that included a set of le-

[26] Denis Crouzet, "Recherches sur la crise de l'aristocratie en France au xvi⁰ᵐᵉ siècle: Les dettes de la maison de Nevers," *Histoire, économie et société* I (1982), 7–50. See also the recent study by Barbara Diefendorf, *Paris City Councillors in the Sixteenth Century: The Politics of Patrimony* (Princeton, N.J. 1983). This work, focusing on the period from 1535 to 1575, shows a substantial portion of the Paris city councillors during this time to have been noble and suggests a relatively minor significance for the noble-nonoble distinction.

[27] For instance, Meyer, *La noblesse bretonne* and Pierre Goubert's conclusion, building from the work of Meyer and others: "The distinction between *noblesse de robe* and *noblesse d'épée* is in large part superficial and mundane, and even falser in the provinces than in Paris." Cf. "Problèmes généraux de la noblesse française," *Treizième Congrès International des Sciences Historiques* (Moscow, 1970), p. 4. This conclusion is stated even more unequivocally by Goubert in *Ancien Régime*, p. 172.

[28] As, for instance, Michel Vovelle has argued for the eighteenth century in "L'élite où le mensonge des mots," *Annales: Economies, sociétés, civilisations* 29 (1974), 49–72; and as is suggested by Jean Meyer's analysis of different conceptions of poverty held by nobles and nonnobles in "Un problème mal posé; La noblesse pauvre; L'exemple breton au xviiiᵉ siècle," *Revue d'histoire moderne et contemporaine* 18 (1971), 161–188.

[29] Richet, "Autour des origines idéologiques." For continuation and reinforcement of aspects of the argument, see also Richet, *La France moderne*; "Elite et noblesse" and "Révolution anglaise et révolution française, 1640 et 1789," in François Bédarida, François Crouzet, and Douglas Johnson, eds., *Dix siècles d'histoire franco-britannique: De Guillaume le Conquérant au Marché commun* (Paris, 1979), pp. 94–113.

gal privileges and some prestige. It was an honor or privilege that was added on to other more important privileges and advantages (obtainable by nonnobles as well as nobles), such as ownership of land and control over other forms of wealth; office and administrative position; family connections; family age and tradition; education; native ability; and the like. In such circumstances nobility would be relatively unimportant in the later ancien régime, a conclusion that fits well with the conclusions of those scholars who, in emphasizing the relative unimportance of the noble-nonnoble distinction, have been working for the past twenty to thirty years to revise our understanding of the origins of the French Revolution.[30] Watching nobility being shorn of its basic military significance in this study should help us understand a little better why these historians have found what they have in the later period.

The Later Seventeenth and Eighteenth Centuries

The above observations about the later ancien régime suggest a closer look is in order on the question of what the problems of nobility during this period look like from the perspective of the sixteenth and early seventeenth centuries. We have seen, for instance, that after relative silence on the subject in the first half of the sixteenth century, there were lively debates on the question of nobility in the 1570s, 1580s, and early 1590s, and then relative indifference once again after the early seventeenth century and on. But important debates about nobility broke out once again in the middle of the

[30] I refer to what are usually called the "revisionist" views of the origins of the French Revolution. The role of scholars such as Alfred Cobban, George V. Taylor, François Furet, Colin Lucas, and numerous others in attacking the traditional view and laying the groundwork for the revisionist ones are well known. A useful survey of the literature on this question can be found in William Doyle, *Origins of the French Revolution* (Oxford and New York, 1980), pp. 7–40 and 214–221. See also Nancy N. Barker, "The French Nobility on the Eve of the Revolution: Was it a Social Class?" unpublished paper read to the Southern Historical Association (November, 1984).

eighteenth century, preceded by some earlier interest, and continued sporadically until the Revolution. How should we now understand these mid-eighteenth-century debates? Do they, for instance, reflect another major transformation of the idea of nobility like the one that took place in the late sixteenth and early seventeenth centuries? To answer this and related questions, we now need to look at writings on nobility from the mid-seventeenth century on, and relate them to the conclusions of this work and to the revised views of the origins of the French Revolution referred to above.

There is no systematic overall study of the concept of nobility from the mid-seventeenth century on. But numerous aspects of the question have been studied, and often well, and we know a good deal about the matter. It appears that the ideas of the early and mid-seventeenth century regarding birth and culture, especially birth, became even more solidly fixed as the reign of Louis XIV continued. Pierre Goubert, for instance, looking for a way to define nobility for the ancien régime, fell back on birth and blood as being the only possible satisfactory definition.[31] That the belief in birth and blood appears to have spread and grown even stronger toward the end of the reign of Louis XIV is suggested by the work of André Devyver.[32] It is also suggested by the actions of Louis and his ministers to tighten up on the nobles and clear out imposters. These "harassments," which is what they often were, and which were carried out mostly for fiscal reasons,[33] certainly helped force the nobles, whether they liked it or not, to accept birth as their defining feature. For, as we know, in order to prove their nobility they were encouraged or forced to take more of an interest in genealogies, to become collectors of parchments and the like,[34] and thus inevitably, it would

[31] Goubert, *Ancien Régime*, pp. 159–163.

[32] Devyver, *Le sang épuré*.

[33] Ford describes these in chap. I (pp. 3–21) of *Robe and Sword* and puts them into the context of Louis' other "harassments" of the nobles.

[34] Cf., for instance, Cubells, "A propos des usurpations" (especially p. 300), where this point is made.

seem, they came to consider their noble birth to be more important than before.

The main assumptions concerning birth of the early and mid-seventeenth century, then, appear to have continued and to have become more emphasized throughout the reign of Louis XIV and well into the eighteenth century. Goubert has pointed out how nonnobles as well as nobles accepted the aristocratic world view,[35] and there seems indeed to have been little serious debate about the matter among nonnobles. They were apparently not bothered very much by having birth determine nobility and culture help define it, and were willing to accept the small inconveniences such a situation might bring in order to profit from the advantages of the absolutist regime.

Toward the middle of the eighteenth century, however, difficulties with this view began to emerge. Great changes were at last being wrought by the rise to dominance of a capitalism and of a capitalist system that, while important before, had not quite broken its way through in the sixteenth and seventeenth centuries.[36] And of course the Enlightenment was at work helping to transform people's attitudes. In this context, the modern idea of nobility of the early and mid-seventeenth century began to run into problems. These problems are reflected particularly in the well-known debate concerning the so-called *noblesse commerçante* and to some extent in the debate concerning nobles and the military.

The *noblesse commerçante* debate came to the forefront of people's attention—even if there had been substantial discus-

[35] Goubert, "Problèmes généraux," p. 2.

[36] For Goubert in *Ancien Régime*, for instance, and for numerous other historians, the rise, or breaking forth, of a different or more "modern" capitalism lies behind much of the great wave of changes taking place in French society toward the middle of the eighteenth century onward. One of the most famous examples of this capitalism *not* finally emerging in the sixteenth and seventeenth centuries can be found in Le Roy Ladurie, *Paysans de Languedoc*.

214

sion on the matter in the centuries before,[37]—with the treatise of the Abbé Coyer of 1756, which argued that nobility and commerce can and should go together, and with the rejoinder of the same year by the Chevalier d'Arcq, which argued that they should not.[38] The Abbé Coyer's work is especially useful because it reflects the strongest and most effective statement of the time of the argument for joining nobility and commerce and thus helps us compare this debate, especially in terms of what might be new in it, with those of the late sixteenth and early seventeenth centuries. The context of Coyer's writing is indeed clearly different and new. His approach is essentially an economic one in the sense that he is concerned primarily with the wealth of the nation. His arguments are deeply embedded in a foundation of the Enlightenment,[39] of the rise of capitalism,[40] and of a belief in progress[41] that cannot be found in earlier writings on the subject.[42] His is a "happy" century in which reason is

[37] Cf., for instance, Zeller, "Une notion."

[38] See Gabriel François Coyer, *La noblesse commerçante* (Paris and London, 1756), and Philippe Auguste de Sainte-Foix, Chevalier d'Arcq, *La noblesse militaire, ou Le patriote françois* (n.p., 1756). A good number of other works on the subject appeared in the following few years. For a list of the main ones, see Henri Lévy-Bruhl, "La noblesse de France et le commerce à la fin de l'ancien régime," *Revue d'histoire moderne* 8 (1933), 221–222. See also Emile G. Léonard, *L'armée et ses problèmes au xviiiᵉ siècle* (Paris, 1958), pp. 178–190, and Edgard Depitre, "Le système et la querelle de la noblesse commerçante (1756–1759)," *Revue d'histoire économique et sociale* 6 (1913), 137–176.

[39] For instance, Coyer, *Noblesse commerçante*, p. 11: ". . . since the time that the flame of Philosophy has enlightened and dissolved our prejudices. . . ." Note also the tone throughout.

[40] For instance, ibid., pp. 91–92: "The nation truly rich is that which, in working hard consumes a great deal; the government which fosters consuming encourages production." See also pp. 11, 35–36, and once again throughout.

[41] For example, ibid., pp. 116–117: a long list of prejudices that have been overcome and are no longer believed in and acted upon in his century.

[42] Cf., for instance, Montchrestien's *Traité de l'économie politique* and Mayerne Turquet's *La monarchie aristodémocratique*, which in some ways call for the same thing as Coyer.

spreading.[43] Reason now simply needs to be applied to the question of whether or not poor nobles—and poor nobles only because the rich and powerful would not want to—should be allowed to carry on commerce for their own good and for the good of the state. He very deftly shows how irrational it would be not to allow this. He argues convincingly that everyone, and above all the nobles, would profit from such an arrangement, and no one would suffer.

Coyer's work, then, is not an attack on the nobles per se. In some ways he even wants to strengthen their position in society by increasing their possibilities for making money. Birth remains the basic determiner of nobility in his mind, and he does not question this. Here he remains, in terms of his fundamental assumptions, in the traditional line from the early seventeenth century on. What he wants to do is simply diminish even further the distinction between noble and nonnoble, to make "nobility" become even less important by not allowing it to restrict the development of commerce. Indeed, he feels that France is already well ahead in this area, as opposed, for instance, to Germany and Poland, where the nobles are much more restricted.[44]

Coyer thus simply gives an extra push to a longstanding movement that was diminishing the significance of the distinction between noble and nonnoble, and the implications of the debate in the middle of the eighteenth century concerning the military and the nobility suggest a similar continuation of earlier directions. Because nobility was assumed to be based upon birth, and because the military was an autonomous institution in a society that was becoming steadily more "enlightened," ways had to be found of allowing that institution to draw upon the most capable members of society, regardless of rank. Some believed that nobility of birth restricted such efforts, thus helping to lead to the famous edict

[43] For example, Coyer, *Noblesse commerçante*, p. 215: "Let our century be the one of *Philosphie, Commerce* and *bonheur*," and p. 11: "Our reason has made a long step. . . ."

[44] Cf. ibid., pp. 11–12.

of 1750 allowing for some ennoblement through the military.[45] On the other hand, these pressures were probably not as strong as those in the case of commerce. Most nonnobles, including the Abbé Coyer, for instance,[46] seemed willing to leave the military to the nobles, as long as enough good nobles could be found to do the job well. Not only the Chevalier d'Arcq but also the Abbé Coyer clearly "understood" that being brought up in a noble family tended to encourage high performance in the military. With their ancestors pushing them on and their fathers talking constantly about honor and courage, young nobles were more inclined to become good military men. (That at least is how most eighteenth-century people, noble and nonnoble, seem to have viewed the matter.)[47] If this push from the ancestors did *not* work, however, then both the Abbé Coyer and the Chevalier d'Arcq—the first with pleasure, the second with regret— would accept nonnobles in leading positions in the army in order to strengthen it; they would even accept their eventual ennoblement.[48]

In both cases, then, although more so in the case of commerce than in the case of the military, a birth-based nobility was seen as a potential deterrent to progress. More than in earlier periods, people now believed that "nobility" must not restrict commercial, military, and other kinds of development. The ancien régime was discovering that its idea of nobility could cause serious problems unless ways could be found

[45] Cf., for instance, Marcel Reinhard, "Elite et noblesse dans la seconde moitié du xviiiᵉ siècle," *Revue d'histoire moderne et contemporaine* 3 (1956), especially 5–12.

[46] For instance, see Coyer, *Noblesse commerçante*, pp. 16–17.

[47] On this see also the important article by David D. Bien, "La réaction aristocratique avant 1789: L'exemple de l'armée," *Annales: Economies, sociétés, civilisations* 29 (1974), 23–48, 505–534, and especially 521–525.

[48] For instance, Coyer, *Noblesse commerçante*, pp. 16–17, and Arcq, *Noblesse militaire*, pp. 56–57. Ennoblement for nonnobles is only hinted at or implied in Arcq's passage, but it does seem to be suggested in the way that he accepts the fact that one may have to rely on some of them in the military.

to make nobility even less important than it had been. And such ways were found as the eighteenth century progressed. Nobles did in fact become active in commerce during that time—indeed, some would say they were in the forefront of the development of capitalism—[49] and some nonnobles were ennobled for commercial activities and for having had distinguished careers in other areas.[50] Moreover, nonnobles could always purchase an ennobling office if they had the money. The view that nobility of birth should be significant continued to have its supporters, to be sure, and they apparently won a victory of sorts with the issuing of the notorious Ségur edict of 1781, which set up genealogical barriers in the army for nonnobles and for those recently ennobled. But even this was done partially for a more effective and professional military.[51] This edict thus had its forward-looking aspects as well, and on the whole it seemed that those favoring a diminishing importance of nobility were winning their case.

These debates and discussions of the middle and late eighteenth century do not, then, reflect a "bourgeois" view of nobility that one might surmise would set the stage for a revolution that would pit bourgeois against noble. Rather, they indicate a continuation of earlier directions growing out of the changes of the late sixteenth and early seventeenth centuries, which favored not considering the noble-nonnoble division as a major one within society. The Abbé Coyer and the others do plainly reflect a certain shift in attitudes that was spurred on by the Enlightenment and the rise of capi-

---

[49] For instance, Guy Chaussinand-Nogaret, "A propos d'une entreprise française au xviiie siècle: Les sociétaires de la compagnie de Guadalcanal," *Revue d'histoire moderne et contemporaine* 20 (1973), 185–200, with expansion in his *La noblesse au xviiie siècle*, pp. 119–161, and Guy Richard, *Noblesse d'affaires au xviiie siècle* (Paris, 1974).

[50] Cf. Reinhard, "Elite et noblesse," 13–26.

[51] Bien, "La réaction aristocratique." As we have seen above, such an edict would not seem to have been particularly shocking to the Abbé Coyer, since he recognized the potential value of being brought up in a noble family and thus being constantly reminded of one's duties of honor, courage, and the like.

talism, but this shift was not a basic one. As far as we can determine, no one involved in these debates questioned whether birth should be the basis of nobility. They do not seem to be arguing for a total nobility of merit by which one would become ennobled only for one's lifetime;[52] instead those who were ennobled would pass their status on to their children in the old way. Birth, therefore, remained central to everyone's conception of nobility, and the only factor that was seriously questioned was how important that nobility would be.

People throughout the eighteenth century, then, appeared willing to let birth define nobility, as long as nobility did not make any serious difference in allowing nobles to act like anyone else in society, and in allowing nonnobles not to be especially restricted just because they were not nobles. And, of course, nobility would remain accessible to the outstanding few. These ideas and realities were not new, however, and thus the fundamental assumption about what defines nobility—birth, with ennoblement in a few special cases—did not change in the mid- and late eighteenth century as it did in the late sixteenth and early seventeenth centuries.

Into the French Revolution

Seeing these debates in the mid-eighteenth century and later as reflecting a further step—in a process several centuries old—toward the diminishing importance of nobility[53] adds an-

---

[52]Cf., for instance, the Abbé Coyer in his rejoinder of 1757, *Développement et défense du système de la noblesse commerçante* (Amsterdam and Paris, 1757), pt. 2, pp. 146–149, where he makes clear that this is not what he is arguing for at all.

[53]Nobility, of course, still had some "importance" in this period. The ennobling office of *secrétaire du roi*, for instance, cost around 120,000 *livres Tournois* on the eve of the Revolution (my thanks to George V. Taylor for having reminded me of this), and that is no small sum; and yet wealthy nonnobles were willing to pay that much in order to add that possession to their others, so it must have been important to them. But, of course, the fact remains that if they had the money they *could* buy it.

other piece of evidence to the well-known and very convincing research of the past twenty to thirty years that has concluded that we must look elsewhere than to the noble-bourgeois or noble-nonnoble question for a real understanding of what brought on the Revolution.[54] One reason many historians for so long have tended—wrongly, it now seems—to assume that nobility *was* a basic division and that nobles did constitute a social class in the ancien régime is that nobility seems to have been such a key factor in the French Revolution, where so many expressions of antinoble feelings are clearly documented. On this point this study offers an interesting irony, one that concerns the events that followed the calling of the Estates General in 1788. The French, for want of a better institution, were forced to turn to the Estates General, an institution that was organized in sixteenth-century, or at least in 1614, terms with three estates. These terms reflected assumptions that nobility was a profession—a crucial one, the military—and that it was thus especially important and deserved its own estate. The evolution of the ancien régime tended toward a society where nobility was of declining importance, but, thanks to the fact that the Estates General had not been called since 1614, this institution had not evolved along with the rest of society. There were forward-looking leaders such as Brienne and others in 1787 and 1788 who seemed aware of this and wanted to find a better and more up-to-date institution to meet their needs, but their attempts failed.[55]

All that was left, then, was the Estates General. It was called, and the rest we know. But what we have perhaps not

---

[54] Cf. the scholars mentioned and works cited above in note 30. And see Doyle, *Origins of the French Revolution*, pt. 2 (pp. 43–237), for a useful synthesis of much of this recent literature, telling the story of the origins of the Revolution without relying on noble-bourgeois differences or antagonisms as any sort of basic key.

[55] Richet, *La France moderne*, pp. 165–178, especially pp. 169–173; and also, for greater detail, Jean Egret, *The French Prerevolution*, trans. Wesley D. Camp (Chicago and London, 1977), 1st French ed. 1962.

realized is that its tripartite organization gave "nobility" a far greater political significance than it actually had in the 1780s. One of the results was the surfacing of an enormous amount of antinoble feeling. This feeling, however, might never have emerged had a more equitable institution been found, an institution that would not have set the Third Estate against the nobles and that would instead have allowed for the expression of more of the liberal tendencies so prominent among many nobles of the time.[56]

The problem in this case, then, was the lack of an up-to-date institution. Nobility as a profession helped produce a French Revolution and an aftermath much more antinoble (and thus quite different) than it might have been otherwise. This was because it had bequeathed a sixteenth-century Estates General that had not been used by the absolutist government after 1614 and thus had not evolved along with the rest of society.

The irony that the three-estate system was called upon in 1789, which led directly and indirectly to many of the struggles and divisions of the Revolution and later, may also have been a factor in contributing to an overrated belief in the nineteenth and twentieth centuries—in France and elsewhere—in the importance of nobility, in people's own times as well as in their past. For instance, it may well have helped lead to the apparent misconceptions about the importance of the noble-bourgeois struggle, both before and during the Revolution, that have come under so much attack recently. In any case, it suggests that "nobility" in fact continued to play a quite similar role, and thus did not reflect a particularly important division in the social struggles of the time, in the period after the Revolution. Joined with hereditary monarchy, and attempting to defend a certain kind of world, nobility might have taken on a significance it did not actually have in the old regime. Even here, however, Patrice Higon-

[56] On these liberal tendencies among the nobles, see Chaussinand-Nogaret, *La noblesse au xviiie siècle*, especially pp. 181–226, and also Richet, *La France moderne*, p. 174.

net, in a recent study, has shown us noble and nonnoble upper classes in France that, even though they were at odds in different ways during much of the early Revolutionary period, had already learned by 1799 that it was better to emphasize what would keep them together than what would drive them apart.[57] On the whole, then, nobility in France after the Revolution seems to have remained essentially what it had been before, while elites, surprisingly similar to those of the later part of the ancien régime, continued to dominate.[58]

We end, then, with an interesting carryover from the sixteenth century—the peculiar organization of the Estates in 1788–89—and the suggestion that had it not been for this anachronistic organization, people in the nineteenth and twentieth centuries might have given less importance to the status and concept of nobility. Although such thoughts concerning the post-Revolutionary period go beyond the scope of this study, they suggest that the sixteenth-century views presented here, and the story of the change from these views to more modern ones, may also present clues for the study of nobility in more recent periods. Perhaps when these questions are examined in more depth, we will find that the difference between noble and nonnoble was never again of nearly the same significance once nobility, by the late sixteenth and early seventeenth centuries, had lost its essential military purpose and function.

[57] Patrice Higonnet, *Class, Ideology, and the Rights of Nobles during the French Revolution* (Oxford, 1981).

[58] Cf., for instance, Robert Forster, *Merchants, Landlords, Magistrates: The Depont Family in Eighteenth-Century France* (Baltimore and London, 1980), and also Chaussinand-Nogaret, *La noblesse au xviii*ᵉ *siècle.*

Bibliography

Manuscript Sources Cited in Notes

A. Academies and Pluvinel

Archives Nationales (A.N.)
Maison du Roi, 0^1 915–917. (This series is concerned with the noble academies throughout France in the seventeenth and eighteenth centuries.)
Chambre des Comptes, P. 74^2 (Pluvinel).

Bibliothèque Nationale (B.N.)
Manuscrits Français, 22884 (Academy).
Manuscrits Français, 28790 (Pluvinel).
Manuscrits Français, Nouvelles Acquisitions, 150 (Academy).
Cabinet d'Hozier, 272 (Pluvinel).
Carrés d'Hozier, 499 (Pluvinel).
Dossiers Bleus, 528 (Pluvinel).
Fonds Baluze, 147 (Academy).

Bibliothèque Mazarine
Manuscrits, 2117 (Academy).

Bibliothèque de l'Arsenal
Manuscrits, 4114 (Academy).

B. Popular Rebellions

Bibliothèque Nationale
Manuscrits Français, 23194 (Rebellions of 1594).
Fonds Dupuy, 62 (Rebellions of 1594).
Collection Périgord, "Livre noir" (Rebellions of 1594).

C. Cahiers

Bibliothèque Nationale
Manuscrits Français, Nouvelles Acquisitions, 2808 (Nobles of Chaumont-en-Bassigny for 1614).

D. Mayerne Turquet

Bibliothèque Nationale
Carrés d'Hozier, 423.
Pièces Originales, 1903.

Published Sources Cited in Notes or Consulted Extensively

Agricola, Johannes. *Die Sprichwörter-Sammlungen.* Ed. Sandor L. Gilman. 2 vols. Berlin and New York, 1971.

Arcq, Philippe Auguste de Sainte Foix, Chevalier d'. *La noblesse militaire, ou le patriote français.* N.p., 1756.

Aristotle. *The Politics.* Trans. T.A. Sinclair. Penguin Books. Baltimore, 1962.

Aubigné, Théodore Agrippa d'. *Les aventures du Baron de Faeneste.* Paris, 1855. 1st ed., 1616–1617.

Bacquet, Jean. *Traicté des droits de francs-fiefs, de nouveaux acquests, d'anoblissemens, et d'amortissemens,* in *Les oeuvres.* Paris, 1644. 1st ed., 1580–1582.

Bara, Jérôme de. *Le blason des armoiries, auquel est monstrée la manière de laquelle les anciens et modernes ont usé en icelles.*

[Barnaud, Nicolas]. *Le cabinet du roy de France dans lequel il y a trois perles précieuses d'inestimable valeur: Par le moyen desquelles sa majesté s'en va le premier monarque du monde et ses suiets du tout soulagez.* N.p., 1581.

Bassompierre, Maréchal de. *Mémoires.* Ed. M. de Chanterac. 4 vols. Paris, 1870–1877.

Bauffremont, Claude de. *Proposition de la noblesse de France.* Paris, 1577.

Belleperche. *L'académie du roy pour l'instruction de la jeunesse.* Paris, 1598.

Béroald de Verville, François. *Dialogue de la vertu.* Paris, 1584.

Boccaccio, Giovanni. *Il Decameron.* Ed. Guiseppi Petronio. 2 vols. Turin, 1950.

Bodin, Jean. *Les six livres de la république.* Paris, 1583. 1st ed., 1576.

Boulainvilliers, Henry, comte de. *Essais sur la noblesse de France, contenans une dissertation sur son origine et abaissement.* Amsterdam, 1732.

Boyssat, Pierre. *Recherches sur les duels.* Lyon, 1610.

———. *Remerciement au roy par les anoblis de Dauphiné.* Paris, 1603.

Bracciolini, Poggio. *De Nobilitate.* In *Opera,* pp. 64–83. Basle, 1538.

Brant, Sebastian. *The Ship of Fools.* Trans. and ed. Edwin H. Zeydel. New York, 1944.

Brantôme, Pierre de Bourdeille. *Oeuvres complètes.* Ed. L. Lanne. 11 vols. Paris, 1864–1882.

Castiglione. *Il Cortegiano.* Ed. Vittorio Cian. 3rd ed. Florence, 1929.

Caumont, Jehan de. *De la vertu de noblesse, aux roys et princes très chrestiens.* Paris, 1585.

Champier, Symphorien. *Le fondement et origine des tiltres de noblesse et excellentz estatz de tous nobles et illustres: Quant à la différence des empires, royaulmes, duchez, contez, et autres seigneuries.* Paris, 1535.

————. *Les gestes ensemble la vie du preulx chevalier Bayard.* Paris, 1525.

————. *Petit dialogue de noblesse, auquel est déclaré que c'est de noblesse et les inventeurs d'icelle. Où le jeune prince demande, et le docteur luy respond.* Paris, 1535.

Chappuys, Gabriel, trans. *Conseils militaires fort utile à tous généraulx, colonnels, capitaines et soldats.* Paris, 1586.

Charron, Pierre. *De la sagesse.* 2 vols. Paris, 1782. 1st ed., 1601.

Chasseneux, Barthélemy de. *Catalogus gloriae mundi, laudes, honores, excellentias, ac praeeminentias omnium fere statuum.* Geneva, 1617. 1st ed., 1529.

Cheffontaines, F. Christophe. *Confutation du poinct d'honneur sur lequel la noblesse fonde aujourd'huy ses querelles et monomachies.* Paris, 1568.

Cherin, L.N.H. *Abrégé chronologique d'édits, déclarations, règlemens, arrêts et lettres-patentes des rois de France de la troisième race, concernant le fait de noblesse, précédé d'un discours sur l'origine de la noblesse, ses différentes espèces, ses droits et prérogatives, la manière d'en dresser les preuves, et les causes de sa décadence.* Paris, 1788.

Chevalier, Guillaume de. *Discours de la vaillance.* Paris, 1598.

————. *Discours de querelles et de l'honneur.* Paris, 1598.

Chorier, Nicolas. *L'estat politique de la province de Dauphiné.* Vol. III. Grenoble, 1671.

Clichtove, Josse. *De vera nobilitate opusculum.* Paris, 1520. 1st ed., 1512.

Coignet, Matthieu. *Instruction aux princes pour garder la foy promise, contenant un sommaire de la philosophie chrestienne et morale, et devoir d'un homme de bien.* Paris, 1584.

Corda, A. *Catalogue des Factums.* 10 vols. Bibliothèque Nationale. The following *Factums* were consulted: 4° Fm 1388 (n.d.); 4° Fm 5835 (1644); 4° Fm 26388 (1612); 4° Fm 35506 (1632).

Corlieu, François. *Instruction pour tous estats, en laquelle est sommairement déclairé, comme chacun en son estat se doit gouverner, et vivre selon Dieu.* Paris, 1559.

Corneille. *Théâtre complet.* Ed. M. Rat. 3 vols. Garnier Frères, Paris, n.d. Mainly consulted were *Le Cid, Cinna,* and *Polyeucte.*

Coyer, Gabriel François. *La noblesse commerçante.* Paris and London, 1756.

———. *Développement et défense du système de la noblesse commerçante.* Amsterdam and Paris, 1757.

Cromé, François. *Dialogue d'entre le Maheustre et le Manant: Contenant les raisons de leurs débats et questions en ses présens troubles au royaume de France.* N.p., 1593. Original version: B.N. Rés. 8°L^{35} b 509.

———. *Dialogue d'entre le Maheustre et le Manant: Contenant les raisons de leurs débats et questions en ces presens troubles au royaume de France.* N.p., 1594. Royalist version: B.N. 8°Lb^{35} 509A.

———. *Dialogue d'entre le Maheustre et le Manant.* Ed. Peter M. Ascoli. Geneva, 1977. Published version.

Curtili, Bonus de. *Tractatus Nobilitatis.* Lyon, 1528.

Dallington, Sir Robert. *The View of Fraunce.* Oxford, 1936. 1st ed., 1604.

Dampmartin, Pierre de. *De la connaissance et merveilles du monde et de l'homme.* Paris, 1585.

Della Casa, Giovanni. *Galateo, Ovvero de' costumi.* Ed. P. Pancrazi. Florence, 1947.

Dorléans, Louis. *Le banquet et après disner du conte d'Arète, où il se traict de la dissimulation du roy de Navarre, et des moeurs de ses partisans.* Paris, 1594.

Du Fail, Noël. *Oeuvres facétieuses.* Ed. J. Assezat. 2 vols. Paris, 1874.

Dupleix, Scipion. *Les loix militaires touchant le duel: Divisées en quatre livres.* Paris, 1602.

Du Souhait. *Le parfaict gentil-homme.* Paris, 1600.

Elyot, Thomas. *The Book Named the Govenour.* Ed. S.E. Lehmberg. London and New York, 1962. 1st ed., 1531.

Ernaud, Loys. *Discours de la noblesse, et des justes moyens d'y parvenir.* Caen, 1584.

Faret, Nicolas. *L'honneste homme ou l'art de plaire à la cour.* Ed. M. Magendie. Paris, 1925. 1st ed., 1630.

Fiaschi, Cesare. *Trattato del modo dell' imbrigliare, maneggiare, e ferrare cavalli.* Venice, 1563.

Flurance, David de Rivault de. *Le dessein d'une académie, et de l'introduction d'icelle en la cour.* Paris, 1612.

————. *Les estats, desquels il est discouru du prince, du noble et du tiers estat, conformément à nostre temps.* Lyon, 1596.

Froissart, Jean. *Chroniques.* Société de l'Histoire de France. 13 vols. Paris, 1869–1957.

Froydeville, Eymar de. *Dialogues de l'origine de la noblesse où est déclaré que c'est d'icelle et ses inventeurs.* Lyon, 1574.

Gentillet, Innocent. *Discours sur les moyens de bien gouverner et maintenir en bonne paix un Royaume ou autre principauté—contre Nicolas Machiavel, Forentin.* N.p., 1576.

Godefroy, Théodore. *Le cérémonial de France.* Paris, 1619.

Godet de Soudé, François de. *Dictionnaire des anoblissements, Extrait des registres de la Chambre des Comptes depuis 1345 jusqu'en 1660.* Ed. E. Barthélemy. Paris, 1875.

Gouberville. *Le journal du sire de Gouberville.* Ed. E. de Robillard de Beaurepaire. Caen, 1892.

Grenaille, M. de. *L'honneste garçon ou l'art de bien élever la noblesse à la vertu, aux sciences, et à tous les exercices convenables à sa condition.* Paris, 1642.

Grisone, Federigo. *Gli ordini di cavalcare.* Naples, 1550.

Guazzo, Stefano. *Le civil conversatione.* Venice, 1551.

Guyon, Loys. *Les diverses leçons.* Lyon, 1604.

La harangue par [pour] la noblesse de toute la France, faite au roy très-chrestien Charles IX, sur l'estat de ce royaume. Paris, 1574.

Haton, Claude. *Mémoires.* Ed. Felix Bourquelot. 2 vols. Paris, 1857.

Hénault, Charles-Jean-François. *Nouvel abrégé chronologique de l'histoire de France.* 5th ed. 2 vols. Paris, 1756.

Henri III. *Lettres.* Ed. M. François. 2 vols. Paris, 1959–1965.

Hotman, François. *Franco-gallia.* Geneva, 1573.

Humphrey, Lawrence. *The Nobles or of Nobilitye.* Amsterdam and New York, 1973. Facsimile of the 1563 ed.

Hurault, Michel. *Premier discours sur l'estat de la France.* Avec certaines lettres du roy: & autres du duc de Guyse, de l'an 1588. Suivy d'un second, sur le mèsme subiect, de ceste année 1591. N.p., 1591.

Isambert, François-André, ed. *Recueil général des anciennes lois françaises.* Vols. XI–XVI. Paris, 1827–1833.

Juvénal. *Quatre satyres de Juvénal: Translatées de latin en françoys, par Michel d'Amboyse escuyer, seigneur de Chevillon, c'est assavoir la viii, x, xi, et xiii.* Paris, 1544.

―――. *The Satires of Juvenal*. Trans. Rolfe Humpries. Blooming-ton, Indiana, 1958.

La Béraudière, Marc de. *Le combat de seul à seul en camp clos*. Paris, 1608.

La Broue, Salomon de. *Le cavalerice françois*. Paris, 1610.

L'Alouëte, François de. *Traité des nobles et des vertus dont ils sont formés*. Paris, 1577.

Lalourcé and Duval, eds. *Recueil des cahiers généraux des trois ordres aux états-généraux*. 4 vols. Paris, 1789.

La Marche, Olivier de. *Traités du duel judiciaire: Relations de pas d'armes et tournois*. Ed. Bernard Prost. Paris, 1782.

La Loupe, Vincent de. *Premier et second livre des dignitez, magistrats, & offices du royaume de France. Ausquels est de nouveau adiousté le tiers livre de ceste matière outre la revue & augmentation d'iceux*. Paris, 1560.

La Noue, François de. *Discours politiques et militaires*. Basle, 1587.

La Perrière, Guillaume de. *Le miroir politique, contenant diverses manières de gouverner et policer les républiques, qui sont, et ont esté par cy devant*. Paris, 1567. 1st. ed., 1539–1540.

La Place, Pierre de. *Traité de la vocation et manière de vivre à laquelle chacun est appellé*. Paris, 1561.

La Primaudaye, Pierre de. *Académie françoise*. 3rd ed. Paris, 1581. 1st ed., 1577.

La Roque, Gilles André de. *Traité de la noblesse*. Paris, 1678.

La Ruelle, Charles de. *Succinctz adversaires contre l'histoire et professeurs d'icelle*. Poitiers, 1574.

La Taille, Jean de. *Oeuvres*. Ed. René de Maulde. 4 vols. Paris, 1878.

La Vacherie, Pierre de. "Le gouvernement des trois estatz du temps qui court." In *Recueil de poésies françaises des xve et xvie siècles, morales, facétieuses, historiques*. Eds. Anatole de Montaiglon and James de Rothschild. Vol. XII. Paris, 1877.

Laval, Antoine. *Desseins de professions nobles et publiques*. Paris, 1612.

Le Masle, Jean. *Discours, traittant de la noblesse, et de son origine*. In *Les nouvelles récréations poétiques*. Paris, 1586.

Le Roy, Loys. *De la vicissitude ou variété des choses en l'univers*. Paris, 1575.

L'Estoile, Pierre de. *Journal pour le règne de Henri IV*. Eds. L.R. Lefèvre and A. Martin. 3 vols. Paris, 1948–1960.

Lettre missive d'un gentilhomme à un sien compagnon contenant les causes du mescontentement de la noblesse de France. N.p., 1567.

228

Loque, Bertrand de. *Traité de la guerre*. N.p., 1588.
———. *Traité du duel*. N.p., 1588.
Loyseau, Charles. *Les oeuvres*. Paris, 1666.
Malherbe, François de. *Oeuvres*. 5 vols. Paris, 1862–1869.
Le manifeste de la France aux parisiens et à tous les français. Tours, 1590.
Mandrou, Robert, ed. *Etats-Généraux de 1614, cahier du Tiers Etat (extraits)*. In *Classes et luttes de classes en France au début du xviiᵉ siècle*. Florence, 1965.
Mayerne Turquet, Loys de. *La monarchie aristodémocratique, ou le gouvernement composé et réglé des trois formes de légitimes républiques*. Paris, 1611.
Medwall, Henry. *Fulgens and Lucrece*. In *Five Pre-Shakespearean Comedies*. Ed. Frederick S. Boas. London, 1934.
Mercure François. 1617. Vol. II.
Molière. *Oeuvres complètes*. Editions du Seuil. Paris, 1962. Mainly consulted were *Le bourgeois gentilhomme*, *Le misanthrope*, *Les précieuses ridicules*, and *Dom Juan*.
Monluc, Blaise de. *Commentaires*. Ed. Paul Courteault. 3 vols. Paris, 1911–1925.
Montaigne, Michel de. *Les essais*. Ed. Pierre Villey. Paris, 1965.
Montchrestien, Antoine de. *Traicté de l'oeconomie politique*. Ed. Th. Funck-Brentano. Paris, n.d. 1st ed., 1615.
Moreau, Jean. *Mémoires du chanoine Jean Moreau sur les guerres de la Ligue en Bretagne*. Ed. Henri Waquet. Quimper, 1960.
Mornay, Philippe de. *Mémoires et correspondance de Du Plessis-Mornay*. 12 vols. Paris, 1824–1825.
Moryson, Fynes. *An Itinerary*. 4 vols. Glasgow, 1907. 1st ed., 1617.
Mousnier, R., J.P. Labatut, and Y. Durand, eds. *Problèmes de stratification sociale. Deux cahiers de la noblesse pour les Etats-Généraux de 1649–51*. Paris, 1965.
Musset, Louis. *Discours sur les remonstrances et réformations de chacun estat*. Paris, 1582.
Navarre, Marguerite de. *Heptaméron*. Ed. Michel François. Paris. 1964.
Nervèze, Antoine de. *Le guide des courtisans*. In *Les oeuvres morales*. Paris, 1605.
Nouaillac, J., ed. "Documents inédits." From the Bibliothèque Nationale on the rebellions of 1593–1594. In *Les Croquants du Limousin: Une insurrection paysanne en 1594*, pp. 43–49. Tulle, 1906.

Oncieu, Guillaume de. *La précédence de la noblesse, sus un différent en cas de précédence plaidé en audience publique, au souverain sénat de Savoy, entre les nobles, et les scindics du tiers estat d'une parroisse.* Lyon, 1593.

Origny, Pierre d'. *Le hérault de la noblesse de France.* Reims, 1578.

Ormesson, Olivier Lefèvre d'. *Journal et extraits des mémoires d'André Lefèvre d'Ormesson.* Ed. M. Cheruel. 2 vols. Paris, 1860–1861.

Paradin, Claude. *Les devises héroïques.* Antwerp, 1967. 1st ed., Lyon, 1557.

Pascal, Blaise. *Pensées.* Garnier Frères. Paris, 1960.

Pasquier, Estienne. *Les oeuvres.* Amsterdam, 1723.

Pelletier. *La nourriture de la noblesse où sont représentées comme en un tableau, toutes les plus belles vertus, qui peuvent accomplir un jeune gentilhomme.* Paris, 1604.

Petit traicté enseignant qu'est ce que vraye noblesse: Avec auctorités de Diogènes, de Sénèque, de Boèce, et Ovide, nouvellement imprimé à Grenoble. Grenoble, n.d.

Pibrac, Guy de. *Les plaisirs de la vie rustique.* Paris, 1575.

Pluvinel, Antoine de. *Le maneige royal.* Paris, 1623. The original edition.

———. *L'instruction du roy en l'exercice de monter à cheval.* Paris, 1625. Revised edition of above work.

Poncet, Maurice. *Remonstrance à la noblesse de France, de l'utilité et repos que le roy apporte à son peuple: Et de l'instruction qu'il doibt avoir pour le bien gouverner.* Paris, 1592.

Pontaymery, Alexandre de. *L'académie ou institution de la noblesse françoise.* In *Les oeuvres.* Paris, 1599.

Rabelais, François. *Oeuvres complètes.* Ed. J. Boulenger. Pléiade. Paris, 1955.

Rapin, Nicolas. *Les plaisirs du gentilhomme champestre; Augmenté de quelques nouveaux poèmes et épigrammes.* Paris, 1583.

Response à une lettre. Escrite à Compiègne du quatrième jour d'aoust, touchant le mescontentement de la noblesse de France. N.p., 1567.

Richelieu, Cardinal de. *Testament politique.* Ed. Louis André. Paris, 1947.

Rubys, Claude de. *Les privilèges, franchises et immunitez octroyées par les rois très chrestiens, aux consuls, eschevins, manans, et habitans de la ville de Lyon, à leur postérité.* Lyon, 1573.

Sainct-Didier, Henry de. *Traité concernant les secrets du premier livre sur l'espée seule, mère de toutes armes.* Paris, 1573.

Saint-Simon, Louis de Rouvroy, duc de. *Mémoires*. Ed. Adolphe Chéruel. Pléaide. 7 vols. Paris, 1953–1961.

Sallust. *The Jugurthine War*. Trans. S.A. Handford. Baltimore, 1963.

Salluste. *La guerre jugurthine*. Trans. Hiérosme de Chomedey. Paris, 1581.

———. *L'histoire de C. Crispe Saluste touchant la coniuration de L. Serge Catelin, avec la première harangue de M. Tulle Cireron contre luy: Ensemble la guerre iugurthine, et la harangue de Pertius Latro contre Catelin: Traduittes de latin en françois, par Loys Meigret, lyonnais*. Paris, 1547.

La Satyre Ménippée ou la vertu du catholicon. Ed. Ch. Read Paris, 1892. 1st ed., 1594.

Saulx, Jean de, Vicomte de Tavannes. *Les mémoires de Gaspard de Saulx-Tavannes*. Eds. Michaud et Poujoulat. Paris, 1838.

Savaron, Jean. *Traicté contre les duels*. Paris, 1610.

Seneca. *Ad Lucilium Epistulae Morales*. Trans. Richard M. Gummere. 3 vols. Cambridge, Mass., 1961.

Serres, Olivier de. *Le théâtre d'agriculture et mesnage des champs*. Paris, 1804. 1st ed., 1600.

Seyssel, Claude de. *La monarchie de France*. Ed. J. Poujol. Paris, 1961.

Sorel, Charles. *Histoire comique de Francion*. Paris, 1965. 1st ed., 1623.

Tallemant des Réaux. *Historiettes*. Ed. L. Cerf. Paris, 1929.

Thierriat, Florentin de. *Trois traictez sçavoir*. 1. *De la noblesse de race*. 2. *De la noblesse civille*. 3. *Des immunitez des ignobles*. Paris, 1606.

Tiraqueau, André. *De Nobilitate*. Lyon, 1559. 1st ed., 1549.

Tommaseo, N., ed. *Relations des ambassadeurs vénitiens sur les affaires de France*. 2 vols. Paris, 1838.

Très-joyeuse, plaisante et récréative histoire composée par le Loyal Serviteur, des faicts, gestes, triomphes et prouesses du bon chevalier sans paour et sans reproche, gentil seigneur de Bayart. In *Nouvelle collection des mémoires pour servir à l'histoire de France*. Eds. Michaud et Poujoulat. Vol. IV, pp. 479–607. Paris, 1837.

Le trésor de tous les livres d'Amadis de Gaule. Vol. I. Lyon, 1575.

Urfé, Anne d'. "Description du pays de Forez." In *Les d'Urfé*. Ed. A. Bernard. Paris, 1839.

Urfé, Honoré d'. *L'Astrée*. Ed. H. Vaganay. 5 vols. Lyon, 1925–1928.

Index

absolutist state: under Henry IV (1594–1610), xv, 95, 122-24, 128, 129; first half of the seventeenth century, 137-38, 144, 146, 169, 172-73, 187-88, 190, 194, 195, 208; seventeenth and eighteenth centuries, 108, 115. See also *solution Henri IV*

academies for nobles, xvi-xvii; accomplishments of, 195-96; in Aix-en-Provence, 188-91, 193; in Angers, 191; Benjamin's, 184, 192-93; calls for, 72, 85, 176-77; curriculum of, 190-92; foundations and early development, 181-95; Italian academies as models, 184-86; need for horses in, 190n; originality of, 186, 195-96; Pluvinel's, 129, 131, 132, 133, 181-84, 186-88, 192, 193; praise of, 131, 133, 182-84

Adam and Eve, 28, 81

Agricola, Johannes, 19

Aix-en-Provence: academy for nobles in, 188-91, 193; provincial estates of, 188-89

Alençon, Duc d', 9, 67

Amadis of Gaul books, 7

ancients, 36, 38; as sources for sixteenth-century France, 48-52, 61; views of nobility among, 39-44

Angers, academy for nobles in, 191n

antimilitary attitudes, 204-205

antinoble sentiment, 101-102, 103-12, 220-21

Arcq, Chevalier d', 215, 217

Ariès, Philippe, 87n

Aristotle, 44; on nobility and virtue, 39-40, 43; as source for sixteenth-century France, 51-52, 60

arms and letters, as new basis of nobility, 177-79; in academy at Aix, 189-90; in academies of Richelieu, 193-95

Artois, 31

Ascoli, Peter, 107

L'Astrée, 131

Aubigné, Agrippa d', on the duel, 170-72

Augustus. *See* Corneille

Bacquet, Jean, on virtue and nobility, 99

ban and *arrière ban*, 13n

Bara, Jérôme de, 87; on nobility as virtue, 76

Barnavi, Elie, 97, 107

Bassompierre, Maréchal de, 185

Bauffremont, Claude de, 89n

Bayard, 27, 89; anonymous history of, 30

Bayeux, *élection* of, 35, 210

Beauce, region of, 32, 35, 87, 156

Belleforest, François de, 81

Bercé, Yves-Marie, 102

Besançon, academy for nobles in, 191n

Bibliothèque Nationale, 48, 49

Billacois, François, 210

Biron, Maréchal, 141

birth, as the basis of nobility: from 1594 to 1610, 115-34; from 1610 to 1660, 134-44; in the late seventeenth and eighteenth centuries, 213-19

Bitton, Davis, 86, 101

Bloch, J.-R., 86

233

Index

Index

Faret, Nicolas (*continued*)
bility as a profession, 205; on
separating virtue and nobility,
139-40
Febvre, Lucien, xviii, 104
Ferguson, Arthur B., 68n
Ferrara, seat of riding academies,
185
feudal-military view of nobility,
30, 36, 37, 38, 44, 48, 51, 106-
107, 180; its dominance, 38-39,
52-62, 67, 86, 94, 99-100; its
origins, 21-27
Fiaschi, Cesare, treatise on horsemanship, 185-86
fief, holding of as *marque de noblesse*, 147, 152-53, 155-57
Florence (Italy), 45; republic, 45-46
Flurance-Rivault, David de, 129,
132, 133, 134, 179, 203; on academies for nobles, 192; on nobility, 129-30; on nobility as a
profession, 10
Foix-Navarre-Albret family, 209
Ford, Franklin, 161
Forster, Robert, 210
Fossier, R., 24
franc-fief, exemption from paying,
as *marque de noblesse,* 147, 147n-
148n
Francis I, 89
François, Michel, 16
French invasions of Italy (1494), 46
French Revolution, xv, 147n, 213,
219n, 221, 222; antinoble feelings
in, 220-21; origins of, 212, 213,
220
Froissart, Jean, 44
Froydeville, Eymar de, 72, 176; on
nobility as virtue, 70
function, nobility as, 3, 16-18, 173,
202. *See also* profession, nobility
as
Furet, François, 212n

Gaston de Foix, 89
genealogies, writing of as a *marque
de noblesse,* 153-54
gentilhomme, as designation for no-
ble, 83, 148n, 178n, 193n
Gentillet, Innocent, 54-55
Germany: nobles in, 216; views of
nobility as a profession in, 18-20
Gimel, Sire de, 128, 141
Godard de Donville, Louise, 152
Godet de Soudé, François de, 91n,
154n
"good" and "bad" nobles, separa-
tion of, 124-28
Goubert, Pierre, 213, 214
Gouberville, Sire de, 13n, 31-32
governors, provincial, 14
Grassby, R. B., 157-58
Greeks, ancient, 39-40
Grenaille, M. de, 140
Grisone, Federigo, treatise on
horsemanship, 186
Guazzo, Stefano, courtly treatise
by, 46
Guise, Duke of (François), 90
Guise, Duke of (Henri), 67, 90
Guyon, Louis, 118, 119, 120; on
nobility, 116-17; on nobility as a
profession, 203

Harangue pour la noblesse (anonymous): on nobility as a profession, 7; on separation, 88
Harding, Robert, 14, 210
Haton, Claude, 32, 77n, 125, 148;
on clothes as a *marque de noblesse,*
151; use of virtue argument, 95-
96
Hénault, Charles-Jean-François, on
nobility as a profession, 17-18
Henneman, John Bell, 12-13
Henry II, 65, 151
Henry III, 49n, 51, 67; on nobility
as a profession, 9

Library of Congress Cataloging-in-Publication Data
Schalk, Ellery, 1938–
From valor to pedigree.
Bibliography: p.   Includes index.
1. France—Nobility—History—16th century.
2. France—Nobility—History—17th century.
3. France—Social life and customs—1328–1600.
4. France—Social life and customs—
17th–18th centuries.   I. Title.
HT653.F7S33   1986   305.5′223′0944   85-43308
ISBN 0-691-05460-6 (alk. paper)

242